MW01088589

Hope Under Oppression

Studies in Feminist Philosophy is designed to showcase cutting-edge monographs and collections that display the full range of feminist approaches to philosophy, that push feminist thought in important new directions, and that display the outstanding quality of feminist philosophical thought.

STUDIES IN FEMINIST PHILOSOPHY

Recent Books in the Series:

Hope Under Oppression

KATIE STOCKDALE

OXFORD
UNIVERSITY PRESS

OXFORD
UNIVERSITY PRESS

Oxford University Press is a department of the University of Oxford. It furthers the University's objective of excellence in research, scholarship, and education by publishing worldwide. Oxford is a registered trade mark of Oxford University Press in the UK and certain other countries.

Published in the United States of America by Oxford University Press
198 Madison Avenue, New York, NY 10016, United States of America.

Library of Congress Cataloging-in-Publication Data
Names: Stockdale, Katie, author.
Title: Hope under oppression / Katie Stockdale.
Description: New York, NY, United States of America : Oxford University
Press, [2021] | Series: Studies in feminist philosophy series |
Includes bibliographical references and index.
Identifiers: LCCN 2021003871 (print) | LCCN 2021003872 (ebook) |
ISBN 9780197563564 (hb) | ISBN 9780197563571 (paperback) |
ISBN 9780197563595 (epub)
Subjects: LCSH: Hope. | Oppression (Psychology)
Classification: LCC BD216 .S76 2021 (print) | LCC BD216 (ebook) |
DDC 152.4—dc23
LC record available at https://lccn.loc.gov/2021003871
LC ebook record available at https://lccn.loc.gov/2021003872

DOI: 10.1093/oso/9780197563564.001.0001

1 3 5 7 9 8 6 4 2

Paperback printed by Marquis, Canada
Hardback printed by Bridgeport National Bindery, Inc., United States of America

Dedicated to Dave

Contents

Acknowledgments

This project began its life when I was a doctoral student at Dalhousie University. I was initially interested in forgiveness, then anger, then finally hope. At some point, I realized that I wouldn't have much to say about forgiveness until I thought more about anger. And it was reading Sue Campbell's influential "Being Dismissed: The Politics of Emotional Expression," then tracing back to Lynne McFall's "What's Wrong with Bitterness?" cited in that article, that brought me to feminist approaches to hope in the first place. If bitterness involves a loss or absence of hope, as I found myself thinking, then what is hope? I am grateful to the Department of Philosophy at Dalhousie for being so supportive of me and my early work investigating these questions.

I am especially grateful to Chike Jeffers, Greg Scherkoske, Susan Sherwin, and Lisa Tessman, who helped me develop early versions of the ideas in this book. They have all been sources of insight, support, and guidance for many years. I also owe a great deal of thanks to Cheshire Calhoun, who originally suggested that I think about a book at the 2016 Nature and Norms of Hope Workshop at the University of Notre Dame. Cheshire's feedback on the manuscript, and ongoing support, made writing a book seem like something I could actually do.

During my time as a residential dissertation fellow in the Hope and Optimism: Conceptual and Empirical Investigations project at Cornell University, I learned much about hope from conversations with Luc Bovens, Andrew Chignell, Alex Esposito, Nicole Hassoun, Miriam McCormick, Michael Milona, Hannah Tierney, and Andre Willis and through conferences and workshops that brought hope scholars in different disciplines together from across the world. I used to be more critical of hope than I am today, in part thanks to my experience in this project.

David Hunter, Mercy Corredor, Michael Milona, and Catherine Rioux all read the manuscript in full as part of a Zoom book club generously organized by David during our collective COVID-19 isolation. I am very grateful for these philosophers' valuable feedback on the manuscript, which helped me reframe and strengthen many arguments and examples in the final stages of writing. Colin Macleod and Audrey Yap also provided feedback on multiple chapters that helped me strengthen the book significantly.

Many other scholars have contributed to ideas in this book through conversations and written feedback that have shaped my thinking about this project. Thanks especially to Clifford Atleo, Claudia Blöser, Barrett Emerick, Matt Hernandez, Chris Howard, Graham Hubbs, Alice MacLachlan, Ben Mitchell-Yellin, Colleen Murphy, Maura Priest, Titus Stahl, Olúfẹ́mi Táíwò, students at the University of Victoria, students at Sam Houston State University, and anonymous reviewers at various journals. I also received valuable feedback from audiences at the New Directions in the Philosophy of Hope conference at Goethe University (2018); the Philosophy, Politics, and Economics Society Meeting in New Orleans (2018); the Hope and Optimism Midpoint Conference in Estes Park (2016); the Hope, Social and Political Perspectives Workshop at the University of Groningen (2016); and the Notre Dame Hope and Optimism Workshop at the University of Notre Dame (2016). I am also grateful to audiences who attended my colloquium talks at Dalhousie University, Sam Houston State University, and the University of Redlands, and my job talks at various institutions that shall remain unnamed.

I was very lucky to have had Lucy Randall and Cheshire Calhoun as editors, who both believed in this project from the beginning and whose encouragement kept me going as the book evolved. The reviewers at Oxford University Press, Adrienne Martin and an anonymous reviewer, were also the best reviewers for the book I could have hoped for. Their suggestions and criticisms on multiple drafts transformed the book into something I am very proud of. I am particularly indebted to Adrienne for her ongoing mentorship throughout my writing process and for pushing me to continue working on parts of the book that needed improvement even when I felt as though I had nothing left to say. I did have more to say, and the book is now much stronger. Thanks also to Hannah Doyle for editorial assistance and Lisa Fedorak for help preparing the index. All remaining errors are very much my own.

I am grateful to family and friends for continuing to encourage me throughout these many years of writing, especially my mom Kristine, stepdad John, and sister Sarah, who were much more optimistic that I'd finish and publish this book than I was. And I owe everything to Dave Dexter, the love of my life and best person I know. Dave read multiple drafts of the manuscript in their entirety, and his insights have contributed to every chapter and argument in the book. Dave's love and unshakable faith in me have sustained

me since I was a first-year doctoral student trying to find my path in philosophy. I would be lost without him.

Sections from "Hope's Place in Our Lives" and "The Value and Risks of Hope" were published in the *Journal of Social Philosophy* 50, no. 1 (2019): 28–44. Parts of "Losing Hope, Becoming Embittered" were published in *Hypatia* 32, no. 2 (2017): 363–379. I am grateful to these journals for their permission to reuse these works in the book.

Introduction

Oppression and the Question of Hope

I'm sure that all readers can remember times at which they were told to "be hopeful," to "never give up hope," and that "there is always room for hope." Hope, we learn at a very young age, is always good to have. Fortunately, too, there is apparently always hope to find. If we focus hard enough, we are supposed to be able to sustain hope—even when the world around us is frightening, dark, and unjust. Losing hope, or being suspected of losing hope, is often met with condemnation. "You shouldn't get bogged down in negative thinking like that. Stay hopeful!" we often hear from our family, friends, and the media. But what is this thing "hope" that ends up in so many sayings, news headlines, and inspirational quotes? And why is hope so valuable that we are so often urged to preserve and protect it?

This book is about the role of hope in human life, particularly in the lives we lead as moral, social, and political beings. It is about the nature and value of hope in the real world in which we live, a non-ideal world that includes suffering, disadvantage, luck, violence, harm, and loss. I want to understand what human agents hope for in this world, whether hope is valuable to us as we navigate our vulnerabilities and the hardships of life, and the relationship between hope and other elements of our psychologies including expectation, trust, anger, and faith. This project is, ultimately, an inquiry in moral psychology: a field concerned with how "we function as moral agents" and the roles of cognition, perception, and emotion in moral agency (Walker 2004, x).[1]

The approach to hope I take is quite different from how philosophers have traditionally approached the subject. Discussions of hope in the

---

[1] As Margaret Urban Walker (2004) explains, philosophical moral psychology is part of ethics. It is a descriptive and normative project that "discovers our real possibilities and limits, and assesses morally our adequacy for living our lives" (xiii). Although it is not itself empirical, philosophical moral psychology "can and should take a searching and critical view of scientific claims" (xiii). Walker's description of moral psychology captures how I characterize my work.

Hope Under Oppression. Katie Stockdale, Oxford University Press. © Oxford University Press 2021. DOI: 10.1093/oso/9780197563564.003.0001

philosophical literature have typically taken place in the existential and pragmatist traditions. Until recently, hope had earned surprisingly little attention in analytic philosophy, the field in which I situate my work.[2] But beginning in the 1950s, analytic philosophers began to see the relevance of hope to areas of the discipline such as epistemology, rational decision theory, and moral psychology. Hope, most of us agree, involves some combination of belief and desire; and realizing that hope involves cognitive and conative elements, philosophers interested in rationality and motivation were naturally drawn to think about hope. In 2014, Adrienne M. Martin published her highly influential *How We Hope: A Moral Psychology* and proposed a sophisticated theory of hope, its relationship to faith, and the role of hope in interpersonal relationships. The John Templeton Foundation launched the Hope and Optimism: Conceptual and Empirical Investigations project at the University of Notre Dame and Cornell University that year, bringing together philosophers, social scientists, and religious studies scholars from around the world to explore hope, optimism, and related states.

Although investigations of hope once lay at the periphery of analytic philosophy, there is growing interest in different facets of the subject. My own interest in hope emerged as I engaged more with feminist approaches to moral, social, and political philosophy. Feminist perspectives have helped to make visible the ways in which persistent, widespread, and multifaceted forms of oppression structure certain individuals' lives, oppressions based not only on gender but also on race, class, sexual orientation, disability, and other features of social difference. Oppression is commonly theorized as a type of structural or social injustice that confines, restricts, or immobilizes people in virtue of their membership in certain social groups (Frye 1983; Young 1990; Cudd 2006). As Marilyn Frye (1983) famously argues, the experience of oppression is analogous to that of a bird locked away in a cage. If you look closely at just one wire, you do not see the other wires, and you may wonder why the bird doesn't just fly around it and escape. To understand that the bird is caged in, you must step back and look at the cage macroscopically. Only then does it become obvious that the bird is caught within a network of systematically related barriers and forces (Frye 1983, 5).

Taking a macroscopic perspective involves a shift in focus from the individual to the collective and institutional. We might ask: How is a particular

---

[2] Hope had also earned surprisingly little attention in psychology. Matthew W. Gallagher (2018) notes that "with other positive psychology constructs, hope was largely ignored as a topic of study for much of the 20th century" (3).

moral injury connected to and facilitated by a broader system of oppression? For example, how is the murder of a particular Indigenous woman in Canada connected to the systemic injustice of widespread missing and murdered Indigenous women, girls, and two-spirit people? Or how is a suicide of an LGBTQ+ youth connected to the systemic injustice of suicides by LGBTQ+ youth, and how has structural oppression led to this devastating pattern? Taking a step back to examine moral problems macroscopically is necessary to understand and address oppression, but it can be as discouraging as it can be enlightening for the moral agent who does so. Shifting one's perspective so that one can better see just how pervasive and often hidden these injustices are may cause the moral agent to doubt whether oppression will ever be eliminated.

The situation becomes worse when one notices the limitations of the bird-cage analogy. It is not the case that individuals who are oppressed are locked in the same cage, experiencing the same forces and barriers in their everyday lives. As Kimberlé Crenshaw (1989) and feminists who take intersectional approaches to feminism have made clear, many individuals occupy multiply marginalized social locations (for example, Black women) that cause them to experience multiple and sometimes fundamentally different oppressions than individuals who occupy singly marginalized social locations. When one comes to realize that there are multiple and intersecting systems of oppression at work, the possibility that oppression will end can seem much farther out of reach. Even worse, oppression operates in the lives of members of oppressed groups along multiple dimensions: politically, in the denial of certain rights; socially, in the practices and norms that become dominant in a society; economically, in unequal pay and employment discrimination; epistemically, in the dismissal and silencing of people's testimony; and psychologically, in the psychological and emotional burdens and harms that members of oppressed groups face.

Reflecting on these insights about the nature and scope of oppression can lead one to feel overwhelmed, discouraged, and even hopeless.[3] Unsurprisingly, perhaps, the language of hope and hopelessness is common in news headlines about the injustices facing those who are oppressed in our world. Consider these sadly familiar examples: "From Horror to

---

[3] Similar reflections led Sandra Bartky (1990) to remark: "Because of the interlocking character of the modes of oppression, I think it highly unlikely that any form of oppression will disappear entirely until the system of oppression as a whole is overthrown" (32).

Hopelessness: Kenya's Forgotten Somali Refugee Crisis" (Human Rights Watch 2009); "Report: Syrian Refugees Face a 'New Level of Hopelessness' as Border Controls Tighten" (Naylor 2014); and "Losing Hope, Some Migrants are Starting to Leave Europe" (Decamme 2016). They concern over 79.5 million people around the world who have been forcibly displaced from their homes, including 26 million refugees fleeing war, violence, and persecution in countries such as Syria, Afghanistan, South Sudan, Myanmar, and Somalia. The Americas, too, have seen an increase in refugees and asylum-seekers hoping to escape violence in El Salvador, Honduras, Guatemala, and Venezuela (UNHCR 2019). But those who reach the United States to request political asylum have found themselves in detention facilities plagued with filth, overcrowding, and inadequate nutrition and healthcare and subjected to abuse and neglect (Gumbel 2018). Dulce Rivera, a transgender detainee, testified that in these dehumanizing conditions "you have no hope" (Rappleye et al. 2019).[4] Rivera's testimony was before the coronavirus pandemic, which left detainees among the most vulnerable to infection and death (Openshaw and Travassos 2020). Human rights violations in US detention facilities have also been exacerbated by the Trump administration's "zero-tolerance" policy on immigration consistent with Trump's own racist, white nationalist, and anti-LGBTQ+ rhetoric.

The United States has joined, and exacerbated, the rise of ethnic politics worldwide. In India, a surge of Hindu nationalism has left Muslims in fear that they will be lynched if they are found walking alone; in Sri Lanka, the rise of nationalist and sectarian politics was linked to the bombing of Christian churches and hotels that killed nearly 300 people by the terrorist organization National Thowheeth Jama'ath; and political parties with nationalist, anti-immigrant agendas have gained prominence across Europe (*BBC News* 2019a; Beech, Bastians, and Schultz 2019). In Myanmar, the political oppression of the Rohingya people by the Buddhist state has caused over 742,000 refugees to flee to Bangladesh following an outbreak of military violence including murders, torture, and gang rapes of Rohingya women and girls (UNCHR 2019; Human Rights Watch 2017). Human Rights Watch (2017) interviewed Rohingya women who reported walking to Bangladesh in agony up and down hills made slippery by monsoon rains, including pregnant women who were forced to give birth on the journey. Survivors suffer from

---

[4] Dulce Rivera, like many other LGBTQ+ and disabled detainees, was placed in solitary confinement for no other reason than her social identity (Rappleye et al. 2019).

depression, post-traumatic stress disorder, physical injuries, and infections, but they do not have access to basic physical or mental health care.

The differences between my own life, as a privileged white woman living in Canada, and Rohingya refugee women's lives abroad are striking and profoundly unjust. Whereas I find myself hoping for tenure and a happy, healthy future, what might these women *hope* for, from the oppressive conditions in which they live?

The monsoon rains in Bangladesh, along with droughts, landslides, flooding, and tropical storms, are among the many harmful outcomes of human-caused climate change, a now very obvious threat to our planet—and, I would add, a threat to hope. As political theorist David Moscrop explains, the overwhelming amount of news from scientists, journalists, and scholars about the devastating effects of climate change can result in feelings of anger, fear, and hopelessness on the part of those who are paying attention (Moscrop 2018). And while some of us can ignore climate change from our privileged geographical and social locations, the most disadvantaged in our world are feeling its dramatic effects (Environmental Justice Foundation 2018).[5] Indigenous peoples across the world who have already been displaced from their lands, cultures, and ways of life due to settler colonialism are among the most likely to be harmed, and Indigenous women and girls are particularly at risk (Vinyeta, Whyte, and Lynn 2015). In Guatemala, Maya Q'eqchi' women and girls were beaten and gang raped in their village of Lote Ocho by police, military, and security personnel with direct ties to Hudbay Minerals—a Canadian oil company with a mining project in the region (Kassam 2017). In Fort McMurray, Alberta; Fort St. John, British Columbia; and Williston, North Dakota, hundreds of men from out of province/state come to work for resource extraction companies in what are known as "man camps," whose existence has led to an increase in sex crimes against local Indigenous women (Sweet 2014; Amnesty International 2016; Estes 2019).[6]

Examples like these ones help to illustrate that climate injustice is inseparable from colonialism and sexist oppression, which themselves (and together) harm so many lives on this planet. And while harmful resource

[5] Approximately 8 million people have been impacted by severe flooding leading to a loss of homes and damaged schools and farmlands, and hundreds of thousands of people have been forced into emergency shelters (Vidal 2018).

[6] There are, relatedly, thousands of missing and murdered Indigenous women, girls, and two-spirit people across Canada and the United states (Urban Indian Health Institute 2018; National Inquiry into Missing and Murdered Indigenous Women and Girls 2019). Indigenous people have known about the crisis, and have been attempting to address it, for decades.

extraction activities continue, expand, and exacerbate other injustices, the planet is itself at terrifying risk. The United Nations Intergovernmental Panel on Climate Change has warned that the world has just twelve years to stop the global temperature from rising beyond 1.5°C, with the cochair of the working group Debra Roberts declaring that she hopes the report "mobilises people and dents the mood of complacency" (Watts 2018). Climate change, Roberts notes, can itself lead to feelings of helplessness and despair. Yet despite repeated warnings from climate scientists, and despite hurricanes, droughts, flooding, extreme heat, forest fires in the arctic, sinking island nations, and more, the problems of complacency, willful ignorance, and strategic political denial persist. Politicians in the United States motivated by an interest in maintaining their own political power continue to accept millions of dollars from the oil and gas industry, then find themselves denying climate change or significantly downplaying its harms as well as humanity's role in the crisis.

Hope can be hard to come by for many of us when we take a hard look at the magnitude and severity of climate injustice. Yet many politicians, activists, and scientists continue to call for hope (e.g., Solnit 2018; Climate One 2019; Davey 2019).[7] As atmospheric scientist Katharine Hayhoe argues, "What we need is rational hope. Rational in that we understand the magnitude of the problem that we have but hope in that we are motivated by the vision of a better future" (Climate One 2019). We witnessed similar calls for hope during the COVID-19 pandemic as scientists and governments mobilized to find a safe and effective vaccine (UN News 2020). In a virtual press conference, United Nations Secretary-General António Gutteres, reflecting on the hundreds of thousands of lives lost, said, "We despair that many more [deaths] will follow," but he then emphasized that "our voice has been clear, calling for solidarity, unity, and hope." One wonders whether these agents in positions of power actually are hopeful themselves, or whether they just believe that hope is a necessary political strategy to motivate action and keep citizens calm—that hope is our only way through.

In my own moral reflections, confronting these and many other persistent, widespread, and multifaceted forms of oppression in our world has led me

---

[7] Christiana Figueres, former executive secretary of the United Nations Framework Convention on Climate Change, has launched Global Optimism, an initiative that aims for the "transformation from pessimism to optimism" to bring about social and environmental change (Global Optimism 2019). As we will see, optimism involves more confidence than hope. It is an even stronger attitude to call for in the face of climate change.

to struggle with hope. How can we hope to build a just world in the face of
so many overlapping forms of oppression that are not going away any time
soon? How can we sustain hope in the face of persistent individual, collective, and institutional failures on the part of privileged members of society
to respond in appropriate ways to past injustices and those that are continuing? How can we hope for just outcomes in the future when injustices in
the past have been left unaddressed? Is it even rational to hope under these
conditions? And as I struggle with hope from my own position of privilege,
I wonder how individuals with far less social and political power than I can
hope for change in their own lives within the confines of their oppressions.[8]
And as Ann C. Cudd (2006) reminds us, "Oppression often seems to flourish
when kept in place . . . by willing, or at least grudging, compliance by the oppressed" (11). Oppression can become internalized in the minds of the oppressed. So how might oppression shape what people hope for or diminish
their hopes, preventing them from forming hopes for a better life and world?

These are some of the questions that have inspired the topic of this book,
some of which call for empirical investigation, while others are appropriate
subjects of philosophical analysis. They have led to me to explore the very
nature and value of hope, the risks and dangers of hope, the relationship between hope and other elements of our psychologies, and the role of hope in
collective struggles against oppression. I wondered: If we begin from the recognition that all human beings exist, deliberate, choose, and act from within
complex systems of privilege and oppression that structure our world, what
insights might we gain about hope? This question has been at the back of my
mind since I began thinking about this project, and it guides the motivation
and approach I take to the issues explored all the way through.

Despite the very real barriers to hope in the face of oppression, people
are still engaging politically. In 2016, the NoDAPL grassroots movement brought together thousands of Indigenous Water Protectors from
the Standing Rock Sioux tribe and their allies to protest the construction
of the Dakota Access Pipeline, a 1,172-mile-long pipeline that would run
through unceded territory, crossing under the Missouri River and threatening Standing Rock's water supply (Estes 2019, 2). Although NoDAPL
was ultimately unsuccessful at preventing the construction of the pipeline,

---

[8] My own struggles with hope are not unique among feminist scholars. As Rebecca Coleman and
Debra Ferreday (2010) point out: "In recent years, feminism has seen the production of a prevailing
mood of hopelessness around a generational model of progress, which is widely imagined to have
'failed'" (313).

many Water Protectors testified to a new hope that has inspired continued resistance to colonial violence and environmental injustice (Hayes 2018).[9] Extinction Rebellion, too, has arisen as a powerful international force fighting ongoing climate injustice across the world. Similarly, despite the systemic violence against Black people in America and elsewhere in the world, Black Lives Matter is still hard at work resisting anti-Black racism. And the MeToo Movement, founded by Tarana Burke in 2006, has emerged as a powerful movement challenging sexual violence against women, with Oprah Winfrey declaring at the 2018 Golden Globes that "a new day is on the horizon" (Demille 2018).

These are just a few examples of groups that have emerged in what might otherwise seem like a hopeless political climate to resist the serious, persistent, and far-reaching forms of oppression in our world. What seems clear is that people are obviously motivated to challenge the powerful agents sustaining and worsening conditions for members of oppressed social groups, whether they have hope that their actions will make much of a difference or not. This is an example of the kind of phenomena I am interested in, of the ways in which people form and lose hopes for their own lives and the lives of those they care about, how they pick up the shattered pieces of their lives and continue fighting for what they believe is morally right and just, and what is going on with moral character as agents face oppression. This book is, as one might guess, personal as well as political. It explores an attitude that many of us struggle with in our own lives while at the same time offering conceptual resources for understanding what it looks like to experience, lose, and rebuild hope in our current world.

The arguments in this book developed and evolved over the past several years. In 2016, I joined the Hope and Optimism project at Cornell University, where I had the opportunity to benefit from thinking about hope alongside some of the leading scholars of hope in the world—philosophers, psychologists, sociologists, and religious studies scholars. My own approach to hope has been profoundly influenced by this experience. Although I write as a philosopher, I engage with literature across these various disciplines as well as scholarship in feminist theory and critical race theory. I see the project of understanding the nature, value, and risks of hope in human life as necessarily interdisciplinary, and I hope that this book speaks not only to

---

[9] Menominee writer and activist Kelly Hayes (2017) remarks that "for Native people, 2016 was a year of tension, hope, and action."

philosophers interested in hope, oppression, and moral psychology but to scholars drawn to these topics from other fields as well.

In addition to a multidisciplinary approach to hope, this book is guided by three key methodological commitments. First, I do not think that it is necessary to find a perfect theory of hope before addressing the experiences, potential value, and role of hope in human life. When the focus of inquiry is not just hope itself but hope under conditions of oppression, it seems apt to examine how hope operates in real people's lives to better understand what, exactly, it is for them. Second, and relatedly, the search for universal features of hope might mask the ways in which individual, social, and political differences shape how people hope, the specific hopes they come to form, and how their hopes are evaluated by themselves and others. For this reason, I spend little time defending a particular theory of hope and spend the earlier chapters highlighting the importance of focusing on the relevance of human difference to experiences of hope. I often rely on testimony of people's lived experiences, which, I believe, is essential to articulating an accurate moral psychology of the emotions. Third, hope must be understood not in isolation but as an attitude that interacts with other mental states to influence how people experience and engage with the world. Throughout the book, I shed light on the relationship between hope and a range of related states including fear, trust, anger, bitterness, despair, and faith.

The first two chapters explore the nature and value of hope. In chapter 1, "Hope's Place in Our Lives," I address the debate about what exactly hope is, highlighting points of agreement between philosophers about the nature of hope and its connection to human agency and wellbeing. I understand hope, roughly, as a way of seeing or perceiving in a favorable light the possibility that a desired outcome obtains. This understanding of hope is consistent with, or at least similar to, many plausible accounts of the nature of hope in the literature (e.g., Walker 2006; Meirav 2009; Martin 2014; Calhoun 2018; Milona and Stockdale 2018). And although there remains significant room for debate about how to precisely characterize hope (a question very much alive in philosophy today), I for the most part set this debate aside. Theorizing the constituent features of hope in the abstract leaves us with many interesting philosophical puzzles and important lines of inquiry but is less apt when the focus of inquiry is experiences of hope in diverse sorts of human lives.

I shift focus, instead, toward the relationship between hope, agency, and the self. This discussion engages with the question of who is hoping and the relevance of power, privilege, and disadvantage to experiences of hope. I show that hope involves an explicit or implicit acknowledgment of the insufficiency of one's own agency in bringing about the hoped-for outcome. In other words, when we hope, we recognize our limitations as agents in our capacities to affect the world. And in societies structured to award privileges to some people at the expense of others, we can see that the hopes of members of privileged groups are often more likely to be realized than the hopes of members of oppressed groups. Oppression can thus be understood as a threat to hope. Beyond shaping the character of people's hopes or what they end up hoping for, oppression creates conditions under which members of oppressed groups must "hope against hope" for outcomes that are highly unlikely to be realized, if they are capable of sustaining hope at all.[10] I then offer an account of what it looks like to lose the capacity for hope: the ability to cultivate and sustain hopes for one's own life and future. Not only can oppression threaten and diminish individuals' hopes for this or that outcome; it also threatens and damages the very ability to form and pursue those hopes.

One of the major challenges for the philosophy of hope is figuring out the value of hope for people as they navigate the unjust and uncertain world in which we live. In chapter 2, "The Value and Risks of Hope," I defend the importance of first-personal assessments to thinking about the value of hope. Given the intrinsic value of hope to many of us, as well as barriers that outsiders sometimes face in understanding the hopes of others, it is often hopeful people themselves who are best suited to appreciate the value of their hopes. But recognizing the importance of first-personal assessments does not mean that people cannot be led astray in their hopes, so long as they endorse them. I argue that hope can be evaluated along multiple dimensions of assessment: epistemic and prudential (or strategic) rationality,[11] fittingness, and moral appropriateness. Each of these evaluative measures are technical terms that capture something significant to us as we face questions about our own hopes, in personal and political life, as well as the hopes of others. They inform the all-things-considered practical question of how, and for what, people should hope. And I suggest that Victoria McGeer's (2004) framework

---

[10] When individuals hope against hope, they hope in the face of evidence that strongly suggests the desire constitutive of hope is unlikely to be fulfilled (Martin 2014).

[11] Some scholars speak of the "prudential value/rationality" of emotions, while others speak of their "strategic value/rationality." I use these terms interchangeably and explain in detail the evaluative language used to assess emotions in chapter 2.

of *hoping well* holds promise for bringing these evaluative measures together in practice, while beginning to illustrate the social and political dimensions of hope's value as well.

In chapter 3, "Hope and Anger," I argue that that we cannot adequately understand how hope operates in conditions of oppression without considering how hope is often cultivated, sustained, and lost alongside the emotion of anger.[12] Many feminist and anti-racist scholars and activists have called attention to the prudential or strategic value of anger in responding to injustice. Inspired by this literature, I develop an account of the relationship between hope and anger. On the one hand, anger often responds to thwarted hopes. We place hope in other people, groups, and institutions to live up to the demands of morality and justice, and when they fail to do so, anger tends to ensue. But on the other hand, anger tends to be accompanied by the formation of new hopes. For example, anger can give rise to the hopes that wrongdoers will be punished, that they will apologize and display remorse, that the criminal justice system will do right by victims of systemic violence, that the injustice won't happen again, and so on. I suggest that these specific hopes all embody the more general hope for repair.

But the anger of members of oppressed groups is not commonly met with uptake, and their hopes for repair are often left unrealized. Philosophers have long been interested in how individuals can move from anger to forgiveness—for example, when their anger is met with a reparative response and individuals acquire moral reasons to forgive. Yet less attention has been paid to what happens to anger when the hopes connected to our anger responses are themselves not realized. In chapter 4, "Losing Hope, Becoming Embittered," I argue that anger can evolve into the emotion of bitterness. Bitterness, on my view, is paradigmatically a form of unresolved anger involving a loss of hope that an injustice or other moral wrong will be sufficiently acknowledged and addressed. In cases where bitterness responds to injustices that have resulted in irreparable damage, the emotion involves losses of hope one had (or might have had) for one's life. And I defend the idea that despite the emotion's reputation as an inherently bad and destructive emotion, bitterness can sometimes be an appropriate emotional response.

---

[12] I actually think that much can be learned by considering the relationship between many emotions, moods, character traits, and other mental states: not only hope and anger but also shame, sadness, depression, grief, etc. But in focusing on hope in contexts of oppression, contexts in which anger is a prominent emotion defended by scholars and activists, developing a philosophical analysis of the relationship between hope and anger is apt.

I then turn to the more uplifting goal of demonstrating the interrelated roles of hope and faith in collective struggles against oppression. In chapter 5, "Hope, Faith, and Solidarity," I develop an account of what I call *intrinsic faith* as a deep belief in the intrinsic value of one's actions or way of life. Intrinsic faith can flow from agents' spiritual faith, faith in humanity, and moral faith, all of which enable resilience to the conditions in which people find themselves. Faith can also serve as a bedrock for the renewal and strengthening of hope, even in the face of seemingly insurmountable setbacks and failures. Faith, in other words, is part of the story of what brings people together in solidarity against oppression. And through what I call moral-political solidarity—that is, solidarity based in a shared moral vision carried out through political action—a new hope can emerge. Joining with others who share one's experiences or commitments for a better life and world and uniting with them in collective action can restore and strengthen hope for the future when hope might otherwise be lost.

The final chapter connects literature on collective emotions to the philosophy of hope. I argue that one form of hope that emerges in solidarity movements is *collective*. There is growing literature on collective emotions that stretches across philosophy, psychology, and sociology;[13] and I draw upon insights about the nature of collective emotions to develop a theory of collective hope. I argue that hope is collective when it is shared by at least some others and when the hope is caused (or strengthened) by activity within a collective action setting. Focusing on hope that emerges in social movements, I suggest that collective hope emerges alongside a collective intention of the solidarity group to pursue a form of social justice. The object of collective hope borne of solidarity is, I argue, justice as a guiding ideal. And I demonstrate different ways in which individuals and groups hope for justice: by hoping for and pursuing the ideal of complete justice (what I call "utopian hope") or by hoping for and pursuing the melioration of injustices (what I call "modest hope"). I argue that both utopian and modest hope can be ways in which we hope well for justice.

Ultimately, this book seeks to offer a new voice to the literature on hope that challenges philosophers to take seriously the implications of the nature and scope of oppression, how its presence threatens the possibility of hope for many of us, and how we might—nevertheless—find ways to live on with hope together.

---

[13] See, for example, Christian Von Scheve and Mikko Salmela, *Collective Emotions: Perspectives from Psychology, Philosophy, and Sociology* (Oxford: Oxford University Press, 2014). This anthology brings together perspectives on collective emotions across these various fields.

1

Hope's Place in Our Lives

Hope is something that nearly all of us experience and struggle with in our lives. It is often quite easy to identify instances of hope: to know when we have it and when we have lost it. We are even quite good at recognizing hopefulness and hopelessness in others through their verbal and behavioral expressions. But while we seem to be skilled at recognizing hope when we see it, it is far less clear what hope *is*: what, exactly, the mental state of hope consists in.

Philosophers have made significant progress in recent decades proposing sophisticated theories of the nature of hope that aim to capture its essential components. This chapter sheds light on the debate about the nature of hope and suggests that hope is a way of seeing or perceiving in a favorable light the possibility that a desired outcome obtains. The understanding of hope I offer is intentionally at a high level of abstraction so as to remain fairly neutral with respect to many competing theories of the nature of hope in the literature. Setting the constitutive features of hope aside, I turn to the ways in which features of human difference influence hope. I develop a feminist approach to hope that attends explicitly to who is hoping and the relative powers of agents in their capacities to affect the world. This approach both enriches our understanding of the nature of hope and opens up space for seeing the relevance of power, privilege, and oppression to hope. Hope, we will see, is often promoted by people and institutions in positions of power to influence human psychology and behavior. It is thus natural for people to invest hope in these agents, acknowledging their power to influence or even realize some of our most important hopes. I end the chapter by exploring the phenomenon of investing hope in others and its relationship to expectation and trust.

Hope Under Oppression. Katie Stockdale, Oxford University Press. © Oxford University Press 2021.
DOI: 10.1093/oso/9780197563564.003.0002

What Is Hope?

In searching for hope, one thing to notice is that we often see the word "hope" alongside optimism, pessimism, and despair. Philosophers tend to agree that when we are optimistic that *p*, we are confident that *p* will occur. For example, it makes sense to say, "I don't just hope that *p*; I am optimistic that *p* will obtain!" where the expression of optimism reveals a higher degree of confidence that *p* will obtain than the hope. It is also possible to be pessimistic that *p* but still hope that *p*. One might say, "You know, I am pretty pessimistic, but I do still have some hope that *p* will occur." Despair, in contrast, is at odds with hope. We cannot both despair of an outcome and hope that it obtains. Hope is thus an attitude that is compatible with pessimism, embodies less confidence than optimism, and is inconsistent with despair. I set aside the question of what it means to be an optimistic, pessimistic, or hopeful person and focus primarily on the attitude of hope (rather than hope as a character trait).[1]

Philosophers also generally agree that hope involves at least the *desire* for an outcome and a *belief* that the outcome is possible (Wheatley 1958; Downie 1963; Day 1969; Ben-Zeʾev 2001).[2] This is what has become known as the standard or orthodox definition of hope, one which traces back to the modern period.[3] But many scholars have argued that the standard account of hope as a combination of desire and belief does not quite capture the nature of our more significant hopes (Bovens 1999; Pettit 2004; Meirav 2009; Martin 2014; Calhoun 2018). The main problem is that desiring an outcome and believing that it is possible that the outcome will obtain is compatible with different degrees of hope, and even despair. Martin's (2014) *Cancer Research* case is commonly cited to illuminate this problem. She considers

---

[1] There is a further question of whether hope is a virtue. It is famously one of the three theological virtues in Christianity (see Lamb 2016 for discussion). Philosophers have also defended hope as an intellectual virtue (Snow 2013), a virtue of character or moral virtue (Kadlac 2015; Snow 2019; Milona 2020), and a democratic, political, and civic virtue (Moellendorf 2006; Mittleman 2009; Snow 2018).

[2] There are a few notable exceptions. See Gabriel Segal and Mark Textor (2015) and Claudia Blöser (2019), who defend hope as a primitive or irreducible mental state. See also Michael Milona (2018), who argues that hope does not require belief but uncertainty. I begin with the more common view that hope involves the combination of desire and belief.

[3] Hobbes, for example, thought that hope is a complex state involving belief and desire (Hobbes 2018). Descartes, Spinoza, Locke, and Hume held similar views. Kant famously asked the question "For What May I Hope?," arguing that human beings may hope for their own happiness proportional to their virtue as well as immortality (Kant 1998). For a discussion of the philosophy of hope in the modern period, see Martin (2014) and Callina, Snow, and Murray (2018). For a discussion of hope in Kant, see Andrew Chignell (2019).

two hypothetical patients, Alan and Bess, both of whom suffer from terminal cancer and have exhausted standard treatment options. Alan and Bess enroll in an early-phase clinical trial of an experimental drug. They know that there is a less than 1 percent chance that they will receive medical benefit from the drug, and they share a strong desire to find a miracle cure. Alan notes that he has enrolled in the trial primarily to benefit future patients due to the unlikelihood of his hope's being realized. Bess, in contrast, appeals to her hope that she will be the 1 percent as "what keeps her going," and notes that she has enrolled in the trial because of this possibility (Martin 2014, 14–15).[4] Martin argues that Bess but not Alan can be described as "hoping against hope": her hope for a miracle cure is strong despite the odds against her. And Bess's hope is stronger than Alan's even though both patients assign the same probability estimate to the miracle cure and their desires for a miracle cure are equally strong. This case shows that to account for the fact that Alan's and Bess's shared hopes differ in strength, there must be some additional feature of hope beyond desire and belief.

Ariel Meirav (2009) points out that it is even possible for two people to have equivalent desires and to assign the exact same probability estimates to the desired outcome (such as in the case of Alan and Bess), while one person hopes and the other despairs. In other words, despair—that is, the opposite of hope—also involves the belief in the possibility that a desired outcome will obtain. Obviously, something is missing from the belief-desire account, and one of the central debates in the literature is about how to resolve this problem.

A number of competing theories have emerged to capture what is distinct about hope, with general consensus that hope involves desire, belief, and something else. Several different suggestions have been made by way of characterizing the additional element. For example, Luc Bovens (1999) suggests that hope involves mental imaging or conscious thoughts about what it would be like for the desired outcome to come about. McGeer (2004) proposes that hope involves engaging one's agency (e.g., in attitude, emotion, and activity) toward the desired outcome's obtaining in the future. Philip Pettit (2004) argues that hope consists in resolving to act as if the desired outcome will occur or is likely to occur. On Adrienne M. Martin's (2014) view, hope involves seeing the probability that the outcome might obtain as

---

[4] The *Cancer Research* case comes from Martin's encounters with real patient-participants in clinical trials during her postdoctoral fellowship at the National Institute of Health.

licensing hopeful activities such as fantasizing about, planning for, and antic-ipating the hoped-for outcome. And Cheshire Calhoun (2018) characterizes hope as a phenomenological idea of the future as one in which the desire con-stitutive of hope has been fulfilled. Although there are clear differences be-tween these and other accounts of the nature of hope in the literature, Martin (2019) suggests that a consensus view has emerged according to which hope consists of desire, belief, and a positively toned "what if" attitude toward the hoped-for end. For my purposes, working with something like the consensus view is sufficient. My goal is not to work out a perfect theory of what exactly hope consists in but to use philosophical insights about the nature of hope to explore experiences of hope in moral, social, and political life.

But one might still ask for some fuller characterization of this "what if" attitude that is partly constitutive of hope. I think of the third element as one that involves seeing or perceiving in a favorable light the possibility that the desired outcome obtains. In this way, hope seems similar to other emotions. In her defense of a perceptual theory of the emotions, Christine Tappolet (2016) identifies key similarities between emotions and sense perceptions that can be extended to capture the crucial "what if" attitude in hope. For ex-ample, both emotions and sense perceptions are conscious states with a phe-nomenological character or "what it is like" experience. There is something that it is like to have the visual perception of an object as blue, just like there is something that it is like to have the experience of fear and to see something as dangerous (Tappolet 2016, 19). However, in both cases, our "what it is like" experiences are not directly chosen or a result of inferences (as in other ac-tive mental states like belief and judgment). Instead, we are struck by them as largely passive responses to our environments. When I walk outside, I see (through my visual perception) mountains in the distance. And when I wit-ness a bike being stolen, I see (through my emotional experience of anger) the act as wrong. Such experiences are analogical: their content is sensitive to variations in what is perceived. When we see red objects, for example, our visual perceptions are sensitive to fine-grained variations in redness (e.g., faint red vs. bright red). Similarly, our emotions come in variations of in-tensity that correspond to degrees in how we evaluate situations. I might be *mildly* angry when a close friend forgets my birthday (seeing the act as only slightly offensive) but *strongly* angry when a friend says something blatantly sexist (seeing the act as strongly offensive).

When we hope—that is, when we see in a favorable light the possibility that a desired outcome obtains—this seeing-as emotional experience can be understood as analogous to sense perception. Hope, like sense perceptions, is a conscious mental state with a phenomenological character: there is something that it is like to be in a state of hope. It is also a largely passive response to situations over which we do not have direct control (Solomon 1976). We find ourselves with hopes that we did not directly choose to have, though we can (as in the case of other emotions) attempt to acquire or abandon hopes through focus, positive thinking, confronting evidence, and so on.[5] Hope has what Elijah Chudnoff (2012) refers to as presentational phenomenology: in hoping, the situation *appears* a certain way to the agent (Milona and Stockdale 2018). In particular, it appears as though the hoped-for outcome might really come about. For example, in *Cancer Research*, Bess sees in a favorable light the possibility that her hope for a cure obtains. She might remark, as Martin (2014) suggests:

> *I know the truth is that I almost certainly won't be cured by this drug . . . but, you know what? A tiny chance is better than no chance! That 1 percent is my lifeline, and I'm going to hang on to it.* (23)

Bess sees the 1 percent chance of a miracle cure favorably, whereas Alan, who is less hopeful, sees the chance of a miracle cure less favorably.[6] Alan's being less hopeful also illustrates that hope comes in degrees. We can be mildly, moderately, or strongly hopeful; and the strength of hope tracks the

---

[5] In contrast, Philip Pettit (2004) argues that in the case of our more substantial hopes, hope is "an intentionally sustained, essentially avowable response" (159). Although Pettit is right that agents do sometimes intentionally (attempt to) sustain their hopes because they find value in having hope, I am not convinced that we have as much control over our hopes as Pettit seems to think. Or, if Pettit identifies a distinct form of hope, then one might agree with Pettit but maintain that hope is paradigmatically a largely passive mental state. And Pettit, too, seems to agree about the passivity of emotions, moods, and feelings. He writes, for example, that when people learn they have a serious disease, they become "swamped by feelings of anxiety and incapacity"; and when we learn about the loss of a loved one, we become "numbed with grief and anger and desolation" (160). I treat hope as more similar to other emotions than Pettit.

[6] On Martin's view, the hopeful person sees the probability that the hoped-for outcome will come about as licensing them to treat their attraction to the outcome (and its desirable features) as sufficient reason for thinking, feeling, and/or planning in accordance with the hoped-for end (65). Not all philosophers endorse Martin's incorporation analysis of hope, but most agree that she is right that hope is a way of seeing, or representing, the hoped-for outcome.

Cheshire Calhoun (2018) also talks of hope as a way of seeing. On her view, substantial practical hope is a phenomenological idea of the future as one involving success. It differs from Martin's (and my own) characterization of hope in that Calhoun thinks of hope as *habituating* the future, taking the "view-from-then" (rather than the view-from-now). Ariel Meirav (2009) similarly characterizes hope as a way of seeing the external factor with the power to realize one's hope as working in one's favor. And Robert C. Roberts (2007) uses seeing-as, perceptual language in his analysis of Christian hope. Sabine Döring (2014), too, describes hope as an emotion that can be understood as a "felt evaluation" (124).

extent to which we see in a favorable light the possibility that the desired out-come will occur. I might, for example, be only mildly hopeful about getting a job because of how competitive I know the job market to be but strongly hopeful about receiving an offer after an interview that went very well.[7]

Hope, then, seems to be analogous to sense perception in a manner par-allel to other emotions (Roberts 2003; Roberts 2013; Tappolet 2016). Hope is a complex mental state that involves seeing in a favorable light the possibility that a desired outcome obtains—a kind of non-doxastic representation of the agent's situation. But as we have begun to see, hope is not just a cognitive state; it is also affective in character. As Peter Goldie (2004) explains, "When an emotion is directed toward its object, then this is a sort of feeling toward the object" (96). The relevant feeling is not a physiological feeling (although it may accompany physiological changes), like the feeling of one's heart pounding or the feeling of sweaty palms. Rather, it is an emotional feeling: a feeling that is directed toward an object in the world "beyond the bounds of the body," a feeling that is bound up with how we take in the world of ex-perience (Goldie 2009, 238). And seeing in a favorable light the possibility that a desired outcome obtains feels a certain way to the hopeful person. As Margaret Urban Walker (2006) suggests, when we hope, "there is a sense, and it can be an actual feeling, of 'pulling for' the yet undetermined resolu-tion one desires" (45). Martin (2014) describes this feeling as anticipating the hoped-for end's obtaining.[8]

Hope, then, can be understood as a way of seeing or perceiving in a favor-able light the possibility that a desired outcome will be realized. But there is also another feature of hope that is not so much experienced as it is im-plicit in hope's occurrence: that is, the insufficiency of one's own agency in bringing about the desired outcome. In other words, the presence of hope indicates that we explicitly or implicitly recognize that our own actions may not be enough to bring about whatever outcome we desire. As Margaret Urban Walker (1991) reminds us, human agency is "hopelessly 'impure'" in a way that Bernard Williams recognized (17). Williams (1981) explains: "One's

---

[7] Michael Milona (2018) argues that the strength of hope manifests along three related dimensions: motivational power (the stronger one's desire, the more inclined one is to help bring it about); attention (the extent to which we fixate on the desire's being fulfilled); and feeling (the affec-tive intensity of the hope).

[8] The phenomenological character of hope need not be pleasant. As I explain later on, how hope feels depends in part on what one is hoping for. If I hope to escape a dangerous situation, I might feel unpleasant anxiety and desperation. Hopes for entirely happy objects will feel different, such as when I feel hopeful excitement that the gift I am opening is the one I wanted. Given the wide range of outcomes for which we hope, it is not surprising that how hope feels to us is quite diverse.

history as an agent is a web in which anything that is the product of the will is surrounded and held up and partly formed by things that are not" (29). Human beings are impure agents, navigating a world in which our actions cannot make certain that the outcomes we desire will come about. In hope, we acknowledge our impurity and vulnerability.

I understand this feature of hope, acknowledgment of the insufficiency of one's own agency in bringing about the desired outcome, as central to hope because of what most philosophers agree is a belief constraint on hope. As Wheatley (1958) puts the point, "To hope, regarding the future, is in part to expect but not to be sure" (127). Pettit (2004) observes that "just as hope requires that one not rule out the hoped-for possibility, so it requires that one does not rule it in as a matter of absolute certainty either" (153). And this belief constraint on hope implies that our own agency is insufficient to bring about the outcomes for which we hope. Our belief in uncertainty with respect to the desired outcome arises in part because we judge that no matter how hard we try, nothing we can do can make certain that the desired outcome will obtain. Such things as luck, environmental conditions, and the agency of other people and institutions can affect the probability that all of our hopes will be realized. The outcomes for which we hope are always, as Meirav (2009) says, "beyond the reach of [one's] causal or epistemic powers" (228). Walker (2006) explicitly connects the uncertainty constraint on belief to agency. She explains that "hope goes to what hovers before us with a sense that all is not decided for us; what is not yet known is . . . open to chance and action" (45). As McGeer (2004) puts it, "Hope signifies our recognition that what we desire is beyond our current (or sole) capacity to bring about" (103).

Thus, hope can be understood as a mental state composed of a number of key elements: (1) the desire for an outcome, (2) the belief that the outcome's obtaining is possible but not certain, (3) seeing or perceiving in a favorable light the possibility that the desired outcome obtains, and (4) an explicit or implicit recognition of the limitations of one's own agency in bringing about the hoped-for end.

Hope also seems to tell us something about the kinds of creatures we are. We are creatures who, because of the constraints we necessarily and contingently face as agents, must depend on factors external to ourselves for many of our desires to be fulfilled. But while hope is one potential response to the inherent vulnerabilities we face, not all of us respond to constraints on our agency with hope. Some people are more prone to respond to agential limitations with frustration, doubt, sadness, and even despair rather than hope.

So there is an important question as to what, exactly, makes people with equivalent beliefs and desires see or perceive a situation differently, such that some of us end up hoping and others do not. How hope manifests in our lives depends upon who we are, both as individuals and as members of social groups.

Hope and Human Difference

One reason we hope differently is that when we hope, our individual subjectivity—that is, the unique angle from which we experience, interpret, and engage with the world—influences how we see the possibility of a desired outcome's obtaining.[9] Our character traits and past experiences all contribute to the emotions we come to have. As Cheshire Calhoun (2003) points out, all of us have "cognitive sets" or "interpretive schemes" that influence our emotions. These sets or schemes make up the unarticulated, pre-reflective portion of our cognitive lives. We passively acquire our cognitive sets as we navigate the world beginning in childhood, picking up new information that comes to bear on how we interpret and respond emotionally to our environments. For example, if I am a pessimist, I may be disposed to be less hopeful than an optimist with respect to any number of hopes I might come to form, seeing in an unfavorable light the very same probability estimates that others see favorably. Or if I have had bad luck with my health in the past, then when I find myself with a new illness, I may be inclined to perceive the possibility of recovery unfavorably and feel less hopeful about my fate. And if I am currently in a happy mood, then I may feel more hopeful about the possibility that certain hopes of mine will be realized than when I am feeling gloomy or depressed.[10]

And beyond these individual differences, our social, cultural, and religious identities can also affect how we hope. For example, living in a supportive community with healthy family, friend, and coworker relationships

---

[9] As Martha C. Nussbaum (2004) explains: "Emotions are not about their objects merely in the sense of being pointed at them and let go, the way an arrow is let go against its target. Their aboutness is more internal and embodies a way of seeing.... It is not like being given a snapshot of an object, but requires looking at it, so to speak, through one's own window" (188).

[10] As Roberts (2003) says of the emotions: "Beautiful surroundings, usual comforts, and the friendliness and calm of one's associates can increase one's joy, gratitude, or hope without being what any such emotion is about. All these factors have their effect, it seems, by contributing to one's impression of the character of the situation" (135).

and being part of a religious or cultural community may foster conditions under which the possibility of being disappointed is less likely to deter one from cultivating or sustaining hope.[11] If I am a member of a supportive community that will catch me when I fall, I might be more likely to embrace the inherent vulnerability that comes with hoping than if I have minimal social support in my life.

Experiences of hope are thus diverse, based on variation in our lived experiences across very different human lives. Many philosophers, though, have attended to commonality in thinking about the nature of hope, for example, by pointing out that hope is something universal to all human beings. As McGeer (2004) explains, "To be a full-blown intentional agent— to be a creature with a rich profile of intentional and emotional states and capacities—is to be an agent that hopes" (101). And, as she says rather strongly, "To live a life devoid of hope is simply not to live a human life; it is not to function—or tragically, it is to cease to function—as a human being" (101). Similarly, Aaron Ben-Ze'ev (2001) suggests that "hope is a kind of background framework that is crucial for human life: a person is someone with hope—someone 'without hope' is close to the grave" (475).

Although these philosophers are right that nearly all of us develop the capacity for hope,[12] focusing on commonality and universality might mask the ways in which individual, social, and political differences shape how we hope. In a world in which some people move about their environments more freely than others and hold more power to affect the future, there is need for perspectives that emphasize human differences in experiences of hope too. As we will see, understanding how social, political, and economic differences can affect hope will also be important in answering normative questions about hope in chapter 2. There we will consider to what extent people can be criticized for failing to hope, failing to act on their hopes, hoping too much or too little, or hoping for the wrong things. If, for example, some people's capacities for hope are threatened and damaged by their social, political, and economic circumstances (as I will argue), then such considerations ought to

---

[11] There are also cross-cultural differences in experiences of hope. James R. Averill, George Catlin, and Kyum K. Chon (1990) found that whereas Americans associate hope with coping, feeling, faith, prayer, belief, and trust, Koreans associate hope (*himang*) with ideal, ambition, pursuit, success, effort, and goal (76). My own perspective on hope is largely limited to North American understandings and experiences.

[12] Some of us with severe cognitive disabilities might not have the capacity for hope, though they very much count as human.

come to bear on whether it is reasonable for them to live without hope, or even to live in despair.[13]

McGeer's (2004) discussion of how the self develops the capacity for hope is a helpful starting point for understanding these differences. She explains that in their early experiences children are constantly confronted with limitations on their agency, leading to responses such as distress, frustration, and anger. Through parents' emotional support of children in the face of challenges that come their way, and through parents' assistance of children in navigating the limitations and potential of their agency in the world, children begin to develop hope as "a fundamental stabilizing and directive force in adult agency" (McGeer 2004, 107). But parental scaffolding is not enough for agents to maintain this capacity to respond to the world with hope. McGeer points out that even for adult agents, "it is others who invest us with our sense of how we can be in the world—who literally make it possible for us to take a hopeful, constructive stance toward the future" (108).

Although she does not situate her view within feminist philosophy, McGeer's attention to the importance of caregiving relationships to developing the capacity for hope echoes feminist philosophers' emphasis on the importance of relationships (especially relations of care) to the formation of the self. We are all born into relationships with others and continue to exist in interpersonal relationships that affect our capacities for and experiences of hope. Some people, in virtue of the support they receive from parents and peers, are more capable of cultivating and sustaining hope than others. This insight lays the foundation for understanding why some people find it more difficult to hope in the face of uncertainty than others whose interpersonal relationships have been more supportive. But I want to suggest that McGeer's analysis is, as it stands, incomplete. It is not only interpersonal relationships that affect how hope manifests differently in our lives. The social, political, and economic positions we occupy in relation to others can and do affect how we hope.

I think that we can strengthen McGeer's argument by taking a more explicitly feminist view, one that attends to who is hoping, including their social identities and relative powers to affect the world. Doing so illustrates the

---

[13] Although I do not take philosophers to be criticizing people outright for living without hope, it is common to critically judge others' hopes in everyday life—as the sayings go, "Don't give up hope," and "Never lose hope." Philosophical insights can help to illuminate what is going on in these encounters and to inform whether they are appropriate. And, as I show in later chapters, the language of irrationality and "hoping badly" can sound like a critique of individuals, when the apt normative criticism may be at the level of society (for fostering conditions under which hope is out of reach).

ways in which social difference affects (1) what people hope for and the degree to which they are hopeful, (2) the forms of agency they can and do engage in hoping, and (3) their capacities for hope. An important implication
of these feminist insights is that oppression is a threat to hope.

Oppression as a Threat to Hope

Feminists emphasize the relevance of human difference to moral, social, and
political thought. They highlight the ways in which systems of privilege and
oppression based primarily on gender but also race, class, ethnicity, ability
status, and other features of social difference structure our lives in important ways. Feminist philosophers working in moral psychology have called
attention to the socially situated nature of persons and the ways in which
relationships shape and constrain how people develop, change, deliberate,
choose, and act (e.g., Card 1996; Mackenzie and Stoljar 2000; Downie
and Llewellyn 2012). These relationships include not only interpersonal
relationships, such as our relationships to family members and friends, but
also public relationships based on social features of our identities—such as
the relationship between women and men. These relational features are not,
as Chandra Talpede Mohanty (2003) puts it, "static, embodied categories
but . . . histories and experiences that tie us together—that are fundamentally interwoven into our lives" (191). About her own identity, Mohanty says,
" 'Race' or 'Asianness' or 'brownness' is not embodied in me, but a history of
colonialism, racism, sexism, as well as of privilege (class and status) is involved in my relation to white people as well as people of color in the United
States" (191). In other words, our complex social identities place us into
relationships with histories, other people, social groups, and institutions.
These relationships all influence who we are and how we interact with
the world.

The relationships in which we are embedded are complex, experienced
together rather than in isolation. As Crenshaw (1989) and others working
within, and inspired by, Black feminism have made clear, the self is *intersectional*: it is a product of multiple social features of our identities interacting
in various ways to produce particular experiences. For example, the societal erasure of violence against Black women in America is unique to Black
women. The stories of police violence against Black citizens that we tend to
hear about and remember are stories about Black men; and the stories of

sexual violence against women that we tend to hear about and remember are stories about white women. Race and gender interact in this societal context, producing an injustice at the intersection of Black women's experiences.[14]

Reflecting on Black women's social location led the philosopher Sue Campbell (1994) to ask what women of color in America can hope for. And I suggest that an adequate understanding of hope requires attending explicitly to the various relations in which people are embedded and their lived experiences resulting from multiple and intersecting social features of the self. The relationships into which we are born and from which our characters develop affect our beliefs, desires, perceptions, and ultimately our hopes. Our beliefs and desires are part of who we are, and they, like other features of the self, are formed within the social and political contexts in which we exist. For example, how we are socialized very much affects the desires we form, including those desires that end up constituting our hopes. What we learn from our caregivers, teachers, and peers influences how we think, feel, and value. They also affect what we come to see as desirable and worth pursuing.

Where we are situated within systems of privilege and oppression can also influence the hopes we come to form. The ways in which oppression operates in particular individuals' lives varies, but the oppressed often find themselves subjected to various kinds of injustices such as employment and housing discrimination, poor education, lack of access to health care, violence, poverty, incarceration, and cultural dislocation. Living under oppression and being subjected to the threat and experience of injustices in virtue of one's membership in an oppressed social group can profoundly affect the content of the hopes one comes to form. For example, members of oppressed groups often form hopes based in their experiences living under the threat or experience of injustice[15]—such as the hopes to be free from violence, harassment, and neglect. People of color may form the hope that they will not be subjected to violence at the hands of police, a hope they form in response to

---

[14] The campaign #SayHerName was launched to create awareness about the prevalence and erasure of police violence against Black women. See, for example, Khaleeli (2016) for discussion.

[15] Empirical literature supports this claim. For example, Hilary Abrahams (2010) discusses women's hopes who experienced domestic violence based on interviews conducted over a period of seven years. One woman she interviewed remarked, "I hope I'm going to be strong enough to say 'too late'" (19). Abrahams suggests that listening to the "early hopes and dreams" of women who have been subjected to domestic violence demonstrates that they hope for "safety and security, to live without fear, to be free to act for themselves, and to be treated with respect and valued—the converse of the situations they had endured previously" (19). Abrahams also documents the connection between women's choices to go back to an abusive partner and "the hope that they can make the relationship change or that this time will be different or that their partner will have changed" (79).

the widespread use of excessive force by police against people of color under conditions of racial oppression. Or women may form the hope that they will not be subjected to sexual violence at some point in their lives, a hope that many women form in response to the widespread instances of sexual violence against women under conditions of sexist oppression. White people in the first case and men in the second generally do not have or need these hopes (*as* white people or men) because their safety is not threatened in virtue of their membership in a certain social group.[16]

And while oppression creates conditions under which members of oppressed groups may find themselves hoping that they will not be subjected to unjust forms of treatment because of their social identities, they may not (for very good reasons) have much hope that they will escape such treatment. History, past experiences, and their knowledge of present conditions may lead them to assign a low probability estimate to the possibility that their hopes will be realized. People of color may decide to avoid police at all costs because they do not have much hope that they will be safe in their interactions with police, and women may decide to avoid walking places alone at night because they lack hope that they will be safe alone on dark streets.[17] Living under oppression can thus shape the content of people's hopes, or what they hope for, as well as the degree to which they are hopeful that the outcomes they desire will obtain.

Interestingly, it is more common to talk of fear in these sorts of cases than it is to talk of hope. People of color fear the police, and women tend to fear men (specific men, as in cases of domestic abuse, or even most or all men, as in cases where women are traumatized by sexual violence in the past). But fear and hope are not at odds, and sometimes hope is based in a fear. When I find myself hoping that I will make it home safely, my hope is formed largely because I fear for my safety as a woman. I experience my hope as a *fearful hope*: a hope tainted by fear, not a hope accompanied by the sorts of pleasant feelings

[16] Class, ability status, sexual orientation, and other social markers will also influence how people hope. For example, a poor man living in a community that suffers from high rates of violence might form the hope to make it home safely at night, a hope that was influenced by his social location. But being a man does not by itself lead him to form the hope to make it home safely, whereas being a woman does itself (in many cases) lead women to form such a hope.

[17] This example will not cohere with every woman's experiences. Not every woman will hope, or even think about, her safety when she leaves home at night. But these women can imagine how trauma from being subjected to sexual violence in the past, living in an unsafe neighborhood without access to safe transportation, or having knowledge about widespread prevalence of attacks on women in the areas in which they live, etc., might (understandably) cause many women to form the hope that they will make it home safely. See Kimberlé Crenshaw (1991) for discussion of the ways in which "routine violence" often shapes the lives of women from multiply marginalized social locations.

that we tend to associate with hope. And it's not just that fear and hope are experienced together, in these cases, as a matter of emotional ambivalence—as when uncertainty gives rise to fear that a hoped-for outcome will not occur. In the case of fearful hope, fear constitutes hope. It changes the phenomenological character of the hope such that the hope is entirely negatively valenced. I have argued elsewhere that fearful hope is a distinct form of negatively valenced (i.e., unpleasant) hope that arises in response to a perceived threat. When one hopes to escape violence, harassment, or neglect, hope will not feel pleasant (at all) in the way that hopes for happy objects do (Stockdale 2019).[18] In other words, my fearful hope that I will make it home safely while walking home at night feels very different than my happy hope that the sushi will be as good as Yelp reviews promise.[19] Of course, hopes formed in oppressive contexts are not the only fearful hopes. A person might fearfully hope to escape death upon finding themselves at gunpoint in a random act of violence. The difference between fearful hopes under oppression and fearful hopes more generally is the systematic nature of fearful hopes in the former case: how one finds oneself fearfully hoping as a member of an oppressed social group.

Hoping under oppression is thus not always, or perhaps even typically, a pleasant experience. Although we commonly think of hope as a pleasant release for the mind, giving people space away from their difficulties to imaginatively inhabit a more pleasant future, hope is frequently an unpleasant attitude through which agents emotionally respond to the possibility of escaping dangerous conditions. And because members of oppressed groups face persistent threats to their safety and wellbeing as they navigate the world, oppression makes more ubiquitous the formation of fearful hopes, hopes that are—also because of oppression—often unlikely to be realized. In fact, oppression renders it unlikely for any number of people's hopes to be realized, not just the fearful hopes they form in response to their oppression. The hope to be successful in business, to live a long and healthy life, to raise one's child in a safe and supportive community—the probability that all of

---

[18] Michael Milona (2018) also makes the point that hope is not essentially pleasant. On Jack Kwong's (2020) view, *hopefulness* is pleasant, while hope need not be.

[19] Vincent Lloyd (2016) makes a similar observation, though not specifically focused on the relationship between hope and fear. He says, "The feeling of hope from a position of privilege is qualitatively difference from the feeling of hope from a marginal position. . . . Seeing a glass half full is quite a different experience when you are at a restaurant than when you are trudging through a desert" (173).

these hopes will be realized is affected by gender, race, class, sexual orientation, ability status, and so on.

Oppression can thus be understood as a threat to hope. It both threatens people's opportunities to form pleasant hopes for happy outcomes and creates unjust conditions under which certain people, in virtue of their social, political, and economic locations, must "hope against hope" for many of the outcomes they desire—if they are capable of sustaining hope at all. Hoping against hope is, as Martin (2014) argues, "hope for an outcome that, first, amounts to overcoming or at least abiding some profound challenge to one's values or welfare; and, second, it is an extremely improbable hope" (14).

To clarify, oppression threatens hope, but it does not necessarily succeed in damaging or destroying it. It is a remarkable fact that certain people are capable of sustaining hope despite the conditions in which they find themselves, and some members of oppressed groups are capable of sustaining hope even when their hopes are not likely to be realized. It is also the case that people who occupy positions of privilege are sometimes less hopeful about their own and others' circumstances than members of oppressed social groups.[20] But it is equally true that oppressive conditions can and do damage many individuals' hopes[21] (while, at the same time, conditions of privilege unjustly bolster possibilities for hope in others).[22] Some people living under oppression find it difficult and sometimes impossible to form hopes for their own lives, for the lives of their loved ones, and for improved social, economic, and political conditions more generally. As E. J. R. David and Annie O. Derthick (2014) argue, "Oppression is perhaps the most important

[20] This difference in how individuals experience the world in which they form hopes can be explained by the diversity of human characters, religious affiliations, education, cultures, degrees of social support, and their senses of community, among many other things.

[21] See, for example, Sarah A. Stoddard et al. (2011) for a discussion of the effects of poverty and violence on hope. On Syrian refugee children's hopelessness, see Leah James et al. (2014). Of nearly 8,000 participants, 26.3 percent reported feeling "so hopeless that they did not want to carry on living" (42). There are many more studies like these ones.

[22] What do the privileged find themselves hoping for? For me, it's tenure, good health, and a long and happy marriage. But these hopes are bolstered by my education, access to health care, socioeconomic status, and freedom to marry the person I love. They seemed out of reach, even for me, at many moments in my life. And others who are even more privileged than I am likely hope for more—the ability to travel the world and visit luxurious destinations, for example. Privilege bolsters possibilities for hope by opening up the range of outcomes that appear within reach to us, even if we can't be certain we will attain them.
Oppression, meanwhile, diminishes the range of outcomes that appear within reach. As Fayez, one Syrian refugee noted, "Our hope for the future is to just be in a safe environment. A country where our children can go to school and be safe and sound. We must hope that things can go from bad to better, not from bad to worse" (Oxfam America 2016). Whereas affluent, white parents might hope that their children get into Harvard, Fayez merely hopes for his children's safety from harm— and that things do not get worse.

sociopolitical factor that influences the entire range of [oppressed individuals'] psychological experiences" (2).

Oppression can threaten and damage hope through diminishing the likelihood that the hope will be realized, through a loss of desire, or both. A Black girl's hope to become an engineer might be threatened by messages girls receive about their abilities in math and science, and by seeing the white-male dominance of the engineering profession. She might end up hoping for other things in life, instead, such as a career in which Black women are more commonly represented. The Black girl's hope to become an engineer is also much less likely to be realized if she is living in poverty than if she comes from an affluent family. Our class status, which is affected by other social factors such as race, significantly affects the opportunities available to us. The teenager living in poverty may not have access to quality education; she may have no choice but to work part-time jobs to help support her family; she may therefore have little time to complete her homework and study; and she may suffer from health issues related to the economic and social problems she faces. Living in poverty creates a range of barriers to the possibility that the teenager's hope to become an engineer will be realized, and it diminishes her ability to engage in activities that will make the desired outcome more likely. The impoverished teenager may have no time, resources, social support, or energy to work toward her goal, and her hope to become an engineer may fade. As Walker (2006) points out, losing one's sense of agency "can lead to hopelessness, even if there remains some desire and sense of possibility" (61). Eventually, the teenager may even give up her desire to become an engineer altogether, believing that there is no point in desiring what will never be realized. Or the desire might diminish naturally as the teenager adapts to her busy, stressful, and demanding everyday life.[23]

Oppression can also threaten and damage individuals' very capacities for hope, or the ability to cultivate and sustain hopes for one's own life and future. Cheshire Calhoun (2008) calls attention to the ways in which certain background beliefs about one's agency, which she calls "frames of agency," must be secured in order for an agent to continue to take an interest in leading their own life and to be secured against conditions such as depression,

---

[23] Oppression might also cause people to form adaptive or deformed hopes based in what many scholars have called "adaptive preferences" or "deformed desires," such as the hopes of oppressed people who adapt to their social and economic situation by entering into gangs, adopting a subculture, and forming hopes that are intertwined with their social identities.

hopelessness, and despair. These frames of agency include having a sense that one's life has meaning, confidence in the efficacy of instrumental reasoning (or that one's actions will produce their intended effects), and confidence in one's relative security from profound misfortune and harm (Calhoun 2008, 198). In the absence of one or more of these frames of agency, agents might become depressed or demoralized, failing to see any point in engaging in the volitional activities of reflecting, deliberating, choosing, and acting altogether. They might, in other words, lose the ability to function as an agent. And since hope necessarily involves exercising agency in some way (e.g., in thought, feeling, and behavior), when one loses the ability to function as an agent, one loses the capacity for hope.[24]

I want to turn to a pressing and timely issue that I think these philosophical insights can help address. Indigenous scholars John Gonzalez, Estelle Simard, Twyla Baker-Demaray, and Chase Iron Eyes (2014) demonstrate the damages to Indigenous people's capacities for hope in North America that result from their experience living on reserves. Such communities tend to suffer from poverty, unemployment, a lack of access to healthcare and transportation, and other social issues brought about by colonialism and other forms of oppression. They explain:

> Internalized oppression . . . exists when indigenous people are *immobilized* and cannot be all that they want to be. This includes fulfilling their purpose in life. . . . In a contemporary context, it is one's inability to sustain one's family, and the truly devastating feelings this situation leaves on that person. It is the *powerlessness* when they cannot buy their child a winter jacket or boots because of the cut-backs to tribal or First Nation welfare programs. It is the *fear* a mother feels when she welcomes her baby into the world, because she knows the reality of child welfare. . . . At times, our internalized oppression is the *pain* and *anger* we feel about our situation in life: *We might not have a job, we are dependent on the reserve to make jobs, they give the jobs to non-natives, they have no job training programs, and so on*—all of which negatively exasperate a person's worth as a man or a

---

[24] What I am calling a loss of the capacity for hope is similar to what Calhoun in more recent work calls a loss of "basal hopefulness." Calhoun (2018) characterizes basal hopefulness as taking an interest in the future generally or globally, rather than taking an interest in pursuing particular future outcomes. Calhoun argues that basal hopefulness is lost in depression. She writes, "The depressed are not dispirited about this or that bit of the future, but about the future generally. They lose a globally motivating interest in The Future" (74).

woman. . . . In the end, internalized oppression is the *profound despair* when choosing suicide as the only option. (45)[25]

This passage suggests that the material and psychological effects of living under oppressive conditions that Indigenous people in North America experience can be so severe so as to lead to "profound despair," with devastating consequences.[26] The social, political, cultural, and economic realities that Indigenous people face can shatter the frames of agency they need to live on with hope, and in many cases, to live on at all. One's sense of purpose, confidence that one's actions will produce their intended effects, and belief that one is secure from profound misfortune and harm are often lost under conditions of poverty, colonialism, racism, and sexism that shape the lives of many Indigenous people.

There is empirical data that reveals the extent of the damages to Indigenous people's hopes. For example, in Pimicikamak Cree Nation, a community of 8,200 people, there were over 140 suicide attempts in a two-week period, and over 150 students in a local high school of 2,000 total students were on suicide watch in the spring of 2016 (Baum 2016). In Attawapiskat First Nation, a community of 2,000 people, eleven people attempted suicide on April 9, 2016, alone, and there were 101 suicide attempts from September to April of that year (Assembly of First Nations 2016). And at least one discussion paper reveals that Indigenous girls between the ages of 10 and 19 are 26 times more likely to die of suicide than non-Indigenous girls, concluding that these numbers likely reflect the disproportionate levels of violence with which Indigenous girls live (Federation of Sovereign Indigenous Nations' Mental

---

[25] Martin (2014) argues that suicide is sometime an act of hope, namely, the hope to end one's suffering. If this is right, then perhaps oppression is not a threat to the capacity for hope; it rather results in the formation of a particular hope for the end of suffering. With Gonzalez et al., I understand suicide in these sorts of cases not as an expression of hope for release from suffering but as a choice that is made out of the conviction that one can in fact end one's suffering through suicide. As one 16-year-old Indigenous girl, Karina, with suicidal thoughts remarked, "I felt like I had no other option; I felt hopeless" (quoted in Randhawa 2017).

    Even when people do formulate their suicidal thoughts and actions using the language of hope, we can still understand their capacities for hope as damaged inasmuch as the only particular hope they have left is to end their suffering. It is likely that offering hope or encouraging the person to maintain hope for their future (in the present life) would not do much good—and this is exactly what a damage to one's capacity for hope looks like.

[26] See, for example, Lisa M. Poupart (2003) for further discussion of the internalized oppression of Indigenous people. Jennifer White and Christopher Mushquash (2016) also discuss how colonialism and other forms of social injustice have caused, and exacerbated, suicide in the Canadian context as well as recommendations for suicide prevention and life promotion strategies. The authors point out that social inequities cause "high levels of hopelessness" (2), and they defend an approach to wellness from a First Nations perspective—of "fostering purpose, hope, belonging, and meaning" (3).

Health Technical Working Group 2017). These are devastating numbers, and the problem is widespread among Indigenous communities across the country and elsewhere in the world.[27]

Hope also features prominently in discussions about what is lacking in these communities and what is required to remedy the public health crisis. In response to the crisis in Attawapiskat First Nation and Pimicikamak Cree Nation, National Chief of the Assembly of First Nations Perry Bellegarde appealed to hope in his call for action:

> We need a sustained commitment to address long-standing issues that lead to hopelessness among our peoples, particularly the youth. And, we need to see investments from the federal budget on the ground in our communities immediately—to support our families to enjoy safe and thriving communities that foster hope. (Assembly of First Nations 2016)

Similarly, in his call for an emergency House of Commons debate to discuss the situation in Attawapiskat, New Democratic Party Member of Parliament Charlie Angus suggested that "the heartbreaking tragedy" should be turned into "a moment of hope-making . . . to start to lay the path forward to give hope to the children in our northern and all our Indigenous communities" (Parliament of Canada 2016).

But it is important to reflect on what it would mean to "make hope" or "give hope" to Indigenous Canadians and Indigenous people elsewhere in the world. While the philosophy of hope can help to shed light on what, exactly, the mental state of hope is, a feminist perspective helps call attention to the ways in which interrelated systems of oppression are responsible for bringing about the overwhelming sense of despair in these communities. It thus connects philosophical insights to what Indigenous scholars and activists have long been arguing (Talaga 2018) and suggests that if hope is something that individuals and communities need, then what should be offered is *reasons* for hope. Indigenous communities require not only the

[27] For example, in 2015, on Pine Ridge Reservation in South Dakota, home to the Oglala Sioux tribe, there were nine suicides and at least 103 suicide attempts by people ages 12–24 in a four-month period alone (Bosman 2015). In Australia, cultural dislocation, trauma, racism, alienation, and exclusion have been found to contribute to the disproportionate numbers of mental health issues, substance abuse issues, and suicides across Indigenous communities (Department of Health 2013). And in Brazil, Indigenous people are committing suicide at an average rate of 22 times higher than non-Indigenous Brazilians (Nolen 2017).

provision of culturally appropriate mental health resources[28] with the goal of encouraging individuals to cultivate hope for their own wellbeing but also committed social justice efforts that effectively address poverty, colonialism, sexism, and racism. Facilitating reasons for hope would involve dismantling systems of oppression that are directly tied to the devastating circumstances in which so many Indigenous people exist.[29]

We have yet to see evidence that these calls for hope, along with current public health strategies in place, have made a meaningful impact at the national level in Canada.[30] But what is clear is that we cannot understand Indigenous people's losses of hope without attending explicitly to the significance of colonial violence and other forms of oppression on their lives.

The Politics and Marketing of Hope

Politicians' responses to the suicide crisis in many Indigenous communities illustrate one way in which the language of hope figures into political discussions about how governments and citizens should address social, political, and public health issues. And perhaps hope really is part of what individuals and communities need in certain cases—it might be beneficial for individual and collective wellbeing, for example. But this example also sheds light on the fact that politicians and, as we will see, corporations and other agents in positions of power employ the language of hope to further their ends. Hope is not just a mental state that exists in individual minds. It is also a political and marketing tool that influences human psychology and behavior.

---

[28] Whereas Western mental health treatment focuses on the absence of mental illness, First Nations communities "see a strong connection between mental wellness and strong physical, spiritual, and emotional health; a connection to language, land, beings of creation and ancestry; the support of caring family and environment; and an interconnectedness enriched by hope, belonging, purpose, and meaning" (First Nations Information Governance Centre, quoted in the National Inquiry into Missing and Murdered Indigenous Women Final Report 2019, 465).

[29] As Poupart (2003) argues, "Indian people, as all Others, must refuse to participate in a mental-health industry that benefits from treating our social ills (substance abuse, depression, physical and sexual abuse) as individual pathologies or familial dysfunctions that are detached from Western cultural and historical forces. Such treatment programs, instead, ensure our complicity in patriarchal power and further promote our disempowerment by denying and invalidating the structural nature of our oppression" (97).

[30] For example, God's Lake First Nation declared a state of emergency in August 2019 after four youth committed suicide and 22 other suicide attempts were documented in the summer, with Chief Gilbert Andrews insisting that without a comprehensive plan in partnership with the federal government, the crisis would not end (Hirschfield 2019).

One of the most widely discussed recent politicians who has inspired hope is Barack Obama, who emerged as a symbol of hope for America beginning with his 2004 keynote address at the National Democratic Convention as a senator. The speech gained widespread attention, inspired Obama's 2006 book *The Audacity of Hope: Thoughts on Reclaiming the American Dream*, and ultimately helped him to win the 2008 presidential election. In his book, Obama explains what he means by the "audacity of hope," which is similar to how Martin (2014) characterizes "hoping against hope." The audacity of hope, a term borrowed from the pastor Rev. Jeremiah A. Wright Jr., refers to "the best of the American spirit" (Obama 2006, 356). It is

> having the audacity to believe despite all the evidence to the contrary that [Americans] could restore a sense of community to a nation torn by conflict; the gall to believe that despite personal setbacks, the loss of a job or an illness in the family or a childhood mired in poverty, [they] had some control—and therefore responsibility—over [their] own fate. (356)

Obama cites the audacity of hope as the spirit of his own family and the American story as a whole, offering a narrative of hope that functioned as a powerful political message that encouraged Americans to place their hopes in him. Evidence also suggests that Obama's politics of hope even increased American citizens' optimism about improved race relations in the country—a mental state that embodies more confidence than hope. In 2008, it was reported in the *Economist* that 80 percent of African Americans polled believed that Obama's victory was "a dream come true," and 96 percent thought it would improve race relations (Teasley and Ikard 2009, 418). And a 2009 *CBS News/New York Times* poll found that 59 percent of African Americans thought that race relations were "good," compared to 29 percent who thought so prior to Obama's election (Teasley and Ikard 2009).[31]

Of course, Obama is just one notable example of politicians who have used hope to drive their campaigns and political agendas. Justin Trudeau, the prime minister of Canada, declared in his 2015 victory speech that "a

[31] The hope of Obama was, it seems, largely lost under Donald J. Trump's presidency, with Trump declaring that "real power is—I don't even want to use the word—fear" (Tackett and Haberman 2019). If Trump inspires hope, it likely takes the form of a fearful hope, such as the hope to remove, exploit, or marginalize perceived threats to the economic prosperity of his base (e.g., immigrants and people of color). For discussion of the relationship between fear and hope in the formation of a political group's intention to perpetuate injustice (with a focus on genocide in particular), see Neta C. Crawford (2018).

positive, optimistic, hopeful vision of public life isn't a naïve dream; it can be a powerful force for change" (*MacLean's* 2015), with the slogan Hope and Hard Work driving the Liberal Party's political vision. And beyond these successful political campaigns, countless organizations and charities with particular moral and political goals have been established in hope's name. For example, in 2015, the Canadian Women's Foundation's Move for Hope and Shop for Hope campaigns fundraised $390,000 to "raise hope for women" who have experienced physical or emotional violence (Canadian Women's Foundation 2015). In 2000, the Aboriginal Healing Foundation in Canada established the Legacy of Hope: a national charity that aims to educate and raise awareness about the Indian residential schools and their ongoing impact on the relationship between Indigenous and non-Indigenous Canadians (Legacy of Hope Foundation n.d.). More recently, Indigenous youth have created #HopePact through the We Matter Campaign, which is a pact Indigenous youth can take in which they agree to "have hope together" (We Matter n.d.).[32] Not-for-profit organizations have recognized the power of hope in motivating people to respond to and resist injustice.

But it is not only charitable organizations seeking, in some way, to make the world a better place that use hope in marketing. For-profit corporations in capitalist societies have caught on to the benefits of offering hope in selling their products. In the cosmetics industry, Charles Revson of Revlon cosmetics declared, "In the factory we make cosmetics. In the drug store we sell hope" (Mastony 2009). Revson was aware that in a social order in which women are expected to conform to strict beauty norms and where their body parts are under regular scrutiny for how well they measure up to unachievable beauty standards, his cosmetic company could sell women hope. Lipstick and other products designed to correct, mold, or enhance women's appearance were marketed as the key to achieving their beauty goals. The brand Philosophy is much more explicitly using hope in marketing at the time of writing. They sell an expensive facial moisturizer called Hope in a Jar whose label reads "philosophy: where there is hope there can be faith. where

---

[32] Indigenous youth are acting as "Hope Ambassadors" as part of this campaign. For example, Danika Vessel, a 27-year-old Métis woman from Temiskaming Shores in Ontario is working to launch a local support group for Indigenous youth. She remarked in an interview: "Practicing culture, having that support, being part of a group where you can meet for ceremony are really important to life promotion. It gives you hope" (Deer 2019). Indigenous youth like Vessel who are acting as "Hope Ambassadors" help us to see that hope branding sometimes really does reflect the work an organization is doing, and that hope can come from culture and community—a theme we will revisit in chapter 5.

there is faith miracles can occur" (Philosophy n.d.). For those whose hopes for a "healthy color and glow" are not realized, they can buy Renewed Hope in a Jar, whose label reads "philosophy: live with optimism. renew with hope" (Philosophy n.d.).

Although it is difficult to unpack what, exactly, these messages are meant to convey, the branding is obvious. Philosophy is women's best hope for young, clear skin. Or, at least, it is affluent women's best hope, since they are the only ones who can afford these products. And to the extent that expensive beauty products do in fact work (it is questionable whether they do), the beauty achievements of affluent women are at the expense of poor women who lack the economic means to buy them.[33]

As Peter Drahos (2004) explains: "Companies know that by creating links between their products and individual hopes, they potentially gain the benefit of a powerful driver of human behavior" (19). Although the use of hope in marketing is not necessarily unethical, it can be and often is exploitative. Adrienne M. Martin (2008) discusses the case of Jason Vale, who was sentenced to 63 months in prison for selling Laetrile to cancer patients who had strong hopes for a cure. (The acting commissioner of the Food and Drug Administration stated that Laetrile offers nothing but "false hope" [49].) While Vale was clearly exploiting cancer patients through deception, Martin argues that there is an even more ubiquitous form of exploiting hope in healthcare that does not involve deception. Because hope influences attention and the interpretation of information, sick people who have hope for a cure are on the lookout for one. They may ignore, discount, or explain away risks involved in certain forms of treatment, thus impairing their autonomy— and this makes patients vulnerable to exploitation (52).[34] Researchers can take advantage of the fact that patients' hopes to be cured enable them to downplay the risks involved in participating in research trials. For example, hope is commonly used in the names of research institutions (The City of Hope in Los Angeles and the National Institute of Health's House of Hope) and advertisements ("New Hope in the battle against . . .") and even ends up on consent forms ("We hope that this drug will . . .") (52). These messages

[33] Although facial moisturizers might not make much of a difference, extremely expensive procedures such as breast implants and other forms of plastic surgery do. These procedures exacerbate barriers between women, making life more difficult for those who cannot keep up with the increasingly demanding beauty norms of many societies.

[34] Martin points out that hope can, in other cases, enhance autonomy—as when a patient's hope to be cured helps her play down the risks involved in a research trial, when the patient strongly believes she should take on risks so that she can contribute to clinical research (51–52).

of hope can diminish, even further, patients' capacity to deliberate autonomously about the benefits of clinical research to their own lives, which serves researchers' (rather than patients') best interests.[35]

Patients who are autonomous can still be exploited, too, through excessive drug prices such as for Avastin—a breast cancer treatment that costs roughly US$8,300 per month (Martin 2008, 53). Although patients might value Avastin even at such a high price, as Martin points out, their hopes for a cure (or the hope that the drug will help them maintain hope itself) might cause them to place a high monetary value on the treatment. Patients end up willing to pay much more money for drug treatments, because of their hopes, than they otherwise would.

Other examples are not hard to come by. Private in vitro fertilization (IVF) clinics in the United Kingdom have come under fire for "trading on the hope" of older women, failing to provide realistic assessments of success, and charging £20,000 for IVF treatment cycles (four times as much as they should cost) (BBC News 2019b). And it is not just women whose hopes are directly exploited who are harmed (economically, and potentially through disappointment) in these situations. By driving up drug prices in response to the high hopes of patients who can and are willing to pay, the possibility of a cure—and the *hope* for a cure—is threatened for other patients without the same economic resources.

From political campaigns and activism to marketing and health research, hope is uniquely used in society to influence human psychology and behavior—sometimes in ways that can ultimately exacerbate oppressive conditions. What these cases remind us is that there are powerful if not always obvious social, cultural, political, and economic forces at work directing and enhancing our hopes. We find ourselves with hope not just because of desire and uncertainty but also because individuals and institutions in positions of power influence how we think, feel, value, and act. And it is most often agents in positions of social and political power who promise

---

[35] In their study of hope and the multibillion-dollar direct-to-consumer advertising industry, Marjorie Delbaere and Erin Willis (2015) found that advertisements for drug treatments for arthritis and diabetes featuring positive messages (e.g., images of puppies and the slogan "Having less diabetic nerve pain . . . it's a wonderful feeling") were more effective in activating hope in participants than negative messages. Interestingly, they did find that some negative messages (e.g., "Pain is a thief") also resonated with participants, eliciting a perception of the brand's credibility (32). Perhaps Donald J. Trump's dark, fear-inducing messages similarly led to a perception of his political credibility in 2016.

hope to individuals occupying disadvantaged positions in society—to those who are most dependent on others to realize many of their significant hopes.

Reflection on the politics and marketing of hope helps us to see the ways in which hope is often placed or invested in other people, groups, and institutions to bring about whatever their hopeful messages are offering. When citizens hope that a politician will deliver on their promises, when consumers hope that a company's product is the key to achieving their goals, and when patients hope that a drug will cure them, people are investing hope in politicians, corporations, physicians, and researchers who they see as holding the power to bring about what they desire. Later on, we will see that investing hope in individuals and institutions in positions of power is not the only option for the oppressed, who so often find ways to engage their agency directed toward a better life and for justice. But for now, it will help to see how hopes are invested in others and how these hopes are connected to what we expect and trust others to do.

Hope, Expectation, and Trust

When we invest hope in people, groups, or institutions, we acknowledge that their agency is necessary to fulfill our desires. Often, too, we invest *moral* hope in others, such as the hope that women place in men to stand up for women in the workplace, the hope that poor people place in affluent members of society with the economic power to improve their lives, and the hope we place in the criminal justice system to do right by victims of systemic violence. Moral hopes are hopes with moral content, unlike nonmoral hopes absent of moral content like the hope for clear skies or a snowy winter. Moral hopes are the hopes with which people living under oppression (and their allies) find themselves as they imagine a more just world.

But how can we understand the phenomenon of investing hope in others? Martin's (2014) account of what she calls "normative hope" captures a range of cases in which we invest hope in other people to abide by norms we endorse; that is, our *normative expectations*. When we hold others to normative expectations, we demand that they regulate their behavior in accordance with certain requirements or prohibitions (Martin 2014). Normative expectations are different from *predictive expectations*, which involve confidence that some outcome will obtain (whether one desires it or not). On Martin's view, investing normative hope in another person is "to relate some norm to her *aspirationally*, to hold it up to her as something with which she has decisive reason to comply, while acknowledging the challenges she faces, externally or internally" (140, emphasis added). We hope in these cases because we believe that a person's compliance with a norm is possible but not certain given the existence of challenges to compliance.

Understanding the relationship between hope and normative expectation is important for understanding our emotional responses to others in whom we invest hope in moral and political life. We respond emotionally to others' behavior through what P. F. Strawson (2008) refers to as the participant reactive attitudes: those attitudes we adopt as a way of holding people responsible for their behavior, including resentment, disappointment, and gratitude. For example, when people fail to live up to our normative expectations, such as when I encounter a stranger who treats me with blatant disrespect, we tend to experience the reactive attitude of resentment. But Martin (2014) argues that when we invest hope in another person to abide by our normative expectations, and when they fail to do so, we might experience a mixture of both disappointment and resentment. We are disappointed because the hope we placed in the person was not realized, and we are resentful because they violated our normative expectation. In other words, disappointment tracks a normative hope's not being realized, and resentment tracks the violation of a normative expectation. If, however, the person in whom we invest hope *does* abide by our normative expectation (e.g., by keeping a difficult promise), we might feel grateful when they do so. Our gratitude signifies an appreciation that the person overcame challenges to keeping a difficult promise and realized our normative hope.[36] Hope is thus intricately connected to a range of other emotions we experience in our interpersonal relationships.

But one thing to notice is that we do not always invest hope in others *aspirationally*. Often, we invest hope in people to meet our moral expectations[37] even when we do not see them as facing challenges to compliance, such as when I hope that other people whom I encounter will treat me with a minimal degree of respect. I will not feel grateful when they do so, since it's not that difficult to treat other human beings decently. But I might generally hope for respectful treatment from others all the same.

---

[36] See Adrienne M. Martin (2019) for further discussion of interpersonal hope and its connection to disappointment and gratitude.

[37] I take moral expectations to be a species of normative expectation, or those expectations we have of other people to act in accordance with distinctly moral norms.

These cases of non-aspirational hope are particularly important for understanding how hope and expectation operate under oppression. When members of oppressed groups invest hope in members of privileged groups to abide by their moral expectations, gratitude following the realization of hope seems out of place, and gratitude might even be reasonably resisted. Brittney Cooper (2015) highlights the problematic demand for gratitude in her discussion of police violence against Sandra Bland. Bland was a Black woman in the United States who was pulled over for a minor traffic violation, subjected to excessive force by a white police officer, and arrested, which led to her suspicious and unjust death. Cooper states:

> Black people, of every station, live everyday just one police encounter from the grave. Looking back over my encounters with police, it's truly a wonder that I'm still in the land of the living.
>
> Am I supposed to be grateful for that? Are we supposed to be grateful each and every time the police don't kill us?
>
> There is a way that white people in particular treat Black people, as though we should be grateful to them—grateful for jobs in their institutions, grateful to live in their neighborhoods, grateful that they aren't as racist as their parents and grandparents, grateful that they pay us any attention, grateful that they acknowledge our humanity (on the rare occasions when they do), grateful that they don't use their formidable power to take our lives.
>
> When we refuse gratitude, they enact every violence—they take our jobs, our homes, refuse us respect, and kill us. And then they demand that we be gracious in the face of it.
>
> Black gratitude is the prerequisite for white folks to treat us like human beings. (Cooper 2015)

Cooper's discussion of white people's demand for Black gratitude is illuminating. The question "Are we supposed to be grateful each and every time the police don't kill us?" urges us to take into account the forces at work imposing moral attitudes on members of oppressed groups in everyday life. As Claudia Card (1988) points out, the powerful and privileged have historically felt as though the powerless should "feel grateful for their 'care'" (124). Such gratitude toward the powerful and privileged is sometimes a manifestation of psychological oppression, helping to keep oppressed people "in their place." Of course, Cooper might hope that a particular police officer she encounters will not use excessive force, and her hope may be realized. But she might reasonably feel relieved and lucky, rather than grateful, if this were to happen. Cooper's potential hope that an officer will refrain from using excessive force on her would be a way of acknowledging that the officer ought to (but might not) meet her justified moral expectation.[38]

The phenomenon of placing hope in others to abide by one's moral expectations raises the question of how hope is different from moral *trust*, inasmuch as both hope and trust are attitudes that we invest in others to behave in ways we think they should. Like hope, trust is an attitude that implies our relative vulnerability and dependence on other people (Baier 1986) and is, on some views, even essential to our moral relationships (Walker 2006). But unlike hope, trust requires a certain degree of confidence in the person (or group, or institution) in whom one invests trust. Karen Jones (1996) characterizes trust is an affective attitude involving optimism about the trusted person's good will toward you as well as optimism about their competence to act as you are counting on them to act. Carolyn McLeod (2000), focusing on moral trust in particular,[39] suggests that moral trust involves a presumption of the person's *moral integrity* to act on shared moral standards (see also Calhoun 1995). McGeer (2008) similarly suggests that trust is "an attitude that we take towards the character of their [the trusted person's] agency" (242). So whereas investing moral hope in a person only requires that I believe it is possible that they will abide by the moral norm I endorse (without any evaluation of their character or the likelihood that they will do so), trust requires confidence that the person can be counted on to meet the moral norm based on relevant features of their character.[40]

---

[38] There is much more to say about what might make gratitude appropriate following the realization of moral hope. Jean Harvey (2004), for example, argues that in the case of a rich person who gives a small amount of money or food to someone suffering from homelessness, gratitude on the part of the recipient might be appropriate (34). On at least some moral theories, the action was morally obligatory; but Harvey contends that, despite the action's being obligatory (let's suppose that it *is* obligatory), the fact that the rich person's sense of self has been shaped by luxury, security, and financial freedom and that he still was moved by compassion to help is sufficient grounds for gratitude. I leave open whether such cases of gratitude are appropriate, while emphasizing that gratitude can be a morally and politically problematic emotional response to the realization of a hope invested in others.

[39] There are cases of nonmoral trust that will be different, such as when we trust librarians to track down books we need and pilots to competently fly airplanes. As Greg Scherkoske (2013) points out, there is even a kind of intellectual trust that involves "reliance on one's own or another's opinions, as well as the faculties and practices that generate and sustain those opinions" (125). I use the language of "moral expectation," "moral hope," and "moral trust" to signify my interest in a specific set of cases: cases where expecting, hoping, and trusting others is bound up with moral assessments about what people should do.

[40] Individuals might have any number of reasons for not acting on moral standards even in cases when they *do* endorse those standards, such as weakness of will, self-interest, or fear. But in trusting

Although moral trust involves confidence in an agent's moral integrity, we do often trust strangers too: people who, for all we know, may not share our moral standards or have the integrity to act in accordance with them. In cases where we trust strangers, we often adopt a stance of default trust, giving them the benefit of the doubt. For example, when I pay cash for coffee, I do not count the change that the employee hands me back. In the absence of evidence that the employee is untrustworthy, I trust that the employee shares my moral belief that stealing money is generally wrong and has the integrity to act on that moral belief. Similarly, when a student comes to my office and explains that a family member has passed away, I trust that the student shares my moral belief that lying is generally wrong and that they would not lie about a family member's passing for their own benefit. I do not request proof of a family member's death to provide the appropriate academic accommodations.

Importantly, too, evidence that is relevant to a person's trustworthiness is not limited to evidence about their character traits, past actions, or moral beliefs and commitments. Relevant evidence may also include things like gender, race, and the person's profession. Women, for example, may approach men on the street at night with default distrust. Although a woman may not know the passerby personally, the fact that women are disproportionately subjected to violence at the hands of men is sufficient evidence to adopt a (prudential) attitude of default distrust. Such distrust helps to explain why women might keep their distance, have their cell phones in hand, or avoid walking places alone at night altogether. Their default distrust indicates awareness of the ways in which sexist oppression and socialization affects men's characters, including their moral beliefs, attitudes, and behavior.

One might, however, hope that a person whom one evaluates as being untrustworthy—for any reason—will do the right thing. A woman might hope that the man who is eyeing her up from the street corner will not act on whatever inclination is causing his suspicious behavior, even if she does not trust him at all. What is required for hope is a belief in the possibility that the desired outcome will come about, not confidence or any sort of assessment of the agent's moral integrity. Thus, as Annette Baier (2012) suggests, "Hope . . . outruns trust, but trust is firmer" (221). While both hope and trust

people to do something, we necessarily trust them to follow through—sometimes, even, that they are willing to make reasonable sacrifices to do so (to one's reputation, to one's relationships, etc.).

can be placed in others to uphold one's moral expectations, it is more difficult to trust others than it is to invest hope in them.[41]

I have argued that hope is threatened and often damaged by oppression. Since trust requires confidence in another person's (or group's or institution's) moral integrity, we should expect that trust is damaged first. And we can see clear evidence of damages to trust in oppressed communities, such as widespread distrust of law enforcement—both individual police officers as well as the criminal justice system as a whole. Henry Luyombya, a participant in Toronto's 2018 Pride Parade and researcher for the Committee for Accessible AIDS treatment, spoke about the LGBTQ+ community's damaged trust of the police in Toronto, Canada. He explained:

> At some point we have to say enough is enough in terms of systematic oppression. The system does not do much to guarantee safety of people who are marginalized. Police need to do a lot of anti-oppression training from grassroots level, and on a consistent basis. Otherwise the trust is broken and will not be repaired soon. (Ngabo 2018)

Luyombya's comments about broken trust were made in connection to the persistent failures of police to adequately handle severe cases of violence against the Toronto LGBTQ+ community. Police have a decades-long history of neglecting missing persons reports involving gay men in the city, an issue that gained international attention when Bruce McArthur was arrested for the murder of eight victims, most of whom were members of Toronto's LGBTQ+ community as well as men of color (Austen 2018). Community members had long suspected that a serial killer might be responsible, but their suspicions were not taken seriously by police. As more and more evidence suggested that the police as a whole and, by implication, individual police officers did not share the same moral standard of treating members of the LGBTQ+ community equal to other missing persons and would not

[41] Although trust and hope are distinct, some philosophers suggest that there is a kind of hopeful trust. Walker (2006) argues that we place hopeful trust in others when we hope that—despite evidence suggesting that it is unlikely—the person will follow through. Investing hopeful trust has instrumental value; it can "activate" a person's sense of responsibility, perhaps increasing the likelihood that they will abide by the norm (82). See also McGeer (2008). Although Walker and McGeer are right that we invest hopeful trust in others for instrumental reasons, I tend to agree with Pamela Hieronymi (2008) that such cases are not fully fledged instances of trust. When our reasons for trusting have to do more with the instrumental value of trust than the agent's trustworthiness, hopeful trust signifies that you do not actually (or at least fully) trust them.

act on the standard of equality (even if they shared it), community members lost trust.

Similarly, Human Rights Watch (2013) found that Indigenous women in Canada will not call police for help because of serious distrust, which comes from their knowledge of the many cases of police neglect and acts of violence against them (Human Rights Watch 2013).[42] In the United States, Canada, and elsewhere in the world, distrust of police officers and criminal justice systems has become a well-known, well-documented response to police violence against people of color more generally. Brian Willingham, a Black police officer with the Flint, Michigan, police department, diagnoses the problem of distrust from firsthand experience. He asks:

> How can citizens in Flint trust the police to protect them when they can't even trust their government to provide them with clean water? This is the kind of question that has placed police officers and African-Americans on a collision course. Police are often seen as outsiders in urban America. White officers are seen as racist, while black officers like me are seen as traitors to our race. (Willingham 2016)

Willingham is in the complicated position of both understanding Black citizens' distrust of police as a Black person *and* experiencing their distrust as a police officer whose occupation is seen as calling his moral integrity into question.

There are many more examples like these ones. They illustrate the ways in which trust, like hope, is influenced by the social and political relationships in which people exist. They also urge us to think about the potential dangers of trust in contexts of oppression in which trusting the wrong person might put oneself at risk, and even at risk of death. Hope might thus not be as risky as trust. If I distrust a man eyeing me up on the street corner, my distrust will trigger protective behaviors even if I have hope that nothing will come of the man's suspicious actions. But if I trust him and I walk by the man as if I am safe to do so, I put myself at risk of violence. Thus, the value of trust should

---

[42] Human Rights Watch (2013) detailed a number of instances of violence against Indigenous women and girls at the hands of police. For example, they documented the case of a 12-year-old girl who was attacked by a police dog, neglect of a 17-year-old girl in need of medical attention after breaking her nose and being choked by her grandmother, women being strip-searched by male officers, women who were injured after being subjected to excessive force and arrest, and rape and sexual assault of Indigenous women by police.

not be overemphasized; and withholding trust—even approaching members of privileged groups with distrust—is often justified and prudent.

Meena Krishnamurthy (2015) even defends the democratic value of distrust for its role in protecting members of oppressed groups from tyranny. She focuses on the democratic value of distrust for Black people who experience racial injustice in the United States, citing Martin Luther King Jr.'s distrust of white moderates from his "Letter from Birmingham Jail." Krishnamurthy points out that King did not trust white moderates even though they too believed in racial equality. King distrusted white moderates because although he believed that they shared the moral belief in racial equality, they could not be counted on to act to promote racial equality. In other words, King did not trust white moderates precisely because he had evidence to suggest that they lacked moral integrity: when they found themselves in contexts that required them to act on their moral belief in racial equality, they failed to do so.

Krishnamurthy (2015) argues that King's distrust was valuable for democracy precisely because distrust motivated citizens to engage in direct action, which promoted democracy and racial justice, and that such distrust continues to hold democratic value in the context of racial justice today. She suggests that Black citizens—aware of the reality of racial profiling and widespread unjustified uses of violence against them—distrust police whom they confidently believe will not act justly. This distrust has, in turn, motivated people to engage in direct action, such as the nationwide (and international) protests against racial injustice in America.

Krishnamurthy (2015) does not discuss King's or Black citizens' hopes directly, but King still hoped that white moderates would act to promote racial equality despite distrusting that they would do so. He speaks of being disappointed in the white moderate, signifying a prior normative hope (in Martin's sense) that they would act as they should. And King also held out hope for racial justice long term, despite his particular losses of hope on the pathway toward racial justice. Black citizens and allies of racial justice today commonly echo King's hope too. Krishnamurthy herself remarks:

> Let us *hope* that Black citizens' sense of distrust will grow and continue to foster the direct action that is needed to ensure that racial justice and genuine democracy are secured. In a world where Darren Wilsons run free and untempered, and Michael Browns are gunned down, we must hope that the distrust of Black citizens will force necessary change and that White tyranny will finally be eliminated. (403, emphasis added)

Krishnamurthy has invested her hope in Black people, whose distrust of white people and direct actions against white tyranny hold the most promise for securing racial justice. Calls for "building trust" are thus premature in such contexts, failing to notice the value of distrust to eliminating oppression. Trust is earned, and white people have obviously not earned the trust of people of color. Krishnamurthy also hints at something I will argue in chapter 5: that investing hope (and trust) in particular people, those who share the intention to eliminate racial justice and who show up in collective action settings, can inspire a new hope for racial (and other forms of) justice—a collective hope borne of solidarity.

Concluding Thoughts

There is much more to be said about the nature of hope, the use of hope in politics and marketing, what it means to place hope in others, and the relationship between hope and other attitudes such as expectation, gratitude, and trust. My aim has been to illustrate how philosophical and empirical insights about these phenomena can help illuminate how people hope in the unjust world in which we live. What we hope for, the strength of our hopes, the character of our hopes, and hope's connection with other elements of our psychologies are all affected by our positions within interrelated systems of privilege and oppression. A feminist perspective encourages us to see where we are situated in the world in relation to others, the opportunities we have and lack, and the desires we form and those that we must depend upon others to help us fulfill. By attending explicitly to features of social difference that have unjustly resulted in privilege for some at the expense of others—gender, race, class, and so on—we have acquired new insights for exploring how, and in what ways, hope can be beneficial or detrimental to our efforts to live well and to our efforts in building a more just world.

2

The Value and Risks of Hope

Part of what is so important about inquiry into hope is understanding the value of hope for people as they navigate a difficult and uncertain world. We often praise people for being "strong" and maintaining hope in the face of adversity, urging those who retreat under difficult circumstances to lift themselves up and continue on with hope. But we also worry about people who are too hopeful in the face of terrible odds and those who spend too much time and energy hoping for outcomes that will never come about. People who are naively hopeful despite the evidence against them seem bound to be crushed by disappointment and defeat.

This chapter aims to understand both the value and risks of hope. As we will see, many people find hope valuable (even essential) to their moral and political lives, even in the face of evidence that strongly counts against the realization of their hopes. Given the apparent intrinsic value of hope to many of us, as well as the barriers outsiders can face in understanding the value of hope for others, I defend the importance of first-personal assessments of the value of hope. But many philosophers have noticed that hope is also risky for epistemic, prudential, and moral reasons. Hope might involve mistakenly believing that something we desire is possible or more likely to occur than it really is. Or hope might lead us to invest ourselves in courses of action that will ultimately be detrimental to the attainment of our goals. And in some cases, people might even endorse their own immoral hopes, such as the hope that an innocent person suffers. I argue that hope can be evaluated along multiple dimensions: epistemic and prudential (or strategic) rationality, fittingness, and moral appropriateness. These evaluative measures are technical terms that refer to different ways in which we already assess the value of our own and others' hopes in everyday life. They help us see what is going on when we endorse hope, worry about it, or urge ourselves and others to pare down or keep our hopes up. And though these evaluative measures can be distinguished from one another, they all contribute to answering the all-things-considered practical question of how, and for what, one

Hope Under Oppression. Katie Stockdale, Oxford University Press. © Oxford University Press 2021.
DOI: 10.1093/oso/9780197563564.003.0003

should hope. I then suggest that McGeer's (2004) framework of *hoping well* holds promise for illustrating how agents might use these evaluative measures for hope in practice, and I build upon her insight that hoping well is, like hope itself, a social phenomenon.

Oppression and Hope's Value

I argued in the previous chapter that oppression is a threat to hope. It creates conditions under which certain people, in virtue of their social, political, and economic locations, must hope against hope for many of their desires to be fulfilled, if they are capable of sustaining hope at all. Oppression is even a threat to individuals' very capacities for hope, or their ability to cultivate and sustain hope for their own lives. This observation is particularly disheartening in light of the existing empirical literature on the benefits of hope to physical and psychological wellbeing. Studies have found that hope contributes to human wellbeing in a number of significant ways. It is helpful for problem solving (Snyder, Rand, and Sigmon 2018); it aids in learning and performing in academic settings (Snyder, Rand, and Sigmon 2018); it has a role in preventing and coping with physical illnesses and disabilities (Dorsett 2010; Hill and Feudtner 2018; Snyder et al. 2018); and it fosters enhanced feelings of self-worth, as well as the ability to cope with trauma and other psychological stressors (Lee and Gallagher 2018; Long and Gallagher 2018; Snyder et al. 2018).[1]

Given these potential benefits of hope to health and wellbeing, members of oppressed groups may be harmed by their losses of hope and diminished capacities for hope—yet another harm of oppression. But while many people understandably lose hope due to the unjust conditions in which they live, others do sustain hope. Many prominent activists have appealed to the value

---

[1] This is a very small survey of empirical literature on hope's benefits to health and wellbeing. One thing to notice is that although there are clear similarities between how social scientists and philosophers define and understand hope (e.g., as involving desire, uncertainty, and motivation in pursuit of goals), how hope is operationalized is relevant to these findings. For example, many social scientists follow C. R. Snyder (2002) in defining hope as, roughly, a positive motivational state involving an exercise of one's agency toward the pursuit of one's goals, along with pathway-thinking about how one can achieve them. This is somewhat similar, but not equivalent to, philosophical accounts of hope. So although empirical research certainly helps us to understand hope and related mental states, there are reasons to be cautious about drawing strong conclusions about the value of hope from the empirical literature alone. Philosophical analyses of the nature of hope might helpfully contribute to the empirical project of uncovering the benefits and risks of hope in human life as well.

and even necessity of hope in the pursuit of justice. Patrisse Khan-Cullors (2018), for example, describes the value of hope for herself and other Black Lives Matter activists in response to racial oppression. For example, in anticipation of finding out about whether Trayvon Martin's killer would go free, Khan-Cullors explains, "We do not speak of our fear about the decision that looms, knowing that our children so rarely receive justice in this nation. We speak about hope because after all, what else?" (173). She reminds us that Black children so rarely receive justice in America and that it took a significant amount of time and hard work for the killer to even be arrested and for activists to make this case known to the broader public. Yet even in the face of this discouraging (and all too familiar) narrative in which the chances of justice for Trayvon Martin are slim, Khan-Cullors sustains hope. She says, "because of this, we know and we are afraid, but still . . . we hold on to hope. Because what else?" (175).

There is, for Khan-Cullors, something irrelevant about the evidence counting against the possibility of justice for Trayvon Martin in seeing the value of hope in this moment. Her ability to sustain hope in such circumstances suggests that hope is often intrinsically valuable, valuable independently of whatever else might happen—whether the hope will be realized or not. Claudia Blöser and Titus Stahl (2017) argue that political activists such as Khan-Cullors often have what they term *fundamental hopes*, which are "hopes that play a particularly important role in people's lives" (350). Fundamental hopes are essential to how people see and interpret the world they inhabit; they are part of people's practical identities. And because such hopes are constitutive of practical identity, Blöser and Stahl (2017) suggest that agents have non-instrumental reasons for sustaining them. In other words, to give up my fundamental hopes is to deny part of who I am; and because I do not want to give up my identity, I have reason to sustain my fundamental hopes.

Blöser and Stahl's insights about the non-instrumental value of fundamental hopes helpfully highlight the priority of first-personal assessments in thinking about the value of hope. Although it is common (in everyday life, and in the philosophical literature) to evaluate emotions as rational or irrational, such assessments can sometimes be suspect. In evaluating the emotions of others, in particular, we might miss an important sense in which hope might hold value to their lives in ways that outsiders are not always well positioned to understand. The first-person point of view often provides a privileged epistemic perspective for understanding the nature, basis, or significance of hope for a person. It is also unclear whether, or to what extent, it is possible to accurately assess the value of others' hopes at all, especially the hopes of people whose lives are very different from one's own. For example, implicit biases and explicitly racist, sexist, and ableist beliefs can factor into normative evaluations in ways that exacerbate harmful stereotypes, distorting our evaluation of the hopes of others. As Vincent Lloyd (2018a) points out, hope is often over-ascribed to Black Americans, who—because of cultural stereotypes—are perceived as emotional, spiritual, and prone to hope. Women, too, are very often charged as being irrational and overly emotional (e.g., Lloyd 1979; Narayan 1988; Jaggar 1989; Held 1990; Jones 2004). There is a risk that these stereotypes might lead to characterizing the hopes of oppressed people as irrational or misplaced, whether the charge is that they are hoping too much or too little.

There is thus a potential worry that evaluative frameworks for emotions such as hope can be (and have been) misapplied and even coopted for immoral purposes. This occurs, for instance, when putatively excessive emotions are attributed to members of oppressed groups as a way of dismissing the legitimacy of their testimony (Campbell 1994). And such judgments can put people into impossible double binds (Frye 1983). If one is too hopeful, they might be seen as childish and unrealistic; but if one is not hopeful enough, they might be seen as a downer, cynic, or killjoy. These charges—childish, cynical, or a killjoy—have been used to condemn the emotions of people of color, women, and people with disabilities. Hope assessments might thus reinforce inaccurate and harmful social understandings about the emotions of oppressed groups more generally. And since members of oppressed groups have a form of epistemic privilege with respect to their lived experiences (e.g., Narayan 1988; Fricker 1999; Collins 1999; Vasanthakumar 2018), those of us who occupy relatively privileged social locations might do better to avoid assessing others' emotional responses to events in their lives.[2] At the very least, there are good reasons for caution rooted in suitable epistemic humility when evaluating the emotions of others.

But there are at least two important benefits of evaluating hope, including the hopes of others. First, advancements in the philosophical literature about the rationality of emotions have helped to undermine the inaccurate

---

[2] Narayan (1988) makes a similar cautionary remark. She says: "By and large, it would probably be good advice to outsiders that they should try and learn from the perceptions of insiders, rather than tell insiders what they ought to do or feel, especially about contexts and issues that they ought to suspect they know less about than insiders" (45).

picture of emotions as at odds with reason, providing frameworks through which members of oppressed groups' emotions (including those in response to their oppression) can be seen as rational responses to unjust conditions (e.g., Jaggar 1989; Little 1995). And because members of oppressed groups are often not taken seriously, it can be politically constructive for members of privileged groups to acknowledge the rationality of oppressed people's emotions. For example, whereas my own unhopeful position might not receive uptake in an academic setting (about, say, my students evaluating me on an equal basis with my male colleagues), a man's validating my unhopeful position might. If a male colleague affirms that, actually, one shouldn't be too optimistic or even hopeful about students' ability to evaluate female professors fairly, it is likely that his testimony will be taken more seriously than mine. And this can be a useful way in which privileged people can work to undermine oppression. Second, a theoretical framework for hope is essential for criticizing the most dangerous hopes: the hopes of white supremacists, men's rights activists, those with anti-LGBTQ+ agendas, and so on. If we do away with the ability to assess others' hopes in all cases, we lose the ability to evaluate harmful hopes.

The project of searching for evaluative criteria, and even (sometimes) evaluating the hopes of others, is thus important enough to proceed. But we might do so with what Uma Narayan (1988) refers to as methodological humility and methodological caution. *Methodological humility* consists in a privileged outsider proceeding on the assumption that because of their social location, they may be missing something important. And what might appear to be someone's "mistake" might make more sense with fuller understanding.[3] For example, if someone less privileged than I am is without hope for their future and I feel inclined to judge their inability to "see the bright side" or the possibility that things could be different, methodological humility requires me to acknowledge that I might be missing an important part of their story. So, to take a specific example, whatever normative claim I might want to make about, say, a poor person's hope to win the lottery, I might acknowledge that because of my privileged economic position, I may be limited with respect to how much I can understand the value of hope for that person. And, notably, this level of assessment is less apt than a criticism at the level of society. It is more productive, in many cases, to

---

[3] As Narayan (1988) says, "Often, the outsider may fail to realize that that the insiders' emotional responses to oppression may be much more complex than his own" (39).

critically evaluate the unjust institutions that exploit the hopes of those who are economically disadvantaged.

Methodological caution, relatedly, consists in a privileged outsider making a sincere effort to carry out evaluative judgments in ways that do not dismiss the validity of the other person's point of view, or in ways that might even look like dismissal (Narayan 1988, 38). This principle acknowledges that outsider judgments can be legitimate. Narayan points out that it can be legitimate, for example, for a white professor to disagree with a professor of color about whether white professors should teach nonwhite perspectives. But knowing that white people are not well positioned to understand the racial dynamics of classroom settings, white professors should validate the legitimacy of the professor of color's point of view in communicating their criticism.[4] Similarly, it might be legitimate for a man to make the judgment that a woman's lack of hope is out of place. If a woman has lost hope about finding a partner who is not abusive given her past experiences, a close male friend might worry that her absence of hope is doing more harm than good given her desires. And methodological caution requires him to have sensitive acknowledgment of the woman's experiences in communicating his evaluative claim. He might remark that while her loss of hope is understandable, he sees reasons for her not to give up on *all* men, since what she desires is to find a male partner, and some of them are good.

Although Narayan is focused on everyday communicative encounters between members of privileged and oppressed social groups, these principles might be extended to philosophical theorizing as well. Although it might be relatively straightforward to determine whether fictional A's hope that *p* is, for example, prudentially rational, real people's hopes are much more difficult to evaluate. Their past experiences, relationships, health, present needs, and so on can all make a difference to the value of their hopes. I do not, then, make definitive judgments about the value of hope for individuals or groups of people (beyond, as I defend below, judgments that derive from the moral constraint on hope). The aim is, rather, to provide a framework through which hope can be evaluated based on the emotion's key features, even if exactly how people should hope is ultimately a matter of wise judgment that varies between contexts and who the moral agents hoping are.

---

[4] She suggests that a response exercising methodological caution would look something like this: "I can understand what you are talking about. Such experiences must be awful. But don't you think that, perhaps, it may be a good thing to push for black writings to be included on syllabuses, regardless of who is there to teach them?" (43).

Such a framework can be helpful to all of us who find ourselves grappling with questions about the value of hope in our lives.

Evaluating Hope

Philosophers have made significant progress theorizing the value of hope. Hope is commonly assessed for *epistemic* and *practical rationality* (and in particular *prudential* or *strategic rationality*, as we will see). But the affective perception involved in hope and the significance of many hopes to moral life are features that subject hope to two additional modes of assessment: in particular, assessments of *fit* and *moral appropriateness*. Each of these criteria are technical terms that highlight specific benefits and risks of hope that are important to many of us as we attempt to understand, and act productively on, our own hopes and the hopes of others. They help to inform the all-things-considered practical question of exactly how, and for what, we should hope. But I argue that there is a moral constraint on hope. When we find ourselves with morally inappropriate hopes, we have sufficient reason to take responsibility to overcome or revise them. I then suggest that McGeer's (2004) framework of *hoping well* holds promise for capturing how these evaluative measures work in practice, while helpfully reorienting the value of hope as a social question. And I build upon her insights to push the analysis further, to begin to capture the political dimensions of hoping well.

Familiar Rational Assessments

Philosophers often assess hope for rationality. Since hope involves a belief—namely, the belief in the possibility that a desired outcome will obtain—the belief part of hope can be evaluated for *epistemic rationality*. For hope to be epistemically rational, it must be in fact possible for the desired outcome to be realized. For example, one cannot rationally hope for an outcome that is logically impossible, such as when one hopes to become a married bachelor (Chignell 2013). One can, however, rationally hope for what is metaphysically possible, such as the hope that God exists. But very often, the question of whether hope is epistemically rational comes down to the question of whether the desired outcome is physically possible. If I had hoped that, after a serious back injury at nine years old, I would still become an Olympic gymnast because of the possibility of a miracle removing the permanent, physical damage to my back, I think my hope would have been epistemically irrational. Once an orthopedic surgeon confirmed that I could not continue training competitively, given the nature of my injury, it was no longer epistemically rational for me to hope to become an Olympic gymnast.

Beyond the requirement that the desired outcome must be possible, assessments of the epistemic rationality of hope involve assessing whether the belief part of hope represents an accurate probability estimate given the available evidence (see, e.g., Bovens 1999). For example, I might hope for a sunny day tomorrow, and it is certainly possible that tomorrow will in fact be sunny. But if I believe that there is a 95 percent chance of a sunny day despite a reliable weather forecast calling for pouring rain, then my hope is epistemically irrational. I believe that there is a 95 percent chance of a sunny day when there is, in fact, a much lower chance of a sunny day (and this is information I have accessed). My hope is epistemically irrational because it involves an irrational belief about the likelihood of a sunny day.

Importantly, it is not the case that hopes that are highly unlikely to be realized are necessarily epistemically irrational. Recall Bess's hope from *Cancer Research*. Bess strongly desired that the experimental drug from the clinical trial would cure her, and she believed (accurately) that there was a 1 percent chance that the drug would cure her. Bess's hope was epistemically rational because her belief (i.e., her probability estimate) is justified given the evidence available to her. Had Bess believed (inaccurately) that there was a 60 percent chance the experimental drug would cure her, her belief and thus the hope based on her belief would have been epistemically irrational. But Bess, in *Cancer Research*, did not make this mistake. She strongly hoped while maintaining her rational belief about the probability that the experimental drug would cure her. Hope, then, is epistemically rational if the belief involved in hope correctly estimates the likelihood that a desired end that is possible will obtain.

Hope can also be assessed for *practical rationality*. Luc Bovens (1999) argues that hope is practically rational in three ways: it can enable us to act to increase the likelihood that our valued ends will be realized; it helps us take risks with payoffs we highly value; and through the imaginative activities constitutive of hope, what we desire becomes clear to us, sometimes leading to new hopes or a restructuring of our goals.[5] Philip Pettit (2004) suggests

---

[5] Bovens (1999) frames this discussion as one about the *instrumental* rationality of hope.

that hope can be practically rational "because it promises to lift us out of the panics and depressions to which we are naturally prey and to give us firm direction and control" (160). In the absence of hope, Pettit says that "we would collapse into a heap of despair and uncertainty, beaten down by cascades of inimical fact" (160). Hope, on Pettit's view, is "the best way of coping" with difficult circumstances so that we can find our way through (161).[6] On Martin's (2014) incorporation analysis of hope, hope involves a licensing stance that is governed by practical norms. In particular, hope consists in a representation of the probability that the desired outcome will be realized as licensing forms of thought, feeling, and activity directed toward the desired outcome. Whether the licensing stance is rational depends on whether engaging in hopeful activities promotes one's rational scheme of ends.

Rational assessments can help us begin to make sense of both the endorsements of and potential worries about hope under oppression. Hope might be practically rational because it is a source of motivation for action, thus increasing the likelihood that people will attain their moral and political ends (Moellendorf 2006; Milona 2018; Huber 2019; Stahl 2019).[7] Derrick Bell (1992a), however, calls attention to the dangers of hope with respect to maintaining particular hopes related to racial justice in America. In the context of civil rights policy, he argues: "The worship of equality rules as having absolute power benefits whites by preserving a benevolent but fictional self-image, and such worship benefits blacks by preserving hope. But I think we've arrived at a place in history where the harms of such worship outweigh the benefits" (Bell 1992a, 101). Bell, as I understand him, is suggesting that some hopes might be beneficial to hopers' wellbeing, but they are not necessarily beneficial (and are sometimes destructive) to the realization of their hopes related to racial justice.[8]

---

[6] I think that Pettit overstates the importance of hope in sustaining agents in their practical pursuits. In later chapters, I show that agents can and do persist in reaching for their goals without hope and that other attitudes (such as anger and faith) contribute to positive action.

[7] Natasha Walter (2018), director of the charity Women for Refugee Women, explains that in the face of personal tragedies and political setbacks, it can feel "impossible to rise above." But though hope might be hard to come by in these difficult times, it is also essential on her view to motivate political action. She worries that without hope, those of us who occupy relatively privileged social locations may retreat into complacency, which is an option unavailable to refugee women and other people who live under extremely oppressive conditions.

[8] Martin has similar worries about the practical risks of hope. As discussed in the previous chapter, sick people's hopes for a cure can lead them to enroll in clinical trials which are risky (Martin 2008). Martin (2014) also worries that suicide can be an act of hope that death will end one's unendurable suffering (73–74). Calhoun (2018), too, raises concerns about the practical dangers of hope. She argues that even though hope might be worth cultivating, it is sometimes worth guarding against, because having hope can lead to crushing disappointment.

More recently, and in a similar vein, Martell Teasley and David Ikard (2010) explore the ways in which the rhetoric of hope in politics can give rise to hopes that are practically irrational. They suggest that the hope that many American citizens placed in Obama and the hope that his election was the beginning of a "postracial era" in the country had the effect of masking the worsening economic conditions for people of color at the time (Teasley and Ikard 2010, 420). As Michael C. Dawson (2012) points out, Obama's election made people hopeful that Americans would be living in a post-racial society in which "one's life chances were no longer significantly determined by race and neither were the basic contours of politics and society" (670). And this hopeful vision about race relations in America distracts from the hard realities of racism. It leads us away from serious inquiry into the relationship between racism and other social and economic problems such as poverty, poor health outcomes, and housing and employment discrimination that disproportionately affect people of color.[9]

These theorists' rational assessments are thus important for understanding the value of hope. But as Claudia Blöser and Titus Stahl (2017) point out, approaches to hope's practical rationality tend to focus specifically on the *instrumental rationality* of hope: whether hope is beneficial for an agent in selecting means to secure her ends. I would add that theories of hope also speak to hope's *substantive rationality*, or whether hope is beneficial for an agent to select ends that are compatible with her interests as a whole. As Andrea Scarantino and Ronald de Sousa (2018) explain, these are both kinds of *strategic* or *prudential rationality*.[10] For the purpose of clarity moving forward, I use the language of *epistemic rationality* in reference to whether the belief involved in hope is rational, and *strategic* or *prudential rationality* interchangeably in reference to the role of hope in securing and selecting our ends.[11] I use the term *practical rationality* when there seem to be strong reasons for hope, all things considered.

---

[9] As Andre Willis (2017) explains, "The USA has just experienced two terms of a Black President who was one of the brightest of lights in the American political firmament. The facts will show, however, that when Barack Obama walks out of the White House in January of 2017 black child poverty will be worse than when he took office" (3). Willis argues that the state of Black child poverty shows that "the democratic promise Obama supposedly represented has left a long shadow on American political and social hopes" (3). Relatedly, in his critique of Obama, Cornel West (2018) speculates that Martin Luther King Jr. "would have shed tears from his grave to see eight years of black symbolic celebration alongside concrete hibernation, of black break-dancing in the air and sleepwalking on the ground—as over one in three black children live in poverty" (513).

[10] See Catherine Rioux (forthcoming), who also characterizes discussions of hope's practical rationality in the philosophical literature in terms strategic rationality.

[11] It's helpful to keep both terms, since sometimes philosophers talk of an emotion's being "prudent," while others use the language of "strategically rational."

But assessments of epistemic and prudential (or strategic) rationality are not sufficient to understand the value of hope. We have seen that hope can also be intrinsically valuable, such as when an activist sustains a fundamental hope for racial justice as part of who they are (Blöser and Stahl 2017). And if we conceive of hope, as I have been suggesting, as an emotion through which we see in a favorable light the possibility that a desired outcome obtains, we can also ask whether hope is fitting. Philosophers of the emotions commonly assess whether emotions such as anger, amusement, and shame are "fitting" (e.g., D'Arms and Jacobson 2000; Tappolet 2016; Milona and Stockdale 2018), "apt" (e.g., Gilmore 2011; Srinivasan 2018), or "correct" (e.g., Teroni 2007). These questions are about the *cognitive rationality* of the emotion, or an emotion's "ability to represent the world as it is and properly relate to other evidence-sensitive processes" (Scarantino and de Sousa 2018). Because emotions are closely connected but not equivalent to our beliefs, assessing the epistemic rationality of beliefs involved in (or causally connected to) hope is not quite what we need to assess the cognitive rationality of the emotion itself.

I want to suggest that an account of when hope is fitting enriches our understanding of the rationality of hope.[12] It also illuminates why many of us have the intuition that something has gone wrong when we maintain strong hopes in the face of very low odds, even when those hopes are epistemically and prudentially rational. So just like we can improve our understanding of the nature of hope by making use of insights in the philosophy of the emotions, so too can this literature improve our understanding of the value of hope.

Fittingness

We have seen that hope involves not only desire and belief but also seeing or perceiving in a favorable light the possibility that a desired outcome obtains. This way of seeing is affective in character, intertwined with a sense of feeling toward the desired outcome. Hope is thus similar to other emotions that involve a way of seeing, or perceptual-like experience of an object. And this

---

[12] One might also use the language of "apt" or "correct," though I follow D'Arms and Jacobson (2000), among others, in using the language of "fittingness" primarily for the purposes of clarity and consistency.

perceptual/affective dimension of hope is not typically subject to assessments of epistemic rationality in the way that beliefs are. In other words, the norms that govern belief are not equivalent to the norms that govern emotions. To make sense of how the perceptual/affection dimension of emotions affects their overall value, philosophers of the emotions have noticed that emotions can be assessed as fitting, apt, or correct.

Justin D'Arms and Daniel Jacobson (2000) argue that philosophers some-times conflate the ways in which emotions can be evaluated: as morally appropriate, as prudentially rational, or whether the emotion is, all things considered, what one should feel. They point out that emotions can also be evaluated for fittingness, which is a distinct form of endorsement. Fitting emotions are emotions that correctly represent their objects as having cer-tain evaluative features.[13] And though there is disagreement about how to best characterize the evaluative representations constitutive of emotional experiences, there is consensus that emotions are perceptions of properties such as the funny (as in amusement) and the fearsome (as in fear). The ques-tion of fit, then, is one about whether the emotional perception correctly represents those properties. So to say that amusement is fitting in response to a joke is to say that the joke really is funny, and to say that fear is fitting in some context is to say that the object of fear really is fearsome. But an emotion can be fitting even if it is not morally appropriate or prudentially rational. It might, for example, be perfectly fitting to laugh at a joke (because the joke is funny) even if it would be immoral and imprudent to do so (because the joke is offensive and laughing could result in repercussions). Moral and pruden-tial assessments are reasons for and against being amused, but they are irrel-evant to the question of whether amusement correctly represents the joke as funny.

The question of whether an emotion is fitting depends on both its meta-phorical *shape* and *size* (D'Arms and Jacobson 2000). An emotion is fitting in terms of its shape if the emotion's object really does have the kind of evalua-tive features the emotion represents it as having. And an emotion is fitting in

[13] They endorse a "fitting attitude theory of value" called rational sentimentalism, according to which we can explain a subset of evaluative concepts (e.g., the shameful or funny) in terms of the *sen-timents* (e.g., shame and amusement). For example, what it is to be funny is for amusement to be a fit-ting response (D'Arms and Jacobson 2000; D'Arms and Jacobson 2010). D'Arms and Jacobson clarify that rational sentimentalism does not presuppose something like a robust form of realism about value, but rather that "sentimental values play a crucial role in the human mental economy . . . which renders skepticism about them moot" (4). Sentiments such as amusement, envy, hope, and fear are natural human responses almost all of us feel and recognize, even if they vary between societies and cultures.

terms of its size if the strength of the emotion is felt to an appropriate degree, given the context in question. For example, it is fitting (in terms of shape) to be amused by a joke if the joke is funny. If one is strongly amused, and if the joke is extremely funny, then strong amusement is also fitting in terms of its size. But it is unfitting (in terms of size) to be strongly amused by a joke that is only mildly funny. Similarly, it is fitting (in terms of shape) to be envious of a friend who has a possession that I desire and lack, a possession that would be good for me to have. If I am strongly envious and my friend's possession would be extremely good for me to have, then my strong envy is also fitting in terms of its size. But it is unfitting (in terms of size) to be strongly envious of my friend if all she has is a slightly better possession than mine. My friend isn't as enviable as my emotion represents her as being.

What about hope? I have argued that hope involves seeing or perceiving in a favorable light the possibility that a desired outcome obtains. Hope, in other words, is an affective perception of its object as favorable. Hope, then, is fitting in terms of its shape just in case the possibility that the hoped-for outcome will be realized really is favorable—that is, both possible and desirable. Consider a job candidate's hope to be offered a position at a small liberal arts college (SLAC) at the initial application stage of a tenure-track search, when the candidate's chances are 1 in 500. The chance is (in some sense) favorable, since being offered the position is both possible and desirable for the job candidate. The job candidate's hope is thus fitting in terms of its shape. But there is a further question of whether the job candidate's hope that he will be offered the SLAC position is fitting in terms of its size, or whether his hope correctly represents the degree to which being offered the position is favorable. This question depends on both the strength of the job candidate's desire for the position and the favorability of the odds. Intuitively, it is more fitting for the job candidate to hope more strongly for the SLAC position than for some other tenure-track position in a city in which he does not want to live, given the strength of his desires. It is also fitting for him to hope more strongly for the less desirable tenure-track position than to hope for a post doc, if what he most wants above all else is to settle down. The strength of our desires helps to determine what it is more or less fitting to hope for.[14]

---

[14] Part of the fittingness of hope thus depends upon whether and to what extent the outcome is desirable. Consequently, it is unfitting to hope for an outcome that is not actually desirable. To borrow a well-known example, suppose that an evil demon threatens the infliction of severe pain on you unless you desire a saucer of mud (for its own sake) (Rabinowicz and Rønnow-Rasmussen 2004, 402). It is unfitting to desire the saucer of mud (for its own sake) because the saucer of mud is not desirable for

But many have the intuition that despite the SLAC job's being strongly desirable for the job candidate, and despite the fact that the strength of his desires structure the degree to which his hopes for various jobs are fitting, if the job candidate is very hopeful about receiving an offer from the SLAC at the initial application stage, something has gone wrong. And what best makes sense of this intuition is that it is unfitting to see a 0.2 percent chance as strongly or even moderately favorable.[15] Emotions (including hope) are fitting in terms of their size if they are experienced to an appropriate degree given the context in question, which includes, in the case of hope, to what extent the available evidence is favorable. It is, for sure, difficult to determine an exact threshold for when the odds of a hope's being realized moves from slightly, to moderately, to strongly favorable. There is space for reasonable disagreement about what constitutes favorable odds. But what is important for our purposes is that it can be unfitting to hope for strongly desirable outcomes that are highly unlikely to be realized.[16]

Importantly, saying that a hope is unfitting is not the same thing as claiming that it is epistemically or prudentially irrational. The job candidate might be epistemically rational in believing that his chance of receiving an offer is 0.2 percent; many activities constitutive of the hope are prima facie harmless; and engaging in hopeful activities might lead him to invest a great deal of effort in his application materials, which might make his application stand out in a positive way. He might even have good reasons for sustaining his hope, all this considered, if hoping is the best he can do to keep his spirits up during a difficult time. But despite these familiar rational assessments, the

---

its own sake. Yet it seems clear that you have decisive prudential reasons to desire the saucer of mud in this context, if only you can bring yourself to do so.

A parallel argument can be made about hope. If the evil demon threatens the infliction of severe pain on you unless you hope for a saucer of mud (for its own sake), your hope is unfitting, because the saucer of mud is not desirable. Yet it seems clear that you have decisive prudential reasons to hope for the saucer of mud, if only you can bring yourself to form such a hope.

[15] Sabine Döring (2014) suggests a similar analysis. She argues that "the cancer patient's hope for recovery or the parent's hope for the safe return of their child may represent a good however great, but if the occurrence probability of the thing hoped for falls below a certain threshold value, we treat the hopes of these persons, like the perception of the Müller-Lyer lines, *as a mere illusion*" (127). Although the language of "illusion" might be too strong, Döring's point that our hopes sometimes misrepresent the world (not through belief but through a "felt evaluation") is helpful. Lisa Kretz (2019) similarly argues in the context of climate change that "the strength of hope, if is to be justified, reflects the probability of it being realized" (163).

[16] This is not to say that it is unfitting to strongly desire to be offered the tenure-track position. It is possible to strongly desire to be offered a position without strongly hoping for it. This is because one can have a desire for the position that functions more like a wish. The candidate might say, "The SLAC job is at the very top of my list! If only I could get it. What a dream."

job candidate's strong hope for the SLAC job represents in a too favorable light the possibility of being offered the tenure-track position given the evidence available.[17] And so, the hope is unfitting in terms of its size.[18]

Returning to Martin's (2014) *Cancer Research* case, many of us have the intuition that Bess's strong hope for a miracle cure in the face of a 1 percent chance is unfitting in terms of its size, even though a miracle cure is a very desirable outcome for her. In other words, her hope represents the possibility of a miracle cure in a far more favorable light than the evidence warrants. And her hope would be even more unfitting if she were to strongly hope for a cure in the face of a 0.0001 percent chance (Milona and Stockdale 2018).[19]

Like the job candidate, it is possible that Bess might have good reasons to maintain her strong hope, all things considered. So one might wonder whether assessments of fit capture anything beyond familiar rational assessments after all. But as D'Arms and Jacobson (2000) point out, "Talk of fittingness of emotions may sound rather recherché, but 'fittingness' is simply intended as a technical term for a familiar type of evaluation" (72). When we say, for example, "The grass is always greener on the other side" in response to someone's envy, we mean that the envied person's situation is not really enviable (that envy is unfitting). It might also be prudentially irrational or morally inappropriate to be envious, but the "grass is greener" response is not criticizing the prudential rationality or moral inappropriateness of the emotion. It is criticizing the emotion's lack of fit. Similarly, "Don't get your hopes up" conveys that a person's hope represents in a too favorable light the possibility that a desired outcome obtains. The criticism is about the emotion itself being out of place, not necessarily the prudential irrationality of the hope. And common expressions such as "Is there still hope?" and "There is hope!" are meant to search for and track the evidence about the likelihood of a hoped-for outcome's being realized, not merely whether the outcome is

[17] Döring similarly suggests that the correctness conditions for hope also cannot be fully captured by assessments of "purely strategic" rationality, which misses "the phenomenal aspect of hope, the 'what-it-is-like' to hope" (Döring 2014, 124).

[18] We can run the same argument for other emotions. For example, if a close friend forgets to wish me a happy birthday, my strong resentment would be unfitting in terms of its size, since forgetting my birthday is not a serious moral wrong. (Perhaps mild irritation might be more fitting.) This is so despite how much I care about my own birthday. And I might have good reasons to not be resentful *at all* if all my resentment does is ruin my birthday even more (my resentment might be imprudent). But it is still fitting to be irritated when a close friend displays a lack of regard for the friendship.

[19] Again, this is not to say that it is unfitting to strongly desire a miracle cure. Bess might maintain a strong desire for a miracle cure that functions more like a wish. She might say, "I would do *anything* for a miracle cure! If only there were better odds." In this scenario, Bess might maintain a strong desire, but only slight hope, for a cure.

possible, and not whether it would be prudentially rational to hope given the person's interests and goals.

Of course, we might also criticize unfitting hope because of how it might lead to other kinds of irrationality. In *Cancer Research*, Bess might originally be both epistemically and prudentially rational in her strong hope that an experimental drug will cure her, as Martin argues. And perhaps it is practically rational for Bess to sustain her strong hope at this very moment, all things considered. But since Bess's strong hope for a miracle cure does not accurately represent to what extent the odds are favorable, her hope might lead to epistemic and prudential irrationality over time. This is because the sense of comfort, assurance, anticipation, and other hopeful feelings we experience in strongly hoping for an outcome can cause us to become irrational in our thinking and behavior. In *Cancer Research*, Bess's strong hope to be cured may cause her to become epistemically irrational if she begins to feel (with the resultant belief) that she will in fact be cured. Bess might then change her behavior, engaging in activities that are detrimental to her self-interest, rendering her hope prudentially irrational too. She might, for example, refuse to talk about her wishes for a funeral for "when the time comes."[20]

Fittingness assessments thus highlight the risks of hopes that are commonly considered to be rational, based on familiar ways of thinking about the rationality of hope in the philosophical literature. They can also help to illuminate concerns about the strength of hope in conditions of oppression. These are conditions in which there is often a very low probability that people's hopes will be realized, and so strong hopes will often be unfitting. For example, although my strong hope that humanity will solve the crisis of climate injustice by 2050 might be fully epistemically and prudentially rational (because I am not mistaken about the evidence and hoping is good for my wellbeing and motivation to see climate injustice eliminated in my lifetime), it is nevertheless unfitting. The emotion represents the very small chance that humanity will solve the crisis of climate injustice by 2050 in a far more favorable light than the evidence warrants. And though

---

[20] One might object that fittingness assessments seem very close to epistemic and prudential rationality assessments, and it's true that the evaluative dimensions of hope are closely related. For example, if a hope is epistemically irrational, then it is likely to be prudentially irrational too. If I irrationally believe that I am likely to win the lottery because "I have a good feeling about it" and purchase a bunch of tickets despite being in a position of financial insecurity, my epistemically irrational hope has led me to engage in prudentially irrational actions. Purchasing a lottery ticket is at the expense of spending the limited money I have on essential resources. Similarly, I am suggesting that unfitting hopes can lead to both epistemic and prudential irrationality. I take this to be a natural consequence of evaluating mental states that are composed of other mental states, as in hope.

the strength of my unfitting hope might contribute positively to my well-being, this fact is itself risky. Seeing in a strongly favorable light the possibility that we will solve the climate crisis by 2050 and thus feeling hopeful about this prospect can eventually lead to a dangerous illusion of comfort about just how severe and complicated the crisis really is. My hope might thus *become* epistemically irrational if feeling strongly hopeful alters my original belief about the likelihood of success, causing me to believe that my desire will (or is likely to) be realized despite the very real evidence to the contrary.[21] And my epistemically irrational hope might lead me to engage in prudentially irrational actions too, such as sitting back and waiting for governments and scientists to come up with a solution (see also Kretz 2019).[22]

Fittingness assessments thus help to enrich our understanding of the rationality of hope. In Andrea Scarantino and Ronald de Sousa (2018)'s terms, they are part of the *cognitive rationality* of the attitude, or whether the emotion accurately represents the world as it is (even if not in the same way as belief). Hope is thought to be epistemically rational if the belief part of hope is justified given the evidence available, but this assessment does not bear on whether the affective perception of the hoped-for outcome's obtaining as "favorable" correctly represents the extent to which the possibility of the outcome's obtaining really is favorable. And hope is thought to be prudentially rational if it promotes one's ends, but again this assessment is distinct from whether the affective perception of the outcome as favorable accurately tracks the extent to which it is. Assessments of fit thus help us to make sense of the intuitive thought that something has gone wrong when we maintain strong hopes in the face of unfavorable odds, even when our beliefs about the likelihood of success are rational.

---

[21] Calhoun (2018) seems to have this issue in mind when she argues that hope may "eliminate from our planning view of the future an assessment of the odds of success or may replace an accurate probability assessment with an unduly rosy one" (88). Milona (2018), too, argues that hope can make us prone to wishful thinking, which "occurs when a person's desires cause her to believe that something is true, or likely to become true" (17).

[22] Blöser, Huber, and Moellendorf (2020) similarly suggest that there may be good reasons to criticize agents whose political hopes are for highly improbable outcomes, when changing course and pursuing alternative, more realistic options would be best. Thus, on their view, "There seem to be cases where hope is [epistemically and prudentially] rational but not commendable" (6). Drawing upon Darrel Moellendorf (2006), they suggest that normative criticisms of hope in such circumstances might best be cast in terms of opportunity costs. But this insight can also be captured by assessments of *fit*. Strong hopes for improbable outcomes are unfitting, and unfitting hopes are *risky*, for epistemic and prudential reasons. And so we have reason to be, at the very least, cautious about such hopes as we pursue important political ends.

But hopes might also turn out to be (epistemically and prudentially) rational and fitting even if they seem clearly morally inappropriate. Suppose a person, Suzie, hopes that her ex-partner's new marriage is disastrous. Suzie's hope is fitting if her hope correctly represents the possibility of the outcome's obtaining as favorable—that is, both possible and desirable. But there are different ways in which we might assess the desirability of this possible outcome. On a subjective view of what is desirable, what is desirable is what is good for Suzie, or what she has reasons to pursue, given what she most wants. It is thus fitting, on this interpretation, for Suzie to hope that her ex's new marriage is disastrous. The hoped-for outcome really is desirable, given what Suzie most wants. One might, however, adopt an objective view of what is desirable instead. On an objective view, what is desirable for Suzie is what is objectively good, or what she has reasons to pursue, independently of (and sometimes in conflict with) her expressed desires. It is thus unfitting, on this interpretation, for Suzie to hope that her ex's new marriage is disastrous. The hoped-for outcome is not desirable, since it is an objectively bad outcome. And perhaps it is always unfitting to hope for objectively bad outcomes, including the failed marriages of decent people.

I actually think (perhaps controversially) that the subjective view is correct. It seems perfectly fitting to me for Suzie to hope that her ex-partner's new marriage is disastrous, if what she most wants is to have the opportunity to pursue getting back together with her ex. And we can imagine that getting back with her ex might really make Suzie happy.[23] It might even be fitting for Suzie to strongly hope for this outcome too, if she has good reasons to think that the new relationship is dysfunctional and that her ex still has feelings for her.[24] It certainly seems morally inappropriate for Suzie to hope that her ex's new marriage is disastrous, and it would be morally wrong for her to act on the hope—by attempting, for example, to sabotage the marriage. But the

---

[23] I find it difficult to accept the position that immoral people cannot be happy, or that successfully pursuing morally inappropriate hopes cannot make people happy. See, for example, Steven Cahn's (2004) "The Happy Immoralist." Cahn suggests that when we find ourselves pulled by the idea that an immoral person must be unhappy, what's really going on is that "*we* are not happy with *him*" (1). I'm persuaded by this line of reasoning: that immoral people can be happy, but we are frustrated by this prospect. And I see hope as connected to happiness, inasmuch as what we hope for is so often what we believe will make us happy (e.g., successful careers, relationships, and so on). One might object that these kinds of morally inappropriate hopes, and pursuing them, never actually make people happy in the end. But that's an empirical question, and it's certainly conceivable that her ex-partner's new marriage resulting in disaster, thus setting her up to get back with her ex, might make Suzie happy. Strange things happen in people's romantic lives all the time.

[24] On the other hand, it might be unfitting for her to strongly hope for this outcome, if she has good reasons to think that her ex's new relationship is a good one.

moral criticism of Suzie's hope seems importantly different from whether her hope is fitting.

Other examples are not hard to come by. We can even inquire about the morality of the job candidate's hope to be offered the SLAC position, discussed previously. There seemed to be nothing morally wrong about the hope as presented. But suppose the entire faculty is white and male, and that the candidate is also white and male. Suppose, too, that the white male job candidate's friend, who is an equally qualified Black woman, is also applying for the SLAC position. It is obviously better, from a moral point of view, for the Black woman to be offered the job. But it seems to me implausible to suggest that it would be unfitting for the white male job candidate to hope for the offer, given what he most wants and how happy he would likely be in his dream job—even if it would be morally worse for him to be offered the position. It even seems to me implausible to suggest that his potential, related hope that the SLAC faculty and institution do not take diversity considerations seriously in hiring decisions is unfitting, given his personal situation. Yet this hope seems clearly morally inappropriate.

These examples suggest that at least some hopes might be fitting even if they are morally inappropriate. This is consistent with D'Arms and Jacobson's (2000) suggestion that it might be fitting to be amused by an offensive joke even if it would be immoral to laugh. Although it is unsettling to concede that morally inappropriate hopes can potentially be (epistemically and prudentially) rational as well as fitting, it is important not to conflate these evaluative measures with a moral constraint on hope. As Claudia Blöser, Jakob Huber, and Darrel Moellendorf (2020) explain:

> The practical rationality of hope can be evaluated along different dimensions: on the one hand, the evaluation can concern the object of hope (e.g., whether it is directed at a morally permissible end), on the other hand, it can concern features of the attitude itself (e.g., whether hoping is beneficial to the agent or has an effect on the likelihood of attaining the desired outcome). Both of these possibilities are instances of practical evaluation; the first concerning the goodness of the object, the second the prudential value of the attitude. (6)

Thus, the moral goodness of hope's object and, as I will argue, the quality of moral character that many of our hopes manifest are additional considerations that are relevant to the practical question of what hopes we should cultivate and pursue.

I now turn to moral assessments of hope.

Moral Assessments

Hope is not always a moral issue. When I strongly hope that my miniature schnauzer will not bark when visitors knock on the door (which would be unfitting, as it turns out), or when I hoped that the sun would shine brightly in Texas on my last day in the state (which was fitting, but not realized), my hopes are irrelevant to what is morally good, bad, right, or wrong in the world. But many of our significant hopes do have moral content: Khan-Cullors's hope that Trayvon Martin's killer would be convicted, the hope that a loved one will not betray you, and the hope that a state will not pass anti-LGBTQ+ legislation, for example. We also have moral hopes for wide-reaching outcomes, such as the hope for justice in the aftermath of genocide (Walker 2018). And beyond these moral hopes (i.e., hopes for morally good or bad outcomes), some of our hopes reflect well or poorly on our moral characters because of what they reveal about who we are. For example, Suzie's hope that her ex-partner's new marriage is disastrous seems to be morally inappropriate because of what this hope reveals about Suzie, even though its object is not a morally bad outcome. Failed marriages are tragic and painful, but they are not in themselves moral wrongs.

I want to bring moral assessments of hope into fuller view. In light of the ubiquity of our moral hopes and the significance of hope to moral life, it seems apt to think about how moral considerations affect the value of our hopes. And there is, I suggest, is a moral constraint on hope: when we find ourselves with morally inappropriate hopes, there are decisive reasons to work to overcome or revise them.[25] Hopes are morally appropriate when

---

[25] Some philosophers have made passing remarks that also suggest a moral constraint on hope. For example, Margaret Urban Walker (2018) acknowledges that victims can be wrong about what they perceive to be justice, and so "not morally entitled to what they hope for" (226). Darrel Moellendorf (2019) suggests that "if it is wrong to act in some way, or if an outcome would be bad, then hoping for the success of the act or the existence of the outcome also seems wrong" (252). Nancy E. Snow (2018) points out that if there is a moral virtue of hope, then one cannot have this virtue if one hopes for immoral ends (173). And Michael Milona (2020), in his discussion of hope as a moral virtue, points out that people sometimes "hope entirely for the wrong thing (e.g., to join the Mafia)" (5).

Andrew Chignell (forthcoming) argues that a person, Sadie, who hopes to hurt Vickie has a duty not to. On Chignell's view, hope involves belief, desire, and "focus on the desired outcome *under the*

they reveal that the agent's character is properly oriented toward what is morally good (hereafter, "the good"). The clearest cases of morally appropriate hopes are hopes that involve a desire for morally good outcomes. For example, when a person hopes that a perpetrator of racial violence will be brought to justice, her hope is constituted by a desire for racial justice, revealing that she clearly cares about this important moral good. In contrast, when a person hopes that anti-LGBTQ+ legislation will be passed, their hope is constituted by a desire for an outcome that threatens the moral rights of LGBTQ+ people. It is enough, on my view, that the person harbors the hope that anti-LGBTQ+ legislation will be passed for the hope to be morally inappropriate, independently of whether the person can, at all, affect whether the outcome materializes. To take a different and rather extreme example, if Richard Spencer found himself stranded alone on an island without any chance of escape, hoping that back home other white supremacists were carrying out his racist agenda, his hope would be morally inappropriate despite its futile effect on the world.

These cases help us to see that it is not only the fact that certain hopes lead to immoral actions that make them morally inappropriate. Of course, the fact that morally inappropriate emotions lead to immoral actions is certainly a very good moral reason counting against them. For example, suppose a man, Joe, hopes that a woman, Tina, to whom he is attracted will consume enough alcohol at an upcoming party for him to have sex with her. On some views, what is practically rational for Joe to do about his hope is constrained by morality: what is immoral is also irrational (e.g., Kant 1996). Joe's hope that Tina consumes enough alcohol at an upcoming party to have sex with him is hoping to be well positioned to use her as a mere means to an end, and this immoral hope/intention/action set is practically irrational. Even if Joe does not care at all about the wrongness of using Tina as a mere means to an end (and so there is no sense in which we can appeal to contradictory desires in explaining the practical irrationality of his hope), the fact that Joe's hope/intention/action set is bad is a reason for him to hope/intend/act differently (see, for example, FitzPatrick 2004).[26]

---

aspect of its undefeated possibility" (10). If Vickie is unable to prevent herself from focusing on hurting Vickie, "then she should do so under the aspect of its *impermissibility* rather than its possibility" (17).

[26] Some philosophers of hope have hinted at this line of reasoning. Martin (2014) argues that even though features of individuals' psychology do sometimes prevent them from being moved by certain considerations, this fact does not "block those considerations from providing reasons for those people to revise their mental states" (44). Miriam Schleifer McCormick (2017) also suggests this kind

There is significant debate about the relationship between practical rationality and morality, so I don't want to wade in too deeply here. Crucially, though, it seems clear that moral reasons are decisive in determining what Joe should do, in the sense that they override other considerations (e.g., Joe's pleasure). I take it that plausible views of what counts as a reason for action can accommodate this claim.[27] And the fact that Joe's hope will lead him to perform immoral actions also seems to be decisive reason for him to suppress his hope, despite his current desires. But I want to suggest that the moral wrongness of sexism, racism, and other forms of oppression generates a moral requirement to work to relinquish relevant attitudes independently of what those attitudes might or could dispose a person to do. So in this case Joe's hope is morally inappropriate even if he is blocked from pursuing it (e.g., suppose the party is canceled, or he's arrested for drinking and driving on his way there). In other words, not only are moral reasons decisive in overriding other considerations about what agents should do, but they are also decisive in determining the characters we should cultivate and sustain.[28]

of view in arguing that "if the hoped-for outcome is something obviously terrible, this will tell against the hope's rationality" (132).

[27] For example, a reasons internalist might say that despite Joe's current desires, it is possible for him based on other features of his psychology to take up the value of respect for persons and the value of consent into deliberation in a way that would motivate him to act on these values. Very roughly, *reasons internalism* is the view that normative reasons are ones that agents can arrive at through deliberation from their set of desires. A *reasons externalist*, on the other hand, might adopt a value-based conception of practical reason, arguing that, despite Joe's current desires, the moral prohibition against sexual assault is a reason for Joe to refrain from his action because such a consideration makes his performing the action bad. Reasons externalism is the view that there are some normative reasons for action external to agents' motivational sets. See, for example, Williams (1981), Fitzpatrick (2004), and Martin (2014) for discussion.
   What is important for our purposes is that we agree that all-too-common men like Joe who hope to take advantage of women, disrespect them, and fail to appreciate the value of consent nevertheless have moral reasons to act inconsistently with their sexual desires. It might very well be pointless, as Martin (2014) argues, to insist that full-blown sociopaths have moral reasons for action if they are wholly incapable of appreciating morality. I think that in these cases, we should adopt what Peter F. Strawson (2008) calls the "objective view" toward such people, suspending the participant reactive attitudes and demands to behave morally and instead treating them as outside of the moral community.

[28] Although I remain focused on hope as an emotion, this discussion of morally appropriate and inappropriate hopes may help philosophers think about how to characterize hope as a moral virtue. However, I agree with Michael Milona (2020) that the virtue of hope (like other virtues) cannot be equivalent to the relevant emotion, or else we would be left with an implausible "flood of virtues" (6). Thus, more work is needed to capture the (potential) moral virtue of hope. On Milona's (2020) own "priorities model," for example, whether hopes are virtuous depends upon "how they are situated with the context of the agent's life as a whole, and principally with respect to their other hopes" (9). I leave open how insights about a moral constraint on hope might relate to the priorities model of hope as a moral virtue.

Sarah Stroud (1998) helpfully clarifies what the overridingness thesis about morality (OT) is meant to capture in the context of actions, which states that "if S is morally required to φ, then S has most reason to φ" (171). OT does not say that agents have most reason to be moral saints and to always choose morally praiseworthy acts but that they have decisive reasons to refrain from doing that which is morally impermissible. So to anticipate the application of OT in the context of hope, the idea is not that one ought to cultivate all morally appropriate hopes. Rather, the claim is that morally inappropriate hopes are ruled out, in the sense that morality provides us with sufficient reason to work to overcome or revise them.

But why think that OT is right, even when it comes to actions? Stroud (1998) provides four reasons for why OT is a thesis we should accept. First, we conceive of (and experience) morality as a constraint on our aims, limiting the extent to which we should pursue our projects. If it were permissible (all things considered) to prioritize other practical considerations (e.g., one's self-interest) above moral requirements, then the authority of morality as a felt constraint on our projects would be undermined (Stroud 1998, 176). Second, OT makes sense of our everyday moral practices. We accept that moral requirements defeat other considerations when we reason about what to do. If we do away with OT, then we are left without a defense of agents' responsiveness to moral considerations over competing ones. Third, OT reflects widespread beliefs about sufficient reasons, namely, that a moral requirement to φ is sufficient reason to φ—whereas a legal, prudential, or etiquette reason alone is an insufficient reason to φ (177). Fourth, much of moral theory presupposes OT to begin with. For example, the moral judgment that one must not torture innocent people presupposes that the "must" is *decisive*—that is, not defeasible in the face of reasons to torture the innocent. Although none of these reasons for accepting OT prove that OT is true, Stroud suggests that they are reasons to favor the thesis.

In light of these considerations in favor of OT, and in the absence of compelling reasons to abandon it, I endorse it for my purposes here.[29] But I also

---

[29] Stroud concludes her article with the following claim: "I think we will be more content with a kinder, gentler conception of morality which permits a reasonable degree of *faith* that our aspirations for morality's status will be vindicated" (187–188, emphasis added). In chapter 5, I discuss the phenomenon of moral faith, which sometimes manifests as faith that one's moral convictions are true in the absence of definitive proof. For those of us concerned with the nature and scope of oppression, who want to build arguments that depend upon the claim that moral reasons to undermine oppression override privileged people's prudential reasons for supporting it, perhaps what we need is some degree of moral faith to proceed.

want to suggest that it can be extended to beliefs, desires, and emotions. If one accepts a moral requirement to not be racist, for example, then what people need to do to meet that moral requirement is much more than simply to refrain from performing racist actions. They ought to work to relinquish false beliefs about people of color, unlearn implicit racist biases, and give up racist emotions. And they ought not be racist not only because having a racist character disposes people to perform morally wrong actions (although this is certainly one very good reason) but also because having a racist character is itself morally criticizable.[30] Recall the castaway version of Richard Spencer and his hope that white supremacists back home will carry out his racist agenda. Although he is stranded on an island with no chance of affecting the social world, Spencer's hope is morally criticizable because it is constitutive of his racist character. As Robert Adams (1985) argues:

> The subject of ethics is how we ought to live; and that is not reducible to what we ought to do or try to do, and what we ought to cause or produce. It includes just as fundamentally what we should be for and against in our hearts, what we ought to love and hate. It matters morally what we are for and what we are against, even if we do not have the power to do much for or against it, and even if it was not by trying that we came to be before or against it. (12)

Ethics is about who we are, not only how we act. Even though we do not choose our desires and emotions, they are responses that belong to us and reveal the quality of our moral characters. Adams thus argues that there are what he calls *involuntary sins*, that is, states of mind that are not under our direct voluntary control but for which we can nevertheless be held responsible—such as unjustified anger, jealousy, and self-righteousness. When people harbor morally inappropriate emotions, we tend to think not just that acting out of these states of mind is wrong but that they ought not to have them in themselves (Adams 1985, 5).

The idea that there are involuntary sins, like the overridingness thesis, also helps to make sense of our everyday moral practices. We complain not just that people act wrongly but that they harbor desires and emotions

---

[30] Rima Basu (2019) similarly argues that racist beliefs themselves are wrong, even if people who hold them do not act on those beliefs. She argues that accounts focused on how beliefs lead to immoral actions are too narrow in scope, failing "to capture the more subtle, insidious, and more prevalent forms of racism" (2502).

that are morally inappropriate in their own right—malicious desires, racial resentments, homophobic hatred (Adams 1985), and, I want to add, morally inappropriate hopes. Even when agents do not endorse such desires and emotions at the level of moral belief (as when you believe that you should not hope that your lovely friend suffers despite your hope that he does), they reveal that agents' orientation toward the good is wrong.[31] You feel awful about catching yourself passively engaged in pleasant, malicious imaginings about your lovely friend suffering (even if you would never act on them) because the desire for your friend to suffer reflects on who you are as a person. Similarly, a white clerk might feel guilty upon catching themselves tensing up while fearfully hoping that a Black person entering their store will not steal (even if they don't and would never act on the hope by, for example, calling security) because the hope is indicative of racism.[32]

Notice that the hope that a Black person does not steal is not constituted by a desire for a morally bad outcome. It is thus not as straightforwardly morally inappropriate as the hope for white dominance. But the hope still reveals a defect in the white clerk's moral character, once we consider the relationship between the hope and its *cognitive bases*: that is, the mental states that causally influence the hope (Milona 2018; Milona and Naar 2020). When a white clerk hopes that a Black person does not steal, the hope is caused by the visual perception of a Black person combined with the internalized racist stereotype that Black people are criminals. So even though the hoped-for outcome's obtaining would be morally good (it is good when people don't steal, after all), the hope is still morally inappropriate. It reveals a weakness in the white clerk's moral character, and in particular the internalization of racist stereotypes. And it is the white clerk's self-awareness about how racism negatively affects their moral character that explains their resultant guilt.[33] Hopes are thus morally inappropriate if they reveal that the agent is

[31] Although this description sounds similar to theological understandings of the virtue of hope (see Lloyd 2016 and Lamb 2016 for discussion), I am not suggesting that the good "images God" (Lloyd 2016, 177). I want to allow for agents to be properly oriented toward the good, in their hopes, regardless of religion.

[32] As Shannon Sullivan (2014) argues, racism does not merely operate, and perhaps does not even primarily operate, at the level of belief. It is in white people's hearts and guts, including their affective and physiological reactions to encounters with people of color.

[33] There are also epistemic errors, here, such as the internalization of racist stereotypes. But there are other cases in which it might be rational to hold a racist belief that is nevertheless an immoral belief. Rima Basu (2019) considers the "rational racist" who rationally believes (based on evidence they have accessed and correctly interpreted) that Black diners tip substantially less than white diners at restaurants. Basu persuasively argues that it is both racist and morally wrong to hold this belief, even though the belief is rational. And we can imagine epistemically rational hopes based on such

not properly oriented toward the good, which can be either through an immoral desire or by way of other morally inappropriate mental states involved in the hope.

The Suzie case above represents a third kind of morally inappropriate hope. Suzie's hope that her ex-partner's marriage is disastrous is not for a morally bad outcome (though its obtaining would of course be unfortunate for the married couple), and the cognitive base of her hope is not an unendorsed immoral attitude (as in the case of the white clerk's racist stereotype). Her hope rather reveals the moral vice of selfishness, a vice that is part of the cognitive base of her hope. What all of these cases illustrate is that morally inappropriate hopes reveal ways in which agents are not properly oriented toward the good, either through immoral desires or other immoral attitudes and traits (e.g., racist stereotypes, moral vices) involved in the hope. There will likely be many different kinds of morally inappropriate hopes.[34]

But there are also morally suspect hopes, or hopes that reveal a potential defect in the agent's moral character, but because of the nature of the hope and/or human beings' limited epistemic resources for understanding our own and others' emotions, the moral status of the hope is indeterminate. For example, suppose a citizen hopes that a woman candidate in a political election gets crushed in a debate by their favored (male) candidate. This hope is not for a morally bad outcome, and the male candidate's performing well and winning the election might be the morally best outcome if his policy proposals are clearly morally superior. But the cognitive bases of the hope might, due to the gender dynamics involved, include sexist attitudes, however subtle and unconscious. For example, contempt for women and distrust of women in positions of authority might causally influence the person's hope for the woman candidate to be crushed in the debate, even if her losing is morally better all things considered. But it's too difficult to be certain, in many cases, whether hopes like this one reveal unconscious sexist biases. The

beliefs. For example, one might hope for white customers to visit one's restaurant, rather than Black customers, on the basis of one's beliefs about racial differences in tipping practices. The hope might be rational, but it is nevertheless morally inappropriate, revealing a discriminatory attitude toward Black customers.

[34] I am focusing on morally inappropriate hopes since my goal is to articulate the moral constraint on hope. But there are also different kinds of morally appropriate hopes. Some hopes are morally appropriate not because they are constituted by a desire for a morally good outcome but because they reveal other morally appropriate attitudes and virtues. For example, my hope that a neighbor I run into has a good day is not for a morally good outcome, but it reveals that I care about the happiness of other people. I don't have an on obligation to hope that my neighbors enjoy their days, but my hope reflects good feature of my moral character—namely, care for others.

moral terrain is thus messy, and there will likely be many morally suspect hopes, or hopes that reveal the potential presence of other morally inappropriate attitudes involved in the hope. I do not mean to suggest that we should interrogate people about such hopes, but I do think that self-reflection and, sometimes, receptiveness to others' observations about our hopes is important—or even just how we should best frame them. Although there is nothing morally suspect about hoping that one's favored (male) candidate performs well in a political debate, hoping that he crushes a woman is. And it might be best to focus on hoping for the former outcome.

What unites both morally inappropriate hopes and morally suspect hopes is that they reflect on a person's moral character. Our moral characters are constituted by beliefs, desires, values, and emotions, all of which make up who we are as people and influence one another in complex ways.[35] Although many of these mental states are passive, non-voluntary responses to events in the world, and although they are shaped by our social, cultural, and religious upbringing, we do have indirect control over them. As Claudia Card (1996) points out, "That our motivations and carryings through are embedded in factors beyond our control does not imply that there is no control after all" (27). She argues that agents can take responsibility for themselves and for their histories of bad constitutive luck (i.e., the luck that shapes moral character) in a forward-looking way by working to improve their characters over time. When we take responsibility in the forward-looking sense, we "locate ourselves as morally relevant centers of agency" (28).[36] We can, for example, attend psychotherapy sessions to "work on" our emotions and attend workshops designed to help privileged people unlearn their racist, sexist,

[35] Robert C. Roberts (2009) nicely illustrates how emotions and character traits influence one another in ways that come to bear on the quality of their moral characters. For example, in the case of morally inappropriate amusement, he points out that we morally criticize people for laughing at offensive jokes because amusement is a pleasant emotion that reveals that the person takes pleasure in offense toward others. Roberts speculates that the virtue of compassion would cancel out any pleasure the agent would take in offense toward others, and so the compassionate person would not be amused. Morally inappropriate emotions, then, might also help to reveal the absence of morally praiseworthy traits.

[36] Nancy Sherman (1999), too, defends the idea that people can take responsibility for their emotions in a forward-looking sense. In a way similar to how McGeer (2004) traces children's development of the capacity for hope, Sherman illustrates how children develop the capacity for emotional regulation through interactions with caregivers who support their emotional development. Through activities such as reciprocal smiling, play, and urging children to hold a blanket when a caregiver's hug is not available, children learn to manage distressing and frustrating emotions and to endure experiences of excitement and joy without being overwhelmed. Sherman points out that children learn to become agents of emotional experience, who "have a 'say' in shaping [their] emotional capacities and sensitivities" (322).

homophobic, etc. habits. Inasmuch as our desires and emotions can change in response to our efforts, they are things for which we can be held (to some extent) morally responsible (see also Neu 2010).

Notice that it is not necessary that the belief, desire, or emotion for which we take responsibility is something we produced (as when we attribute responsibility to agents for past actions). I might find myself with morally inappropriate emotions (e.g., racist fears, malicious hopes) through little to no fault of my own, yet the fact that I didn't produce these emotions in myself does not mean that I cannot take responsibility for having them. If it is at least possible for me to know that my emotion is morally inappropriate—such that I could be responsive to moral reasons to work to relinquish or revise it— yet I fail to take responsibility for doing so, it is that failure that is morally blameworthy.[37] By possible, I mean that correct moral evaluations are available to me through my ability to reason, my emotional capacities, socialization, education, access to information, and so on. These conditions enable the possibility for me to endorse correct moral evaluations. Sometimes, people are not blameworthy for failing to meet a moral requirement because correct moral evaluations are unavailable to them. For example, an 8-year-old, home-schooled child of white supremacist parents who does not know that racism is morally wrong and does not have access to the skills and information necessary to form this belief is not blameworthy for failing to take responsibility for his racist hopes. The extent to which it is possible for us to arrive at correct moral evaluations is a matter of degree. The now-grown-up, 20-year-old white supremacist attending a public university who continues to harbor racist hopes despite being equipped with newfound critical reasoning skills and access to less biased education and who is surrounded by diverse people who challenge his racist views is more blameworthy than his 8-year-old self.

Importantly, individual moral responsibility is also often mitigated because others shoulder some of it. Parents, friends, colleagues, the media, and public institutions can all shape the beliefs, desires, emotions, and character traits people have. These agents thus bear some moral responsibility for the conduct and attitudes of the people they have helped to shape.[38]

---

[37] Suzie might revise her hope that her ex's new marriage is disastrous by, for example, attending psychotherapy sessions with the goal of working on her selfishness so that she can hope to find new love for herself and to be happy for her ex.

[38] I am indebted to Susan Sherwin's work and mentorship, which encourages me to always keep this point in view. Responsibility is *relational* in the sense that our responsibilities as individuals are bound up with the responsibilities of other people, groups, and institutions (see Sherwin 2012 and Sherwin and Stockdale 2017).

The 8-year-old's parents are largely morally responsible for providing their son with a racist education (and there are likely other people who are partially morally responsible for the parents' racism too). Public institutions can also certainly do better to equip citizens with the skills and knowledge they need to challenge their racist, sexist, etc. beliefs and attitudes about history and the world. But there *are* overriding moral requirements that are unmet (and violated) when agents continue to harbor morally inappropriate hopes and other emotions. They include the individual's unmet moral obligation to work to overcome such hopes and emotions, and, quite often, others' unmet moral obligation to provide good moral education.

If these reflections are on the right track, then hope is subject to moral assessments, and it is sometimes apt to hold people responsible and to blame them for not working to relinquish their morally inappropriate hopes and other morally inappropriate attitudes (or for failing to provide the necessary moral support of others who are developing their moral characters).[39] It is also sometimes apt to morally praise agents who have hopes that are morally appropriate—even if there is no moral requirement to cultivate them. Agents who harbor hopes for morally good outcomes have integrated moral beliefs and desires: their moral beliefs are correct and consistent with what they desire and hope for. And this, I think, is a significant moral achievement independently of the likelihood that one's hopes will be realized. Of course, and as we have seen, some agents' hopes are damaged by the unjust conditions in which they live. Their losses of hope are often fitting and sometimes even politically useful (Bell 1992a).[40] But there is something morally admirable about hoping against hope, or maintaining hopes related to justice in the face of a low chance of success. And what seems admirable about such hopes is that they supplement agents' commitment to their moral ends.[41]

---

[39] In other words, agents have the responsibility to work to overcome both morally inappropriate hopes and the morally inappropriate mental states (e.g., racist stereotypes) on which even morally inappropriate hopes are based (e.g., the hope that a Black person does not steal).

[40] I cannot overemphasize this point enough. I do not take agents who lose hope under oppressive conditions to be necessarily morally lacking in any way. As Bell (1992a) and, as we will see later on, Coates (2015a) and other activists demonstrate, a loss or absence of hope can be morally, epistemically, and politically valuable as well as compatible with resistance to oppression. In other words, hope is not required to demonstrate a commitment to ending oppression. It is possible to be committed and motivated to end oppression yet hopeless about the possibility that oppression will end. There are different kinds of admirable moral characters people might have.

[41] Matthew Benton (2019) similarly argues that "we may regard one who persists in hopefulness, against very strong evidence that their hope will be fulfilled, as exhibiting a series of *virtues*: being steadfast, brave, faithfully and unwaveringly committed to the increasingly unlikely hoped-for outcome" (145). And this is an assessment of the agent's moral character.

Cheshire Calhoun (2009) argues that commitments are active, sustained intentions to pursue a project or end—ones that are resistant to reconsideration or revision. So when I commit to a project or end, I reason that setbacks, obstacles, or challenges must be quite severe in order for me to give up on my commitment, to varying degrees and depending on the strength of my commitment. Commitments therefore "*safeguard* one's future against psychological vicissitudes" (617).[42] In more recent work, Calhoun (2018) argues that hope supplements agents' commitments, lending additional motivation to their practical pursuits.[43] Hope seems to strengthen, even further, agents' ability to uphold their commitments in the face of setbacks, obstacles, and a low chance of success. And it is this, I think, that is Khan-Cullors's moral achievement, and the achievement of other activists who sustain moral hopes in the face of oppression.[44] Although not all of us need hope to sustain our commitments, some of us do. And when hope supplements our commitments to the most important moral and political ends, it is an especially praiseworthy mental state to sustain in its own right.[45]

I imagine that the world would be much less (morally) decent than it is now without these activists and their hopes. And, as I will show later on, the world would also be much less (morally) decent than it is now in the absence of prominent activists without hope—Derrick Bell, Ta-Nehisi Coates,[46] and others. So I don't mean to suggest that hope is a moral requirement, or that it's better to have hope than to not have hope *simpliciter* in social justice contexts. I think that whether an agent requires hope is best assessed first-personally, as one about what *I* need to go on. Familiar rational assessments

[42] This might sound like Pettit's defense of substantial hope as cognitive resolve, whereby one acts as if the desired outcome will obtain. However, in contrast to Pettit, I don't understand agents as putting certain beliefs (e.g., related to setbacks, obstacles, and challenges) offline. Rather, they keep setbacks, obstacles, and problems in view (as Khan-Cullors does) while holding on to hope nonetheless.

[43] Calhoun (2018) argues that the "as-if" attitude toward the future involved in hope is best understood as a phenomenological idea of the future as one involving success. Her view is not equivalent to how I have been talking about hope, but both of us focus on hope as a phenomenological state that takes a favorable attitude toward the hoped-for end's obtaining.

[44] I am focused on normative commitments. See Calhoun (2009) for reasons to be skeptical about the value of other types of commitments.

[45] McCormick (2017) relatedly argues that "as the practical importance of hope increases, the demand for the level of evidential support lessens" (128). I am suggesting that this is true with an increase in the moral importance of hope in particular, at least for some of us who require hope to go on.

[46] As I show later, Coates's *Between the World and Me* paints an unhopeful narrative about the future for Black people in America. In response to Black Lives Matter protests following the murder of George Floyd in 2020, Coates noted in an interview with Ezra Klein that he sees progress and hope, in part due to the solidarity observed not only in America but across the world (Klein 2020). I explore the ways in which solidarity can give rise to hope in chapter 5.

and assessments of fit are secondary evaluative measures that can help agents as they find themselves with hopes, wondering if those states of mind are correctly tracking the evidence, good for their wellbeing, productive or risky, and so on. We can use these criteria in checking in on the hopes of those we care about too. The advantage of morally evaluating hope is to ensure that the significant personal and political hopes we formulate and pursue are consistent with the demands of morality.

The evaluative measures of importance in assessing hope do float freely from one another, in the sense that it is possible to assess hope for each of them independently. Hope is *epistemically rational* if the belief involved in hope is justified given the evidence available, and *prudentially* (or *strategically*) *rational* if the hope promotes one's rational ends. Hope is fitting if the possibility of the hoped-for outcome's obtaining really is favorable, to a degree that matches the strength of the hope. Finally, in the case of morally significant hopes, hope is morally appropriate when the hope reveals that the agent is properly oriented toward the good. And there is a moral constraint on hope: agents who have morally inappropriate hopes have sufficient reason to work to overcome or revise them, even if those hopes are fitting or strategically rational based on their subjective interests and goals.

But while the above criteria help to inform the all-things-considered practical question of what, exactly, an individual should feel, hope is also a social phenomenon, operating in community with others. I suggest that McGeer's (2004) framework of hoping well holds promise for applying the evaluative dimensions of individuals' hopes in practice, while also helpfully reorienting the value-of-hope question as a social question. But as we will see, the framework of hoping well needs some revision once we attend to the relevance of power and oppression at work influencing people's hopes.

Hoping Well

In chapter 1, we saw how McGeer (2004) understands hope as an attitude that is developed in childhood through parental scaffolding and sustained in adulthood by supportive interpersonal relationships. I argued that we need to extend her analysis to capture the relevance of a broader range of social, political, and economic relationships to our capacities for and experiences of hope. I want to make a similar argument here about McGeer's evaluative framework. Understanding what it means to hope well requires attending to the social, political, and economic conditions in which agents form and pursue their hopes.

McGeer argues that, given the profound significance of hope to human life, questions about the rationality of hope are best cast not in terms of whether or not a person should have hope or not but in terms of how they might hope well. Hoping well, on McGeer's view, involves developing *responsive hope*, or *the hope of care*. This kind of hope requires, first, that agents are responsive to real-world constraints on the ability to form and pursue their hopes. Being too hopeful is risky because it can lead to increased vulnerability, disappointment, despair, or wishful thinking (McGeer 2004, 102). (This is similar to the idea that unfitting hopes can lead to irrationality.) But it is not the case that people who hope against hope, or who strongly hope in the face of bad odds, should give up their hopes altogether. Hoping well involves shifting the target of hope when the world proves to be resistant to some hoped-for end's being realized. So to preserve hope in the face of bleak prospects is not necessarily to continue to hope for the realization of the same specified end (e.g., that racial justice will be attained in our lifetime) but to "invest our efforts toward some state or condition that has meaning and value for us" (McGeer 2004, 109). As Khan-Cullors (2018) explains, "We hold on to hope . . . because what else?" Hoping well in the face of a low chance that racial oppression will end has meaning and value for many who are committed to racial justice and who invest their agency toward it, even while fully acknowledging the evidence available and barriers to success.

Importantly, McGeer points out that the capacity to hope well in circumstances in which the world is unresponsive to the meaning and value of our ends is often dependent on a "responsive other" who supports and endorses our "hopeful struggles" (109). Hoping well, like hope itself, is largely a social phenomenon. We hope well *with* others, as we lean on them for support in pursuing our hopes and as we act as a support for others' hopes too. This practice keeps each of our hopes alive.[47] But caring about and supporting another's hopes does not necessarily mean agreeing with everything the hopeful person says and does. It involves "inviting them to articulate and pursue their hopes in a way that supports their own sense of effective agency," sometimes encouraging them to articulate more clearly their goals and the

---

[47] I think McGeer's insights here help to answer some of Vincent Lloyd's (2016) worries about approaches to hope that are overly individualistic. He argues that when we analyze hopes in terms of the beliefs and desires of individuals, "we forget that hope is cultivated in community, and we forget that hopes may be evaluated in terms other than rational self-interest" (171).

means by which they intend to pursue them, or the meaning and value they find in pursuing certain hopes (123). The evaluative measures identified in this chapter are of help. In supporting the hope of another person, I might encourage them to reframe their hopes in ways that are more fitting based on the extent to which the odds are favorable, especially if I know they value seeing bleak prospects for what they are, or if I see that their hopes make them vulnerable to disappointment. Or I might urge them to work toward giving up morally inappropriate hopes (e.g., hopes that involve internalized, harmful stereotypes), pointing out that however understandable their morally inappropriate hopes might be, sustaining them is morally wrong. And when it comes to our own hopes, hoping well involves being open to others' responses to our hopes and the potential need for gaining clarity about how to best invest in them. Hoping well takes place in community with others who support and challenge our hopes for the better.

I will say more about the ways in which hoping with others for the same ends produces and strengthens hope in chapter 5. But here I want to reflect on the idea that hoping well is not just about getting one's own hopes right but also attending to the hopes of others. McGeer is focused on relationships between loved ones who are obviously well positioned to support (and sometimes challenge) one another's hopes, so I do not take her to mean that we should point out when anyone might do well to redirect their hopes. Philosophers have not focused much on questions about standing when it comes to evaluating hope, but we can borrow insights from the literature on the standing to blame, which asks when someone is well positioned to blame a person morally for what they do. Obviously, blaming and challenging another's hope are quite different activities. But the question of standing helps us to think about the ethics of evaluating others' emotions. What might grant one standing to judge another's hope?

In the context of blame, Macalester Bell (2013) argues that having the standing to blame depends on one's relationship to the target of blame and whether that relationship allows one to hold the other person to certain standards of behavior. In the context of intimate interpersonal relationships, it is standard for each party to care about the emotions of the other—their hopes, anger, jealousy, happiness, fear, courage, and so on. It is also standard to challenge our loved ones' morally inappropriate emotions and those that seem unhelpful given their desires or goals. In our relationships with close loved ones, we often implicitly accept that we are there for one another to help each other overcome destructive emotions (as in my partner's fear of flying) and to cultivate responsive hope (as in my partner's encouraging me to be more hopeful at times, tempered with understanding of my pessimistic, unhopeful character). Communicating evaluative judgments about others' emotions is very much a part of our everyday interactions with people with whom we stand in close relation.

Beyond romantic and family relationships, we might have implicit agreements with friends whom we understand to have the standing to support and sometimes challenge our emotions, as well as fellow activists in social justice pursuits. There will be clear cases in which one can be reasonably confident in one's standing to assess another's hope and to communicate that assessment. There will be other cases in which one is unsure. The nature of one's relationship to the hopeful or unhopeful person is a helpful guide to figuring out one's place to make such evaluative judgments or to refrain from doing so. The relevant relationships are also not just interpersonal ones but include the assessor's social, political, and economic location in relation to the hopeful or unhopeful person. For example, as an outsider who lacks epistemic access to the lived experiences of racism, colonialism, and transphobia, I am not well positioned to assess the overall value of hope for people who are disadvantaged along these axes of oppression. And to make matters more complicated, I might be well positioned as a very close friend but poorly positioned as a white person to challenge a Black friend's seemingly out of place hopelessness in the face of a racial issue. Whether one should (or could permissibly) make an evaluative judgment will depend on particular features of the relationship and context in question. Hoping well requires not only responsiveness to real-world constraints and the support of others' hopes with whom one is in relationship but also awareness about one's own social identity in relation to others as it affects their standing to judge others' hopes.

In line with these reflections about the relevance of social identity, I want to raise one objection to McGeer's understanding of what it means to hope well. McGeer argues that hoping well requires "neither depending too much on external powers for bringing one's hopes about nor ignoring the critical role others play in supporting (or thwarting) one's hopeful efforts" (123). What she calls "wishful hope," on the other hand, is hope that involves a failure "to take on the full responsibilities of agency and hence to remain overreliant on external powers to realize [their] hopes" (110). In wishful hope, individuals passively await, rather than work toward, the fulfillment of their desires. And this is a kind of hoping badly, according to McGeer. For example, she suggests that parents who indulge their children make them prone to wishful hope and that such people grow up with "a sense of their own centrality in the universe" that leads them to focus on what they desire rather than what they need to do to fulfill their desires (113). But beyond problematic parenting techniques, there is a drastically different source of wishful hope. Many people are vulnerable to wishful hope not because they are used to getting what they want without effort but because they are incapable (or feel incapable) of engaging their agency in ways that will increase the likelihood that their hope will be realized. Individuals' social, political, and economic circumstances all combine to affect how much time, effort, and resources (if any) they have to contribute their own agency to fulfilling their desires. A single mother from a low socioeconomic background working multiple jobs to feed her three children may have no time, energy, or resources to invest in gender justice that may increase (however slightly) the likelihood that her hopes for gender justice will be realized.

McGeer's notion of wishful hope helps us to make sense of situations in which individuals may for good reasons believe that *there is nothing they can do but hope* that things will get better, but we should disagree with the claim that wishful hope is necessarily a kind of hoping badly.[48] If the single mother finds value in maintaining hope for gender justice even though she cannot do much to affect the hoped-for outcome (it might be a fundamental hope of hers), it seems perfectly reasonable for her to maintain hope for improved conditions for women. As Walker (2006) suggests, it is in these sorts of conditions in which agents might need hope the most, when hope is "all there is against inertness, terror, or despair" (57).

But this example also illustrates that members of oppressed groups are often forced to rely on the agency of members of privileged groups to realize their hopes, a dynamic that results in yet another danger of hope. Because members of oppressed groups often lack the power, resources, time, and energy to engage in activities that will increase the likelihood that their hopes will be realized, individuals and institutions in positions of power can exploit the wishful hopes of individuals living under oppressive conditions. Politicians, for example, can market themselves as symbols of hope for improved conditions to gain the support of those in powerless positions. And for-profit companies can market hope to those who, because of their strong desires in the face of bleak prospects, are targets of ineffective, unsafe, or highly expensive treatments or products that promise to realize their

---

[48] Although I do agree that wishful hope is sometimes a way in which people hope badly, such as when white people sit back and hope that racial issues will go away.

hopes. The politics and marketing of hope are often exploitative. And when people place their wishful hopes in agents in positions of power and buy into the hopeful messages that powerful agents promise, doing so can end up reinforcing power structures that maintain oppressive patterns.[49]

Concluding Thoughts

There is much work to be done to understand the value and risks of hope. I offer these reflections not to settle the debate about how (and for what) people should hope but to highlight the relevance of hope to moral character and to shed light on the various evaluative measures that capture a range of benefits and risks of hope in human life. I have not spent much time talking about the question of whether particular people or groups *should* hope, all things considered, beyond defending a moral constraint on hope. Answering the question of how a person should hope is, on my view, a contextual matter, only really to be determined in concrete cases (and often by the hopeful or unhopeful people themselves). And though I have tried to shed light on how we might evaluate hope in fraught social and political contexts, doing so is especially complicated. It requires explicit attention to dimensions of power, privilege, and oppression in thinking about the value of hope. Ultimately, my aim has been to open up space for understanding how hope might be valuable for human agents living in an unjust social world.

But the hopes that individuals formulate and pursue in contexts of oppression are often left unrealized. Perpetrators of violence against women, people of color, and the LGBTQ+ community often go free or receive very light punishments; refugees and undocumented immigrants continue to be denied basic human rights; the gap between the rich and the poor grows wider in many societies and globally, and so on. People are, right now, quite angry about these and other circumstances. And it would be a mistake to consider hope in isolation, abstracted away from the complex emotional lives of people living under the threat and experience of injustice. I now turn to the relationship between hope and anger.

---

[49] As Lloyd (2016) argues in the context of politics, "Charismatic leadership is more likely to bring manipulation than salvation. It manipulates hope" (169). Cornel West (2018) directly criticizes Obama on this issue, arguing that Obama "manipulated false consciousness in clever and misleading ways" (513–514).

3

Hope and Anger

I have situated this book around the nature and value of hope in moral and political life and how our various positions within interrelated systems of privilege and oppression affect how we hope. But hope does not operate alone. Many scholars and activists have defended the emotion of anger as a rational and justified response to moral wrongdoing, injustice, and oppression. This chapter explores the relationship between hope and anger. I begin by canvassing the literature on the nature of anger as an emotional response to moral wrongdoing and injustice. I then illustrate how the evaluative framework developed in the previous chapter illuminates the benefits and risks of anger as well. Anger can be prudentially rational, fitting, and morally appropriate—all of which highlight different aspects of anger's value and role in our lives. As we will see, recognizing the full range of evaluative measures according to which anger can be assessed also helps us to better see the epistemic, moral, and political value of anger in contexts and oppression. I then argue that anger in such contexts often indicates the presence of a hope for repair.[1]

What Is Anger?

I understand anger as an umbrella term that encompasses a range of emotional responses such as resentment, indignation, bitterness, and rage (see also Cherry 2017). What all of these emotional responses have in common is that they involve a perception that a wrong or injustice has occurred or is continuing. In other words, anger is about violations of our moral

---

[1] I qualify this claim because we also get angry when people do not live up to our moral expectations even when we did not have hope that they would do so. Sometimes, we are "just angry" even though our anger does not indicate the presence of hopes for repair. Other times, anger interacts with varying degrees of hopelessness to produce the emotion of bitterness. I explore the nature and value of bitterness in chapter 4.

Hope Under Oppression. Katie Stockdale, Oxford University Press. © Oxford University Press 2021.
DOI: 10.1093/oso/9780197563564.003.0004

expectations: that is, expectations we have of one another to abide by moral norms that we endorse. But how anger manifests in various contexts does not always take the same character. The form that anger takes can depend on the individual's standing in relation to the perceived wrong (as in resentment vs. indignation), the intensity of the anger (as in rage vs. low grade resentment), and how anger is colored by the presence of other emotions.

Discussion of anger in the philosophical literature has typically focused on resentment as a moral emotion and what it means to make the emotional transition from resentment to forgiveness. Philosophers' interest in the connection between resentment, interpersonal relationships, and moral judgments can be traced back to Bishop Joseph Butler's sermons on the emotion. Butler was specifically interested in reconciling what he saw as the moral value of resentment with the Christian imperative to love one's enemies. In his well-known sermon "Upon Resentment and Forgiveness of Injuries," Butler argues that resentment is not inherently or always sinful but a natural human passion whose end is justice. The emotion is "a weapon put into our hands by nature, against injury, injustice and cruelty" (Butler 1726, sermon 8).

Many philosophers have followed Butler in understanding resentment as an emotional response to perceived moral wrongs done to oneself, or a form of personal anger (e.g., Hampton and Murphy 1988; Hieronymi 2001; Solomon 2007; Strawson 2008). This characterization of resentment stands in contrast to indignation, or a kind of third-personal anger in response to moral wrongs done to others. The distinction between resentment and indignation is not clean, since we take things more or less personally as a matter of degree. But it captures the fact that we feel anger differently depending upon our relation to the perceived wrong. For example, when I read about the unjust conditions facing refugees across the world, I feel quite indignant. But I do not in any way feel, as refugees might, resentful about what I have learned. My anger manifests as a "spectator emotion" in Paul Woodruff's sense of the term: an emotion that is not about a wrong done to me but to other people (Woodruff 2014). We become resentful when we take a perceived wrong personally and indignant when we perceive the wrong as one done to others.

As Woodruff (2014) points out, spectator emotions "do not call for detachment, and they do not even call for less intense degrees of engagement. The mark of spectator emotions is that they engage the subject less directly (not less intensely) than nonspectator emotions" (71). So I might care very much about the global refugee crisis, consider it a social justice issue about which I ought to do something, and find myself intensely angry upon reading the news and learning about the conditions of war, violence, and persecution that refugees face, and yet my anger is still experienced as indignation (not resentment). The closer I come to the refugee crisis (for example, if a friend or family member is a refugee, or if I meet and become close to refugees in my own community, and so on), the more I might be able to empathize with their plight and feel more resentful than indignant about the injustices refugees face. My anger might evolve from the perception that others (generally) have been wronged to the perception that others *close to me* have been wronged, becoming more personal in the way that resentment is. But I am not a refugee, so my anger is still not about a wrong done to me.

The distinction between resentment and indignation also helps to explain why only some individuals have the appropriate standing to feel resentment in response to certain wrongs and injustices. And I think that this is an important distinction to make. Whereas you would have the appropriate standing to feel resentment if you were the victim of violence, I have the appropriate standing to feel indignation. If I perceive the wrong as one done to me and take the wrong personally, I have made a mistake; and, in some cases, I have made an offensive mistake. For example, if I were to take injustices targeting people of color personally as wrongs done to me, people of color might rightly point out that, due to my whiteness, I cannot take those injustices personally. They might even observe that, as a white person, the injustices benefit me. So though I can be rightly indignant about racial injustice as a way of communicating my moral condemnation, I cannot rightly be resentful. Because we are all positioned differently in relation to moral wrongs that occur, our anger responses do and should reflect these differential positions.

But when we consider more deeply the kinds of anger that arise in social and political contexts, the distinction between resentment and indignation becomes even more difficult to track. Resentment is often about the existence of systemic social and political injustices that target entire social groups, as well as injustices done to members of a social group to which one belongs. For example, Indigenous women might resent colonialism, sexism, racism, and poverty (i.e., they might resent these systems of oppression themselves). They might also feel resentful about particular instances of violence toward other Indigenous women that reflect those systemic injustices.[2] As T. M.

---

[2] For a defense of Indigenous women's anger (including resentment and rage) in response to ongoing oppression and as a way of resisting oppression, see Samantha Nock (2014) and Rachel Flowers (2015).

Scanlon (2008) argues, actions (such as acts of violence) carry meaning: they carry significance for the wrongdoer and for others.[3] The meaning of an act of violence toward an Indigenous woman does not only carry significance for the individual victim; it also carries significance for other Indigenous women who are also disproportionately subjected to the threat or experience of violence under interrelated systems of oppression. All women, in some sense, can be resentful about violence against women—including violence against Indigenous women. But Indigenous women's resentment in response to violence that specifically targets Indigenous women will manifest very differently than non-Indigenous women's resentment. It will be much more personal.

Some philosophers have noticed that the moral wrongs we take personally—that is, moral wrongs about which we feel resentment—stretch far beyond injustices done directly to us by other individuals. Alice MacLachlan (2010) argues that we experience resentment not only about direct moral injuries done to ourselves by some identifiable moral agent but also about social and economic circumstances. For example, individuals experience resentment about such things as having a difficult or unrewarding job, the culmination of events over time, and social practices—such as practices that marginalize women in a patriarchal society. People might resent, in particular, the unfair ways in which their workplaces marginalize them even when it is difficult or even impossible to identify specific people who are responsible for creating these morally objectionable structures. As MacLachlan (2010) points out, even though there may be no individual wrongdoer(s) who can be identified as responsible for bringing about these circumstances, events, and practices, we can and do resent them.

Walker (2006) argues that the object of resentment is also not always an individual wrongdoer; it is sometimes a whole community that does not stand by victims of injustice. And to broaden our understanding of the sources of resentment even further, Thomas Brudholm (2008) draws upon testimony from the South African Truth and Reconciliation Commission to illustrate how experiences of resentment sometimes respond to calls for forgiveness (and not just the original injustice). He explores the ways in which political leaders seeking to repair social and political relationships communicate the expectation

---

[3] Pamela Hieronymi (2001) similarly notes that "an event can make a claim when it is authored, that is, when it is an action. An action carries meaning by revealing the evaluations of its author. The event could not make a claim or carry meaning (positive or negative) if its perpetrator were not capable of making moral statements with his actions" (546).

that victims will forgive perpetrators of mass atrocities and how reconciliation politics function with an aim to shape people's emotional lives. Brudholm points out that individuals sometimes respond to calls for forgiveness with further resentment toward political leaders for pressuring them to forgive.

Traditional philosophical understandings of resentment as a form of personal anger in response to moral wrongs or injustices done to oneself are thus too narrow to capture experiences of resentment in social and political contexts, and I have suggested a further revision to our understanding of the nature of resentment. To capture the range of moral wrongs that we can (reasonably) take personally, we need to pay attention to individuals' social identities, and the socially and politically relevant groups to which they belong. Since we are all socially constituted beings whose identities and relationships (both interpersonal and political) shape who we are, an account of resentment as "personal anger" must be able to accommodate this fact. Since characteristics such as gender, race, class, and ability status are part of our identities, then when we perceive injustices done to members of social groups to which we belong based on these features, we can, and very reasonably, take those injustices personally.

In particular, when we become angry about an injustice done to a member (or members) of a social group to which we belong, we experience a kind of *group-based resentment*. We experience resentment in these contexts not because we are the direct victim of the injustice (we were not) but because the victim of the injustice was targeted in part because of their membership in a social group to which we belong. For example, when another woman is subjected to sexual violence, I experience group-based resentment in virtue of my identity as a woman. I experience resentment not because I was the direct victim of sexual violence (I was not) but because the instance of sexual violence represents a threat to all women as members of a social group who are disproportionately subjected to sexual violence in a patriarchal society (Stockdale 2013). I am resentful because I, too, am a woman who is harmed by that threat. And my resentment calls attention to the persistence of sexist oppression that the particular instance of sexual violence about which I am resentful reflects. So when I resent instances of sexual violence against women, I experience "resentment that is felt and expressed by individuals in response to a perceived threat to a collective to which they belong" (Stockdale 2013, 507).[4] Group-based resentment makes sense of individuals'

---

[4] In my 2013 article, I use the language of "collective resentment" to capture this phenomenon. There is now a growing literature on collective emotions in philosophy and the social sciences, and

experiences of resentment when they are not themselves the direct victim of injustice. For example, it makes sense of Indigenous people's resentment in response to injustices done to other Indigenous people within the context of colonialism, women's resentment in response to injustices done to other women in the context of sexist oppression, poor people's resentment within a context of economic insecurity, and so on.

But some scholars have noticed that anger is not just an episodic emotion; it can also be a character trait or disposition. Lisa Tessman (2005), for example, draws attention to the reality that members of oppressed groups live under conditions in which anger may be a useful (or strategically rational) disposition for individuals engaged in political resistance to cultivate in response to ongoing injustice. She defends the notion that anger is a "burdened virtue," that is, a disposition that is burdensome for the agent to bear, but one that is nevertheless a means to the end of liberation and eventual flourishing (Tessman 2005). In order words, anger is one example of a virtue that is "unlinked" from flourishing but is necessitated by the future possibility of a world in which the flourishing of all people is possible (108).

Macalester Bell (2009) defends an alternative conception of anger as a virtue. She points out that Tessman locates the value of anger as a virtue in its instrumental value (i.e., to bringing about a future in which all human beings can flourish), and thus implies that anger's being a virtue depends on the success of the anger in securing flourishing. To locate the value of anger within the agent's moral character and not whether the anger fulfills its function, Bell draws upon Thomas Hurka's and Robert Adams's approaches to virtue theory according to which a virtuous person is someone who both loves what is good and hates what is evil. Bell (2009) argues that what makes a character trait a virtue is not its instrumental value in bringing about flourishing but "that loving good and hating evil is itself non-instrumentally valuable" (177).

I do not take a stand on whether Tessman's or Bell's conception of anger as a virtue is more plausible (like in the case of hope, I am interested in anger as an emotion that manifests in specific cases more so than anger as a character trait). But both discussions of anger as a virtue raise important questions

---

though there is disagreement about what it means for an emotion to be collective, there is general consensus that collective emotions must be experienced by more than one person. The kind of resentment to which I call attention here is, in contrast, group-based: one can experience the emotion alone, but one's reasons for experiencing the emotion are reasons that all members of the group have. Collective emotions, in contrast, pick out an emotional phenomenon that can be ascribed to a collective rather than just the individuals who constitute the collective. I develop an account of collective hope in chapter 5.

about the value of anger. While they disagree about what exactly makes anger a virtue, Tessman's claim that anger may be useful in political resistance and Bell's claim that anger is valuable to individuals' moral characters because it reflects their "love of the good" suggest that anger plays an important role in our moral and political lives. Tessman's insight helps us to see that anger can be strategically rational, and Bell's insight shows that anger can be morally appropriate in itself, independently of how anger affects the world.

In what follows, I illustrate the ways in which anger can be evaluated consistently with hope: as prudentially (or strategically) rational, fitting, and morally appropriate. It is morally appropriate anger, as we will see, that scholars and activists have commonly appealed to as the kind of anger that is most valuable in struggles against oppression. But in defending the idea that anger can be a morally appropriate and valuable emotion, I am not suggesting that the emotion lacks any negative effects. As Tessman makes clear, the anger of people engaged in political resistance is instrumentally valuable but burdened. Anger can be psychologically and physically costly; it can prevent us from enjoying many goods in life and maintaining healthy and satisfying relationships; it can interfere with our ability to make sound decisions; and it can lead us to engage in harmful behaviors toward ourselves and others. But emotions are often valuable and harmful at the same time: contributing to our wellbeing yet distorting our thinking (as hope sometimes does), attuning us to what we have done wrong yet preventing us from moving forward con- structively (as guilt sometimes does), or alerting us to a potential threat yet preventing us from enjoying what might be worth the risk (as in fear). So a defense of anger need not deny its harms and risks. It should rather show that anger can contribute positively to agents' moral characters and to the pursuit of some of our most important moral and political ends.

Evaluating Anger

Many approaches to evaluating anger focus on the prudential or strategic ra- tionality of the emotion. Patricia Greenspan (2000) argues that emotions can be part of a strategy in agents' rational decision-making. For example, getting angry and expressing anger can be in a person's rational self-interest, such as when a man "works himself into a state of anger" in order to offer a con- vincing threat to leave his marital partner (471). Robert C. Solomon (2007) similarly argues that anger is a strategy: it is a way of emotionally engaging with the world to "serves one's ultimate ends" (26). On Solomon's view, we are even irrational when we fail to get angry in certain cases; in particular, when doing so would have been in our rational self-interest (26). Feminist and anti-racist defenses of anger, too, highlight the strategic value of anger in the pursuit of our moral and political ends (e.g., Frye 1983; Lorde 2007).

But assessments of strategic rationality alone cannot make sense of the value of anger. As Solomon explains, anger can also pick out the right or wrong object (for Solomon, the object of anger is the "offender"), it can be warranted or unwarranted depending on the situation in question, and it can be rightly or wrongly directed (Solomon 2007, 25). And this description of the value of anger begins to look like the one I gave about hope. Like hope, anger can be evaluated as fitting—namely, when the emotion correctly represents its object as having certain evaluative features (i.e., fitting in terms of shape), and to a degree that is warranted by the situation (i.e., fitting in terms of size).[5] As we will see, anger is fitting in terms of its shape when the emotion correctly represents its object as wrong or unjust; and anger is fitting in terms of its size when it is experienced to a degree that matches the severity of the wrong or injustice. So, to anticipate, it is fitting to be intensely angry about the ongoing genocide of Indigenous people, but it is unfitting to be intensely angry about a friend telling you an innocent white lie. The question of whether anger is fitting—that is, whether the emotion correctly represents an action, event, or set of circumstances as wrong or unjust to a degree that is warranted by the situation—is separate from the question of whether it is strategically rational. It might, for example, be prudent to experience only mild or moderate anger in response to the ongoing genocide of Indigenous people if intense anger is harmful to the person's wellbeing, relationships, and behavior.

Both emotions are also subject to moral assessments. I have argued that hope is morally appropriate when the hope reveals that the agent is properly

---

[5] But unlike hope, anger does not necessarily involve a belief in the way that hope does. Since hope involves a belief in the possibility that a desired outcome will come about, philosophers of hope have assessed the belief part of hope for epistemic rationality (whether the belief, or probability estimate, matches the evidence available). Although we can evaluate whether the beliefs that give rise to anger are epistemically rational (e.g., the belief that a person intentionally brought about a harm, the belief that an institution was responsible for a tragic event, etc.), these beliefs are thought of as the cognitive bases of anger (i.e., the mental states that causally bring it about). They are not constitutive of the emotion. This, I take it, is the main difference in how hope and anger are commonly assessed. And this difference raises the question of whether the belief in the possibility that a desired outcome will come about can be best understood as the cognitive base of hope, rather than a constitutive feature of hope. I leave this question aside for my purposes, though I take it to be an important question for further inquiry.

oriented toward the good. Although there is no moral duty to cultivate particular morally appropriate hopes (e.g., the hope that one's neighbor has a
good day, or the hope that a stray dog finds the perfect home), such hopes reveal that the agent cares about, and orients her attention and often activities
around, what is of moral value (e.g., cultivating kindness and compassion toward others). Morally appropriate emotions are constitutive of having a good
moral character.

Hope is morally inappropriate when the hope reveals that the agent is not
properly oriented toward the good. For example, a person's hope might be
constituted by a desire for a morally bad outcome to occur (e.g., continued
white dominance). Or her hope may be based in another immoral attitude
(e.g., racist stereotypes leading to racist hopes, such as the fearful hope that a
Black person does not steal from one's store). Or her hope may reflect a moral
vice (e.g., the selfish hope that one's ex's new marriage is disastrous). Because
there is a moral constraint on the characters that we should cultivate and sustain, we have sufficient reasons to work to overcome or revise morally inappropriate hopes and other emotions.

Anger is morally appropriate when the emotion reveals that the agent
is properly oriented toward the good. As Macalester Bell (2009) argues,
"*Appropriate anger* is a particular way of hating evil or being against the bad"
(177).[6] Although there is no moral duty to cultivate morally appropriate
anger in response to particular wrongs and injustices, such anger reveals that
the agent cares about, and orients her attention and activities around, past
and persistent injustices so as to protest or condemn them. Morally appropriate anger is thus constitutive of a good moral character. In contrast, anger
is morally inappropriate when it reveals that the agent is not properly oriented toward the good. For example, one's anger might be based on incorrect
moral beliefs about what is wrong or unjust (e.g., anger about public health
measures requiring the wearing of masks based on the incorrect moral belief
that one's individual freedom is more important than saving lives in a global
pandemic). Or one's anger may reflect a moral vice (e.g., the moral vice of
irascibility leading to excessive anger). When we find ourselves with morally
inappropriate anger, we have sufficient reasons to take responsibility to overcome or revise it.

---

[6] Although Bell's interest is in the virtue of anger, I take it that this characterization of the moral
appropriateness of anger carries over to particular manifestations of the emotion too.

But there is an important dissimilarity between hope and anger. Anger is a moral emotion involving the perception of moral properties (namely, the presence of wrongness or injustice), whereas hope is often completely irrelevant to morality (e.g., the hope for clear skies or a snowy winter). Consequently, the evaluative question of whether anger is fitting is more closely connected to the question of whether anger is morally appropriate than in the case of hope. This is because the shape of anger is moral. In anger, we perceive an action, event, or set of circumstances as wrong or unjust; and these are moral properties. As such, anger cannot be morally appropriate unless it is fitting *in terms of its shape*. Consider a bystander's anger about witnessing an act of transphobic violence. The bystander's anger is fitting because it correctly represents its object as having certain evaluative features (namely, wrongness and injustice). At the same time, the bystander's anger reveals that they are properly oriented toward the good—that they are against transphobic violence. So their anger is morally appropriate too.

In contrast, unfitting anger is morally inappropriate anger. For example, a man's anger about a rape survivor speaking up and threatening one's reputation is unfitting because it incorrectly represents the survivor's action as wrong. It is actually morally supererogatory for rape survivors to speak up about their experiences. The accused's anger might be based in an incorrect moral belief (e.g., that the woman was morally responsible for her own rape because of how she was dressed or because she consumed alcohol, or a belief about how women deserve to be treated more generally). It might also reveal that the agent has other morally inappropriate attitudes and vices (e.g., the man is a misogynist, or is indifferent to the rights and dignity of women, or is so greedy that his desire for power has made him lose his sense of morality).[7]

So as we can see, the fittingness of anger (in terms of shape) and moral appropriateness of the emotion converge. But what about the size of anger, or the degree to which anger is felt, as it bears on the quality of an agent's moral character? Anger is fitting in terms of its size if the emotion is experienced to a degree that matches the severity of the wrong or injustice. At first glance, it might seem as though morally appropriate anger must also be fitting in terms of its size. This is because if I am only mildly angry about horrific wrongs and injustices, my anger seems to reveal that I don't care enough about moral violations that have occurred, or that I'm relatively indifferent

---

[7] Even D'Arms and Jacobson (2000), who argue that many philosophers commit a moralistic fallacy by conflating the fittingness of emotions with the moral appropriateness of emotions, agree that anger is a distinctly moral emotion whose fittingness is determined in part by moral considerations.

to the significant unjust suffering of others. Or if I am intensely angry about only minor slights, my anger may reveal that I have the vice of irascibility. So whether anger is experienced to a degree that matches the severity of the wrong or injustice seems to track the extent to which the agent is properly oriented toward the good. In particular, the degree of a person's anger seems to track just how much she cares about justice, how much attention she orients toward protesting and resisting it, the quality of her moral perception in distinguishing between degrees of wrongness and injustice, and her underlying attitudes and traits.

But we should hesitate to say that morally appropriate anger must always be felt to a degree that matches the severity of the wrong or injustice. Context matters significantly. Consider a case where anger is unfitting because it is too mild given the severity of the wrong. For example, suppose a bystander witnesses a person yell a hateful, transphobic message at someone through the window of their car as the person is walking down the street, minding their own business. Suppose, too, that the bystander experiences only very mild anger. It is possible, in this case, that the bystander's mild anger reveals that he does not care enough about trans people's lives and wellbeing and is not strongly against the serious wrong. This interpretation may be right in many cases. However, the presence of unfitting, mild anger may not reveal this defect in moral character. The bystander in question might care significantly about trans people's lives and wellbeing, but there may be other reasonable explanations for the low degree of intensity in his anger response. For example, the bystander might endorse a spiritual worldview according to which anger should be moderated. And he may have invested a significant amount of time and energy into regulating his anger through mindfulness techniques, channelling his serious concern about transphobic violence and about the lives and wellbeing of trans people into volunteer work and donations to LGBTQ+ organizations. He might, then, have only mild anger in response to the act that he at the same time rightly judges is very wrong.

So for anger to be morally appropriate, it must be fitting in terms of its shape, correctly representing an action, event, or set of circumstances as wrong or unjust. But we cannot (at least not always) fault people morally for failing to get angry enough. At most, cases where anger is unfitting in terms of its size may be morally suspect in a manner similar to cases of morally suspect hopes. I have argued that morally suspect hopes reveal a potential defect in moral character, but their moral status is indeterminate because of the nature of the hope and/or human beings' limited epistemic resources to fully understand the emotion. In this case of anger, further inquiry would likely reveal an answer to the question of whether the bystander's mild anger was morally inappropriate, or whether his mild anger has a reasonable explanation. But what is important for our purposes is that anger may be morally appropriate even when it is experienced to a degree that does not match the severity of the wrong or injustice.[8]

I have also argued that there is a moral constraint on emotions, such that people have sufficient reason to work to relinquish or revise morally inappropriate emotions—even when those emotions might be strategically rational. So however rational anger might be for a person as a strategy in pursing their ends, moral assessments give us conceptual resources to make sense of how to evaluate and respond to complex political cases of anger. For example, white men might use anger as a strategy in response to the claim that they have "white male privilege," as they work to maintain their social and economic positions at the expense of others. But these white men's anger is not morally appropriate (or fitting), since their anger incorrectly represents its object as unjust (i.e., advancements *toward* racial and gender justice) and reveals that they are not "for" what is morally good—namely, racial and gender justice. Moral assessments not only help us to see that such anger is out of place (as in fittingness); they encourage deeper reflection on the ways in which agents' moral characters—their moral beliefs, attitudes, and traits—have led to the experiences and expression of unfitting anger.

But there is an additional evaluative dimension of anger not yet discussed—that is, whether anger is properly or improperly directed. Anger is properly directed when it is felt and/or expressed toward the right agent(s) who are in fact responsible for bringing about the wrong or injustice. Because anger commonly arises in response to systemic and overlapping injustices under conditions of oppression, where there is not always a direct moral injury caused by an identifiable moral agent who is clearly responsible, it is quite common for anger to miss its mark. In other words, it is common for people to correctly represent a situation as unjust but to misdirect their anger toward the wrong agent(s).[9] This is especially the case in fraught social

---

[8] I'm less certain about whether anger that is too strong, given the degree of wrongness or injustice to which it responds, can be morally appropriate. I hesitate because, and as Lorde, hooks, Tessman, and as other scholars and activists have seen clearly, intense anger is morally risky. There seem to be good moral reasons to cultivate attitudes and traits that limit the range of contexts in which the agent will experience intense anger (such as patience, compassion, and understanding).

[9] Amia Srinivasan (2018) also observes that "one can be aptly angry without always perfectly targeting and proportioning one's anger" (130, footnote 33).

and political contexts in which there are multiple agents at different levels of human organization (e.g., individuals, social groups, and institutions) participating in various and intersecting systems of oppression. Tessman (2005), for example, draws upon Audre Lorde to discuss the ways in which Black women sometimes get angry at one another instead of those responsible for the sexism and racism they experience. She explains that these women's misdirected anger results from internalized oppression, and in particular the internalization of self-hate toward both oneself and others who are like oneself. Lorde (2007) even notes that she too sometimes misdirects her anger toward other Black women even though she knows that Black women are "not the root cause nor the source of that pool of anger" (145). Black women's anger, including Lorde's own, is thus complicated as she describes it. It is certainly fitting anger in the sense that much of Lorde's anger is about racism, sexism, and other injustices she experiences; and it is morally appropriate in the sense that her anger reveals that she is against those injustices. But as Lorde recognizes, *when* her anger is misdirected, it expresses morally inappropriate blame toward Black women who are not responsible for her pain or suffering.[10]

What's more, because many people are members of privileged *and* oppressed groups, all of which inform their lived experiences, it can be quite difficult to direct one's anger toward the right target(s) (Tessman 2005). Tessman (2005) discusses the example of Black nationalists' anger at white people and how it can manifest in misogynistic ways that sadistically target white women. We can also imagine a poor white man's anger about his economic position being misdirected toward people of color and women whom he judges to "free ride" on equity policies that make it appear easier for them to earn or advance in employment positions. He might hold a mistaken, racist belief that immigrants and women are "stealing all the jobs." Although it is certainly fitting for poor white men to be angry about the economic injustice they experience, evaluating these poor white men's anger requires attending to their economic disadvantage *and* their race and gender privilege in a racist and sexist society.[11]

---

[10] Myisha Cherry (2017) similarly points out that anger can reveal a moral error, such as when there are two wrongdoers but the angry person only directs their anger toward one of them. The person's misdirected anger is morally inappropriate in this case because it reveals the angry person's unfairness (51).

[11] Obviously, these cases are very different. But they are all examples of misdirected anger whose moral status is compromised, to varying degrees.

Since poor white men's anger about their economic situation correctly represents their economic situation as unjust, their anger is fitting (and in this way, it is morally appropriate, inasmuch as their anger reveals that they are against economic injustice). But these poor white men's anger can be easily misdirected and incorrectly target people of color, women, environmental activists, and immigrants as the source of their disadvantage. Since oppressive socialization and political rhetoric shape people's beliefs and emotions, it is especially easy to see how anger can be misdirected. I think, for example, of a Lyft ride in 2019 in which our driver, a Turkish immigrant living in Houston, angrily complained about incidents of racism he had experienced, including a recent run-in with the law. But he then remarked that although President Donald J. Trump is racist (against people like him), *Trump was right* that all those immigrants at the border trying to get in illegally are making life more difficult and unsafe for legal immigrants. Why, he asked, should they get to come into the country when others have to go through strict processes to obtain visas legally? This man's anger was clearly misdirected, though he does have a point. His life *is* unjustly difficult due to racism, and it is fitting to be angry about the racial injustices he experiences. But Trump's racist, anti-immigrant rhetoric affected the target of his anger, compromising the extent to which it is morally inappropriate[12] and leading him to misdirect his anger toward undocumented immigrants.[13]

The causes of our anger, how and when anger is felt and expressed, and who we end up directing our anger toward are all influenced by our social, political, and economic circumstances. Like hope, anger can be tapped into and exploited by politicians like Trump to serve their own ends. And given the influence of both intentional and non-intentional social and political pressures on individuals' emotional experiences and expressions, the question of who is to blame for misdirected anger is not straightforward. It is, I think, similar to the question of who is to blame for false moral and other

---

[12] The Lyft driver's anger was clearly about racial injustice, revealing that he is against racial injustice and that he desires racism against people like him to end. And this is a morally appropriate response to racism. At the same time, directing his anger toward undocumented immigrants reveals that he too holds racist and xenophobic biases, which compromises the morality of his anger.

[13] Some philosophers might want to say that the question of whether anger is fitting includes whether it is properly directed. But notice that the direction of anger often comes as an afterthought, or through its expression. We get angry about perceived injustices and other moral wrongs, *and then* we search for who is responsible, or for a target deserving of our anger. If I read that Indigenous students on campus find the climate of the campus to be racist and hostile toward them, the anger I experience in the moment is about racism against Indigenous students on campus. I will then want to know who is responsible and to whom I should express my anger. So these features of anger come apart and can be evaluated separately.

beliefs that are influenced by social, political, and economic circumstances as well (e.g., the belief in the moral superiority of one's own culture and the belief that climate change is not real or serious). Our beliefs and emotions are, in part, products of our socialization, exposure to peer and political pressure, media influence and bias, and information and (sometimes) disinformation we access, and many other things. So in calling attention to misdirected emotions, false beliefs, and so on, I think we should remain mindful of the ways in which individuals' mental states are influenced by the circumstances in which they exist without simply appealing to such circumstances as an excuse for individual culpability.

But like in the case of morally inappropriate hope, individuals can often (and should) take responsibility for their misdirected anger when they notice it, working to ensure that their anger gets all the morally salient features right. This does not mean that it would have been appropriate for me to call out my Lyft driver in that moment, urging him to see how his anger is misdirected and to take responsibility for redirecting it (perhaps even toward Trump!). There is a time and place for correcting others when they clearly display misdirected emotions, and I hesitate to think that this Lyft ride was one of them. Not to mention, being a white Canadian expat in the United States with a steady income whose visa was paid for by a university as well as a stranger to this man denies me the standing to intervene in his life and point out emotional flaws that I perceive—and doing so could have been harmful. Perhaps what cases like this one illustrate is that, even when one is certain that a person's anger has gone wrong, even offensively wrong (as I was), listening and making an effort to understand might still be a reasonable response.[14]

These cases show that assessments of anger, like other emotions, are quite complex—especially in conditions of oppression. Anger is morally appropriate when the emotion reveals that the person is properly oriented toward the good. But the extent to which anger is moral appropriate is affected by whether the emotion is fitting and properly directed. Anger is fitting if it correctly represents an action, event, or set of circumstances as wrong or unjust to a degree warranted by the severity of the wrong or injustice. (Though, as we have seen, we can't always morally fault people for failing to get angry enough.) Anger is properly directed if it is directed at the right target—that

---

[14] I leave open whether there is a correct response, or whether there are more reasonable responses than my own.

is, the agent(s) who are in fact responsible for the wrong or injustice. The distinction between anger's fit and direction captures the intuitive thought that Lorde's anger is both fitting and (even if at times not fully) morally appropriate. It also allows us to affirm that my Lyft driver's anger both correctly perceives racism as unjust and has a moral point while acknowledging that his anger is misdirected (and is in this sense morally inappropriate, since his misdirected anger paradoxically reveals his own racism and xenophobia).[15]

The distinction between an emotion's fit and direction also helps us to make sense of cases in which anger is fitting even when it is not directed toward a target at all. Whereas cases of interpersonal anger take the shape "A wronged me" (as in the case of resentment) or "A wronged them" (as in the case of indignation), cases of political anger are often about persistent structural injustices. For example, women's anger about sexist oppression sometimes takes the form "Men and patriarchal institutions wrong us," but (as Walker and MacLachlan make clear) it can even take the form "*This experience* is unjust." It is not always easy to articulate what one takes to be the cause of the injustice about which one is angry—which men and institutions, and where one's sense of injustice is coming from. Yet this does not make anger about sexism any less fitting and morally appropriate. Anger is fitting just in case it correctly represents an action, event, or set of circumstances as wrong or unjust, and morally appropriate to the extent that the emotion reveals that the agent is properly oriented toward the good.

In conditions of oppression in which experiences of injustice are persistent and severe, it is fitting to experience very strong anger—even rage. This is the case even if members of oppressed groups might reasonably want to overcome their anger or experience less intense anger, because doing so is in their rational self-interest. bell hooks (1995), for example, explores the fitting rage of Black Americans and how that rage can lead to problematic actions. As hooks (1995) argues, the rage of Black Americans is "not pathological. It is an appropriate response to injustice. However, if not processed constructively, it can lead to pathological behavior" (26). Living under white supremacy,

---

[15] The Lyft driver was also epistemically irrational in his beliefs. For example, the cognitive base of the Lyft driver's anger included false beliefs (e.g., undocumented immigrants are making his life worse). But there are other cases in which agents are epistemically rational in their beliefs, yet they experience unfitting anger. This is because emotions can be recalcitrant to reason. For example, I might be angry about receiving a rejection from a top journal after a promising revise and resubmit, seeing the rejection as an offense against me, as I might find myself imagining the editors having personal (immoral) aversions to feminist philosophy. But I might, at the same time, rationally believe that the rejection was not an offense and that (probably) the editorial decision was fair. I hold a rational belief that the decision was not wrong, but I *see* it as wrong by way of my anger nonetheless.

alongside other forms of oppression, can engender uncontrollable rage that risks turning into violence. So even though Black Americans' rage is a fitting response to racial injustice, its intensity can lead to harmful and counter-productive behaviors. Tessman (2005) similarly points out that in contexts of systemic injustice "there may be no moderate state that allows one to be angry all the times one ought to be" (120–121). But she acknowledges that even when some situation seems to warrant "an awesome level of anger," individuals might choose to aim at moderation for prudential reasons (121).

Amia Srinivasan (2018) even argues that the choice between embracing fitting anger and working to give up that anger for prudential reasons is itself an "affective injustice." If we give up our anger because of the risks and harms of bearing it, we also give up one way of seeing injustice *as* injustice (by way of our apt or fitting emotion). Yet if we maintain anger, doing so is risky and, perhaps, even harmful and destructive. On Srinivasan's view, this choice situation is itself unjust because it forces people into an unfair normative conflict through no fault of their own (133). What's worse, when we urge members of oppressed groups to overcome their anger, assessing anger as imprudent, the implication is that it is the responsibility of victims of injustice to "fix the problem" and relinquish their counterproductive emotion, rather than the perpetrator(s)' responsibility to address the harm caused by injustice.

Many feminists have called attention to a further injustice linked to outsiders' responses to anger—that of emotional dismissal (Frye 1983; Campbell 1994; Cherry 2017; Lorde 2007). Sometimes, we do not directly urge people to overcome their anger but instead behave in ways that dismiss others' anger through failing to provide the emotion uptake. Marilyn Frye's (1983) classic carburetor case illuminates the source of this feminist complaint. She imagines a woman who, after gassing up her car, finds a male gas station attendant messing with her carburetor. The woman becomes angry and responds by telling the man to stop. He replies, "Crazy bitch," dismissing outright the possibility that the woman has a point—that she might actually have good reasons to forcefully object to his behavior. And in refusing to take the woman seriously at all, the man fails to give her anger uptake, where uptake would consist in directly confronting the anger (whether the direct response is a good one or not). For example, by explaining himself, apologizing for the misunderstanding, defending himself against the anger by offering reasons for his action, and the like, the man would have taken the woman seriously. Instead, he shifts the focus away from the issue toward the woman's mental stability.

Critiques of anger that shift attention away from the presence of injustice toward the emotion's counterproductiveness or toward the agent's mental stability are ways in which responses to anger help to keep members of oppressed groups in their subordinated place. Reclaiming anger, and especially morally appropriate anger—experiencing and defending it—has thus become a tool of resisting oppression. For example, many feminists, scholars of race, and activists have praised anger for its role in appreciating and marking the world as it is, in Srinivasan's terms, but also for its role in consciousness-raising and motivating justified political action. I want to argue, along these lines, that anger has moral, epistemic, and political value. The claim that anger is valuable is not in tension with the widespread consensus that anger can be harmful to individuals' wellbeing and destructive to their relationships, and can motivate aggressive and other problematic behaviors. As I mentioned above, I do not deny these harms and risks. So the argument that anger has moral, epistemic, and political value certainly does not entail that the emotion is "all good." But despite these harms and risks of anger, the emotion can be valuable in our moral, social, and political lives.

Anger's Value: Moral, Epistemic, Political

Many philosophers have noticed that resentment demonstrates the moral value of respect. Jeffrie G. Murphy (1988), for example, argues that resentment is essentially bound up with self-respect and that individuals who fail to resent moral injuries done to them either lack self-respect or have failed to express it. As he states, "Not to have what Peter Strawson calls the 'reactive attitude' of resentment when our rights are violated is to convey—emotionally—either that we do not think we have rights or that we do not take our rights very seriously" (Murphy 1988, 17).[16] In exploring women's anger, Marilyn Frye (1983) argues that "anger implies a claim to domain—a claim that one is a being whose purposes and activities require and create a web of objects, spaces,

---

[16] I generally endorse Murphy on this point, but context matters. In line with some considerations earlier, if I endorse a spiritual worldview according to which anger should be moderated (or even relinquished), the absence of my anger does not necessarily indicate that I think I don't have rights or take them seriously. The presence of morally appropriate anger indicates that the agent is properly oriented toward the good (that they are against, for example, moral rights violations), but the absence of anger only sometimes, if perhaps often, reveals that the agent is not properly oriented toward the good. It is possible to be against injustice, with a strong sense of self-respect and moral values, yet fail to get angry.

attitudes and interests that is worthy of respect, and that the topic of this anger is a matter rightly within that web" (87). In a manner that is consistent with Frye, Glen Sean Coulthard (2014) defends Indigenous Canadians' resentment on the grounds that it signifies Indigenous Canadians' "purging" of the inferiority complex that many of them have internalized as colonized subjects, prompting Indigenous Canadians to "affirm the worth of their own traditions, of their own civilizations" (167–168).[17] And Elizabeth Spelman (1989) identifies women's anger toward men as an "act of insubordination," a response that signifies one's equality with men and the right to judge them for their morally blameworthy conduct (266). As these views make clear, when we respond to perceived moral wrongs done to us or to members of a social group to which we belong, we demonstrate the moral value of respect.

Anger also has epistemic value. Many scholars have appealed to anger as an emotion that should be "listened to" because it reveals important insights about people's lived experiences. bell hooks (1995), for example, attests to her rage as a catalyst for developing "critical consciousness, to come to full decolonized self-actualization" (16). And she speaks of some Black people's absence of rage as connected to their "experience of the world as infinitely less hostile to blackness than it actually is" (17). Listening to and understanding anger is thus instrumentally valuable for the oppressed to gain knowledge about their own oppression, as well as for listeners to gain knowledge about the oppression of others.

But the claim that anger is epistemically valuable has been met with criticism. Glen Pettigrove (2012), for example, argues that anger is actually epistemically disadvantageous for a number of reasons. (1) It enables people to assess risks as lower than when they are in a "neutral emotional state"; (2) it causes people to focus on the hostile (rather than non-hostile) stimuli in their environments; (3) angry people are more inclined to interpret "unpleasant events" as brought about by responsible agents rather than non-agential causes; (4) they are more inclined to believe that others' actions are a result of "lasting dispositional traits" instead of accidents; (5) they are slower in coming to see positive traits (rather than negative ones) in people from

---

[17] María Lugones (1995), for example, testifies to her own experiences of the harms of anger—how it feels, how it affects her view of herself and others, and how it overpowers other concerns (e.g., about fitting in and being liked and appreciated). But she argues that anger is politically valuable in resisting oppression nonetheless. Coulthard (2014), too, affirms the risks of anger while at the same time defending the emotion's value. He points out that "individual and collective expressions of anti-colonial anger and resentment can be destructive and harmful to relationships; but these emotional forces are rarely, if ever, as destructive and violent as the colonial relationship they critically call into question" (177).

outsider groups; and (6) they are less likely to trust other people (363). So anger distorts, rather than enhances, people's thinking. It is thus more epistemically risky than valuable.

I think that these criticisms of anger do have merit, and that it is important not to deny the epistemic risks of the emotion. But it is not clear that these worries apply to all anger equally, especially in social and political contexts. And here I suspect that the anger of privileged people might be more vulnerable to the epistemic risks that Pettigrove identifies, at least in cases where individuals' privileged positions affect what their anger is about. Consider (2), for example. When white people experience anger toward people of color, they may see people of color in an even more hostile light than they do without their anger, distorting even further their beliefs and perceptions about people of color. Suppose, to take another example, a man does not get a job a woman was offered. His anger might, as in criticism (3), incline him to interpret the unpleasant event as caused by "reverse sexism" rather than the woman's being more qualified for the position than he was or more impressive at the interview stage. And in terms of criticisms (5) and (6) members of privileged groups who experience anger toward members of oppressed groups often "other" them even further, in terms of both negative associations and exacerbated distrust. These are, importantly, not just epistemic but also political risks of anger.

But the anger of members of oppressed groups can sometimes enable them to see things more clearly. Consider criticism (1). If anger enables activists to take on risks that they consider essential for pursuing social justice, and if they most care about social justice over other values, then anger can actually enhance rather than interfere with judgment.[18] As for criticisms (2) and (3), due to internalized oppression, the oppressed sometimes struggle with a range of emotions that can cause them to view themselves as the problem (e.g., self-doubt, guilt, and shame). If anger enables people to see others as responsible, rather than themselves, then anger might help to guard against these psychological harms of oppression. And as for (3) and (4), because oppressors' actions are commonly explained away by forces beyond their control or social norms that somehow make them okay (e.g., "That's just locker room talk"), the oppressed might have a hard time believing that it is not "non-agential causes" but rather responsible action resulting from

---

[18] This is similar to Martin's (2008) claim, discussed in chapter 2, that hope can sometimes enhance autonomy in healthcare settings. She gives the example of a patient who believes that she should enroll in a clinical trial for the benefit of clinical research, and whose hope enables her to see a clinical trial as less risky than it is.

oppressors' "lasting dispositional states" that are problematic. Anger might plausibly work against these barriers as well, helping members of oppressed groups to interpret unpleasant events as injustices, ones for which others are responsible. Finally, as for (5), distrust of the privileged, as we have seen, is often quite appropriate for precautionary reasons.[19]

So because the anger that I take to be epistemically valuable is not any old anger but the anger of the oppressed in response to legitimate injustices done to them, and because this anger operates under conditions in which epistemic risks can become epistemic advantages, Pettigrove's worries seem more apt in addressing the epistemic risks of anger in other kinds of cases. And as we have begun to see, anger's epistemic value also cannot be separated from its political value. Lorde (2007) helps us to make this connection more explicit. She points out that the anger of women is "loaded with information and energy" (127), and when women listen to one another's anger, they can come to understand the true cause of their anger: that is, their experiences of injustice under conditions of sexist oppression. Lorde states, in an oft-quoted passage: "Every woman has a well-stocked arsenal of anger potentially useful against those oppressions, personal and institutional, which brought that anger into being. Focused with precision, it can become a powerful source of energy serving progress and change" (127). This is true, for Lorde, even if women's experiences of sexist oppression are different from one another's because of the ways in which race, class, sexuality, ability status, ethnicity, and other features of their identities all affect how sexist oppression factors into their lives. In other words, anger brings women together in a common struggle against sexist oppression, and so has liberatory potential. Similarly, hooks (1995) argues that "sharing rage connects those of us who are older and more experienced with younger black and non-black folks who are seeking ways to be self-actualized, self-determined, who are eager to partic-ipate in anti-racist struggles" (20). She links rage to courageous action and argues that rage is an essential component of resistance (16).[20]

---

[19] Acknowledging the epistemic harms of oppression is consistent with the standard claim (which I endorse) that members of oppressed groups are epistemically privileged. Even when members of oppressed groups experience internalized oppression, their experiences under oppression— including their experiences of internalized oppression—are what they have privileged epistemic ac-cess to.

[20] Even Martha C. Nussbaum (2016), who believes that anger is inherently normatively prob-lematic, admits that anger can be politically useful in motivating struggles against injustice. See Nussbaum (2016, 39).

Sonali Chakravarti (2014) has taken up these feminist insights to argue that expressions of anger in witness testimonies as part of truth and reconciliation commissions should be listened to. She explores and critiques the approach taken by the South African Truth and Reconciliation Commission in responding to individuals' anger about their experiences of injustice under apartheid. Chakravarti (2014) argues that expressions of anger were often met with "ambivalence and confusion" (59), with the commission seeing "individual expressions of anger and despair only as mental health problems to be gotten over" (75). She defends, instead, an approach to victim testimony that listens to anger for the purpose of uncovering politically important information about citizens' experiences that might otherwise be unavailable.

Many feminists have been inspired by reading Lorde, hooks, and other feminist thinkers who offer optimistic readings of the value of anger for members of oppressed social groups. There is often, it seems, something hopeful about anger. When it is morally appropriate, the emotion provides insights into what will make the world better in the future. It can energize and spring people to positive action against injustice in pursuit of the achievement of their moral and political goals. And it can guide listeners toward actions that can lead to reconciliation and toward social and political change. But the relationship between anger and hope has not, to my knowledge, been explicitly explored in the philosophical literature. I want to make the case that there is an important relationship between hope and anger.

The Relationship between Hope and Anger

There is some discussion of the relationship between different emotions, including forms of anger, and how they interact in the social science literature (e.g., Halperin et al. 2011). Philosophers, however, often remain focused on one emotion at a time: investigating the emotion's nature and evaluative content, and considering its effects on individuals' wellbeing and agency. But understanding people's experiences of and responses to injustice requires attending to the ways in which various emotions, attitudes, and feelings—not just hope or anger but hope and anger together, as well as determination, courage, and so on—all interact to determine how they think, feel, and act. An analysis of the relationship between hope and anger thus contributes to the project of understanding emotional interaction in contexts of injustice.[21]

We have seen that when we invest hope in other people, groups, and institutions to live up to our moral expectations (i.e., those expectations we have of one another to abide by moral norms), we tend to experience resentment or another form of anger when they fail to do so. So anger responds in part to disappointed moral hopes. For example, when I invest hope in another person to abide by my moral expectation for respectful treatment and they fail to treat me with respect, my hope for respectful treatment has been disappointed, and I might become resentful about the moral violation. Notice, however, that even though my hope was not realized in this case, my moral expectation for respect remains intact. I continue to morally expect respectful treatment from others even when they have failed to treat me with respect in the past, and even when I may no longer trust them to be respectful or have much hope that they will treat me with respect in the future.

Beyond the moral expectations that we have of one another to abide by moral norms we endorse (such as the norm of respectful treatment), we also have the moral expectation that when moral wrongs occur, they will be acknowledged and addressed. Following Strawson (2008), Walker (2006) points out that anger is a way of holding others responsible, "bidding them to recognize the existence or the possibility of a kind of relationship, the kind in which parties are responsible to each other" (134). Its "aim" is to activate protecting, reassuring, or defensive responses from others who are called upon to affirm that the victim is within the scope of the community's protective responsibilities (135). Srinivasan (2018) similarly argues that anger "is a form of communication, a way of publicly marking moral disvalue, calling for the shared negative appreciation of others" (132). Thus anger, many philosophers have argued or implied, has a communicative function. It sends a message to perpetrators, bystanders, and sometimes the community at large about what is needed in response to the injustice.

Colleen Macnamara (2015) explores the communicative nature of reactive attitudes such as anger in an illuminating way. She points out that communicative acts paradigmatically involve sending a message to a recipient,

---

[21] There is some psychological literature that explores the relationship between hope and anger. In his discussion of children's anger in response to separation from their parents, John Bowlby (1973) argues that children's anger responses are sometimes "the anger of hope," as when they express anger to their parents with the hope that their parents will not leave or neglect them again, and "the anger of despair," as when children experience repeated separations and become "lost and desperate" (246).

often in the form of verbal or written words. Such messages have a number of important features. First, they have representational content. For example, a No Trespassing sign represents the requirement that passersby respect the borders of private property, and a colleague's email about the time and place of a colloquium represents the colloquium as occurring at that time and place. Second, messages have a purpose or function. They elicit a response from the recipient and, in particular, uptake of the message that was sent. Macnamara argues that, just like pumping blood is the function of hearts (because past hearts have pumped blood), communicative acts function to elicit uptake of messages in recipients (because past communicative acts have done so). Communicative acts are successful when they do evoke uptake in the recipient and unsuccessful when they fail to do so. Even if messages are not sent (e.g., if the No Trespassing sign is never put up), they are still *for* eliciting uptake of content (e.g., keeping people off of private property).

Macnamara argues that because reactive attitudes share the two key features of messages—that is, they have representational content and function to elicit uptake in a recipient—they too are communicative. Emotions are intentional, in the sense that they are about something in the world. They also paradigmatically elicit uptake of their representational content. Whether an emotion is explicitly expressed (e.g., "I am so angry at you!") or whether facial features and other behavioral cues indicate that an emotion is present, the presence of the emotion tends to produce a response in others. In the case of resentment or indignation, Macnamara suggests that emotional uptake consists in wrongdoers' feelings of guilt (559). These are feelings that "catalyze the reparative work" necessary to heal damaged moral relationships (561).

I want to largely endorse Macnamara's argument for how anger is communicative, but it seems to me that her account of the uptake of anger is too narrow as she presents it, for three reasons. First, it is not always wrongdoers who give uptake to anger. Recall that anger is not always directed toward wrongdoers. Although it is always about a perceived wrong or injustice, anger is often about systemic injustices, conditions of oppression, and other circumstances for which no specific wrongdoer(s) are identified. It is therefore not only (or even primarily, in many cases) wrongdoers who give uptake to anger but often bystanders, family members, friends, counselors, colleagues, and anyone who is related to the angry person such that they are positioned to listen and respond. (I get to what constitutes uptake below.)

Second, guilt is not the only form of uptake for anger. Note that Macnamara is using "uptake" differently than Frye, where Frye uses the term to refer to any response to another person's anger that takes the anger seriously. In the carburetor case, Frye recognizes a broad range of potential responses from the gas station attendant that would have constituted uptake of the woman's anger toward him: defending himself, attempting to explain himself, apologizing, and so on. All of these responses take seriously the representational content of anger, namely, that the gas station attendant's behavior was wrong. By defending and explaining oneself, one takes seriously the other person's anger but in a way that attempts to show how the anger was unfitting given the situation. And by apologizing, one endorses anger's message that one has done something wrong and attempts to make amends. Macnamara is right that guilt is another (emotional) way in which people take seriously another's anger. Guilt, like an apology, signifies that the person endorses anger's message that they have done something wrong. But it is one potential way, rather than *the* way, in which anger elicits uptake in recipients. (Defensiveness is often more common than guilt, since it is much easier to defend ourselves than to admit that we have done wrong.) Our responses to others' anger are highly complex and contextual, depending on a range of factors such as our relationship to the angry person and the time and place at which anger is expressed or detected. For these reasons, I follow Frye in thinking that anger tends to elicit uptake of its representational content, but the kind of uptake elicited will vary widely.

Third, not all forms of uptake in receiving another's anger are necessary, or even beneficial for, the aim of anger's communicative function that Macnamara recognizes—namely, repair. For example, defensiveness tends to exacerbate the harm caused by the original wrong. And guilt, especially guilt on the part of privileged people (such as white people) who are recipients of the anger of the oppressed, might be unnecessary and counterproductive to repairing race relations (see, e.g., Sullivan 2014). Given anger's representational content (i.e., that an injustice or other moral wrong has occurred or is continuing), it would be odd to say that anger's function is to evoke uptake in ways that would constitute a further wrong or exacerbate harm caused by the original wrong. It is more plausible to hold that anger functions to evoke uptake in recipient(s) that would genuinely constitute repair, where what constitutes repair depends on the nature of the wrong, its severity, who is involved, and contextual features of the situation. In cases where there is no prior morally good relationship to repair, anger functions to evoke uptake in recipient(s) that would be productive of constructing positive relations for the future.

Along these lines, I want to argue that anger is paradigmatically communicative, in the sense that (in agreement with Macnamara) it elicits uptake of its representational content. But the aim of anger is genuinely reparative uptake. I also want to suggest that anger as a mode of communication often indicates the presence of a hope for repair. Anger communicates that we desire repair, believe it to be possible that repair will come, and see the possibility of repair in a somewhat favorable light—as a process that might in fact occur. Although the hopes that accompany anger are not always consciously felt, they operate in the background of our minds, framing how anger moves us to act and how we express our anger toward others. I might, for example, only confront a person with whom I'm angry if I have at least some hope that they are capable of listening, feeling remorse, and changing their ways for the future. But if I am hopeless about their ability to understand why I am angry and to change, I might decide to distance from them instead. (As I argue later on, in the latter case I might be bitter.)

Aristotle apparently noticed a relationship between anger and hope. As Nussbaum (2016) explains, Aristotle "emphasizes that the forward movement characteristic of anger is pleasant, and that anger is in that sense constructive and linked to hope" (21). Nussbaum defends an Aristotelian account of anger according to which anger always involves a "payback wish," that is, a wish that the wrongdoer suffers. As she says, "The idea of payback or retribution—in some form, however subtle—is a conceptual part of anger" (15). Anger's wish for payback manifests in one of two ways: as (1) the mistaken assumption that the wrongdoer's suffering will restore or at least contribute to restoring some sense of "cosmic balance" in the universe, or as (2) the idea that the perceived wrong has damaged one's status and that the wrongdoer's suffering will lift one's status back up through "down-ranking" the status of the wrongdoer. However harsh or subtle—from the wish that the wrongdoer suffers physical injury, to unhappiness, to social unpopularity— anger involves some kind of payback wish. It "involves, conceptually, a wish for things to go badly, somehow, for the offender, in a way that is envisaged, somehow, however vaguely, as a payback for the offense. They get what they deserve" (23).

Notice that we can characterize the payback wish involved in Nussbaum-style anger as a hope for payback, at least in most cases. Nussbaum does not explore the distinction between a wish and a hope, but it is important for our

purposes here. Hope involves the belief in the possibility that a desired outcome will obtain, whereas we can wish for desired outcomes that are outside
the realm of possibility (see Wheatley 1958). I can wish, for example, that
the Holocaust had not happened. But I cannot hope that it did not happen.
I cannot hope that the Holocaust had not happened because I understand
that my backward-looking desire cannot be fulfilled.

Nussbaum is right that wishes are sometimes tied to our anger responses.
We might wish, for example, that a now-deceased wrongdoer had apologized
before dying, or we might wish that he had suffered more than he actually
did before his death. We can't hope for these outcomes because we acknowledge that the wrongdoer's apologizing and suffering more than he did is outside the realm of what we take to be possible. But most of the possible "wish
for payback" outcomes Nussbaum thinks are conceptually part of anger are
ones for which the angry person hopes. When the wrongdoer is still alive,
the desire that they suffer is within the realm of physical possibilities. That
the wrongdoer suffers physical injury, unhappiness, social unpopularity, and
so on are all outcomes for which the angry person might hope. Nussbaum
even slides between the language of wishing and hoping in describing anger,
indicating that she is using these terms interchangeably. She argues that the
philosophical tradition understands anger as "a retaliatory and hopeful out-
ward movement that seeks the pain of the offender because of and as a way of
assuaging or compensating for one's own pain" (24). And Nussbaum sees her
position as in agreement with "many first-rate thinkers" on anger, including
Aristotle, the Stoics, Joseph Butler, Adam Smith, and psychologists Richard
Lazarus and James Averill (22).

I am unpersuaded by the understanding of anger as an emotional response to perceived moral wrongs that necessarily involves a wish for
payback, nor do I see this understanding as the standard or consensus in
the literature. Notice that, on Nussbaum's view, the target of anger is the
wrongdoer. But as Walker (2006), Brudholm (2008), MacLachlan (2010),
and I (2013) argue (as just a few examples), anger is not always directed
toward a wrongdoer. We can resent social and political circumstances
(without knowing or thinking about who caused them), the community
at large, the criminal justice system, the universe, spiritual beings, and so
on. Once we notice that anger can be directed toward things that stretch far
beyond an individual wrongdoer who is directly responsible for inflicting
a moral injury, it seems implausible that anger always involves the wish
that a wrongdoer suffers. Take, for example, women's anger about ongoing

sexist oppression. If Nussbaum is right that women's anger about sexist oppression involves a wish for payback, it would seem that women's anger would involve the wish that all men who are perpetrators of or complicit in sexist oppression suffer. But most women do not wish for all men who are perpetrators of or complicit in sexist oppression to suffer. Understanding a payback wish as a necessary component of anger appears even more implausible when one considers anger about women, nonbinary people, and people of other genders who are complicit in sexist oppression. When we get angry about systems of oppression, it is unclear who (if anyone) we wish to suffer.

Instead, women's anger about sexist oppression involves the perception that sexist oppression is a serious and ongoing social injustice combined, very often, with the hope that the oppression will someday end (a hope for repair). Women's anger may imply particular hopes, such as the hope that wrongdoers are brought to justice. I might feel group-based resentment, for example, when I hear about an instance of sexual violence against another woman. My anger response might indicate the hope that the community will stand up for the victim of sexual violence and that the criminal justice system will adequately deal with the case. It might even be connected to the hope that the wrongdoer suffers, but not necessarily so. Instead, anger indicates that I am morally against sexual violence against women, and the hopes accompanying my anger tend to reflect my moral convictions and commitments. As Sara Ahmed (2004) explains:

> If anger is a form of "against-ness," then it is precisely about the impossibility of moving beyond the history of injuries to a pure or innocent position. Anger does not necessarily require an investment in revenge, which is one form of reaction to what one is against. Being against something is dependent on how one reads what one is against (for example, whether violence against women is read as dependent on male psychology or on structures of power). The question becomes: What form of action is possible given that reading? (174–175)

Ahmed's description of anger captures the fact that the hopes and/or actions bound up with one's anger response will depend upon the context in question and will not necessarily be revengeful. Nussbaum's narrow conception of anger, as involving a wish (or hope) for payback, misses the widespread variation in anger responses.

Payback wishes are thus not a necessary feature of anger, though Nussbaum's insights do begin to capture the relationship between hope and anger. Anger often, or typically, functions to elicit reparative up-take in recipients, and it indicates the presence of hopes for the future. In experiencing anger, I might hope that a wrongdoer apologizes and displays remorse, that justice will be done, that our communities will help to prevent similar wrongs from occurring again, and, encompassing all of these hopes, the hope for some kind of repair.

Nussbaum (2016) attempts to isolate this forward-looking response to moral wrongdoing, which does not necessarily involve a wish (or hope) for payback, as something that does not count as genuine anger. She defends an account of what she calls Transition-Anger, that is, a transitional form of anger that begins the shift away from "the terrain of anger toward more productive-forward looking thoughts, asking what can actually be done to increase personal or social welfare" (6). Nussbaum explains:

> In a sane and not excessively anxious and status-focused person, anger's idea of retribution or payback is a brief dream or cloud, soon dispelled by saner thoughts of personal and social welfare. So anger (if we understand it to involve a wish for retributive suffering) quickly puts itself out of busi-ness, in that even the residual focus on punishing the offender is soon seen as part of a set of projects for improving both offenders and society—and the emotion that has this goal is not so easy to see as anger. *It looks more like compassionate hope.* (30–31, emphasis added)

On Nussbaum's view, then, Transition-Anger focuses productively on so-cial welfare and one's hopes for the future, whereas fully fledged anger is connected to narcissistic concerns about one's own social status. Again, drawing upon Aristotle:

> When someone looks to the future with "decent hope"—by which Aristotle seems to mean the hope characteristic of a decent or fair-minded person (not, therefore, a hope of riding roughshod over others), he is less vulner-able to payback wishes—or to competitive anxiety. (54)

So hope, unlike and without anger, is preferable because it does not involve payback wishes for the wrongdoer to suffer, or anxiety about one's own status in society.

Nussbaum is certainly right that angry people often "cool down," moderating their anger upon reflection and considering more constructive ways of moving forward. But is this necessarily a shift away from anger? I'm not convinced that it is, and Nussbaum herself seems unsure. She asks: "Is Transition-Anger a species of anger? I really don't care how we answer this question" (36). But I think that we should care very much, inasmuch as we are trying to understand the nature of anger and the various ways it manifests in our lives. If what Nussbaum calls "Transition-Anger" is in fact a legitimate form of anger, then anger does not necessarily include a payback wish (or hope). Only some forms of anger do. This seems to me quite plausible and coheres with my own understanding of anger.

So we should reject the notion that anger always involves a payback wish (or hope) while acknowledging that anger does sometimes manifest in this way. The understanding of anger as implying hope more generally also extends to social and political contexts in more plausible ways than Nussbaum's view can account for. Chakravarti (2014) points out that "feminist proponents of the role of anger in the process of consciousness-raising have hoped for, among other things, the uptake of better legal policy with respect to sexism as well as the acceptance of anger as legitimate" (130). She thus links the epistemic value of anger from consciousness-raising to the hope for improved legal policies. Myisha Cherry (2019) similarly argues that anger strives for change (as Lorde too teaches us). Anger about racial injustice is thus about not revenge but reform, where anger expresses the need to repair damage.

There are many examples of anger responses in social and political contexts that fit this analysis. For example, in expressing group-based resentment about the widespread cases of missing and murdered Indigenous women in Canada and the United States, Indigenous women participate in consciousness-raising about the systemic injustices that many Indigenous women face (including sexism, racism, colonialism, and poverty). Indigenous women's resentment aims to prompt a genuinely reparative response so that the crisis will be addressed, and in resenting, Indigenous women may hope that social justice efforts will be pursued. They know that their own agency, both individually and collectively, is insufficient to dismantle the inter-related systems of oppression that so often lead to violence against them and death. Indigenous women might thus hope that individuals and institutions with the authority, economic resources, and political power will take interest in, fund, and carry out effective inquiries into missing and murdered Indigenous women, follow through on recommendations, and allocate resources and implement services to address the unjust conditions in which they live.

But Nussbaum is right that sometimes the hopes implied by our anger responses are vindictive. Her view of anger as involving the wish (or hope) that wrongdoers suffer thus makes sense of some anger responses. Brudholm's (2008) discussion of a quotation from Peter Maass, a witness to a massacre of civilians in Sarajevo, illustrates a drastic example of this type of anger. Maass explains:

> My first thought was for the commander who gave the order to attack. I hope he burns in the hottest corner of hell. My second thought was for the soldiers who loaded the breeches and fired the guns. I hope their sleep is forever punctuated by the screams of children and the cries of their mothers. (quoted in Brudholm 2008, 1)

Maass's revengeful hopes are understandable given what he witnessed, and they raise interesting questions about how revengeful hopes can be evaluated. If revenge is always morally wrong, then Maass's hopes are not morally appropriate. And if such hopes do not contribute to Maass's wellbeing or to improved social and political conditions, his hopes may also be imprudent. I leave aside the question of how Maass's revengeful hopes should be evaluated (which requires discussion of whether revenge is necessarily, or always, unjustified).[22] But this example reminds us that the hopes implied or expressed through our anger responses can be directed toward a wide range of outcomes, some of which might be worthy to pursue and others not. In anger, we might hope that wrongdoers will be brought to justice, that our communities will not tolerate such injustices in the future, that wrongdoers' lives will be ruined, and so on. The crucial point is that anger can be understood as an emotion that often communicates the hope for repair.

---

[22] See Jeffrie G. Murphy (2000) for a qualified defense of vindictiveness. We will also see, later on, that a kind of faith in humanity seems inconsistent with revenge, as conceived by some social justice activists who appeal to faith in humanity as fundamental to their pursuits.

Concluding Thoughts

I have argued in this chapter that we cannot adequately understand hope in conditions of oppression without considering its relationship to anger—an emotion that many scholars and activists have advocated as a justified and useful response to injustice and oppression. But the value of anger can be quite difficult to determine. Anger is strategically or prudentially rational when it promotes the agent's rational ends. The emotion is fitting when it correctly represents its object as wrong or unjust to the degree warranted by the severity of the wrong or injustice. There is a further question of whether anger is properly directed, that is, directed toward the right agent(s) who are responsible for the wrong or injustice. And anger is morally appropriate when it reveals that the agent is properly oriented toward the good. Fully morally appropriate anger is both fitting (in terms of its shape) and properly directed, revealing that the agent is both against injustice and holds correct moral beliefs and attitudes about what agents are responsible and blameworthy for the injustice. The all-things-considered practical question of whether a person should be angry, about what, and how angry they should feel is—like hope—a contextual matter, only to be determined in concrete cases. But we can nevertheless see that anger can have moral, epistemic, and political value in our personal and political lives.

While philosophers have long been interested in how individuals can move from resentment to forgiveness—for example, when wrongdoers offer a reparative response and individuals acquire moral reasons to forgive—less attention has been paid to what happens to anger when it is not met with uptake. And this happens most often to members of oppressed social groups. As Macalester Bell (2009) points out, members of oppressed groups "will likely experience greater and greater alienation from the wider community and their anger will remain, in some sense, incomplete" (172). I want to understand what happens to anger when it is incomplete: when our anger remains a part of our emotional lives in cases where it has not been met with an adequate reparative response. In the next chapter, I argue that the loss of hopes accompanied by our anger responses can result in the emotion of bitterness.

4

Losing Hope, Becoming Embittered

> The accusation of bitterness implicitly acknowledges that a great
> many people have never been granted the social goods likely to lead
> to the luxury of cultivating sympathetic emotional lives. Bitterness
> does not always involve gender as one of salient determinants of who
> is most likely to be accused. The angry disadvantaged of a society—
> visible minorities, aboriginals, the working class, the disabled, the
> ill, the divorced, and the old—are all targets of this critique.
>
> Sue Campbell

Feminist philosophers have increasingly recognized that it is individuals at
the margins of society who are most likely to be accused of bitterness. To call
someone "bitter" is an accusation because it is assumed that the person is not
merely angry but still angry, and that the point of the anger has expired. The
accusation implies that it is time to move on and let go. This understanding
of bitterness as an inherently inappropriate and destructive emotion stands
in contrast to other forms of anger that have earned much attention and, as
we have seen, moral praise in the philosophical literature. Resentment, for
example, is commonly praised when it demonstrates self-respect and an appreciation for morality.

Discussions of bitterness are far less common and have taken place most
frequently by feminist philosophers who have noticed the tendency to cate-
gorize people who are socially and politically disadvantaged as bitter and not
just angry. In her widely cited 1991 article "What's Wrong with Bitterness?,"
Lynne McFall defends the view that bitterness is sometimes rationally and
morally appropriate. Bitterness, on her view, is a refusal to forgive and forget
injustices that have disappointed one's important hopes. This article paved
the way for Sue Campbell's discussion of bitterness in her influential 1994
article "Being Dismissed: The Politics of Emotional Expression," which
explores the ways in which the accusation of bitterness is used politically as

Hope Under Oppression. Katie Stockdale, Oxford University Press. © Oxford University Press 2021.
DOI: 10.1093/oso/9780197563564.003.0005

a form of emotional dismissal. Following Campbell, philosophers such as Susan Babbitt (1997), Diana Tietjens Meyers (2004), Macalester Bell (2005), Sylvia Burrow (2005), Margaret Urban Walker (2006), and Kathryn Norlock (2009) have built upon McFall's account to continue discussions of the significance of bitterness to feminist moral and political thought.[1]

But while there is much to be learned from McFall's discussion of bitterness, there are significant problems with her view that have gone largely unnoticed. The purpose of this chapter is to expose these problems and to offer an alternative account of bitterness that more accurately traces the character and effects of the emotion. I argue that bitterness is not primarily about the disappointment of important hopes but about violations of moral expectations: those expectations we have of one another to abide by moral norms. But hope is still important to understanding bitterness. Bitterness is paradigmatically a form of unresolved anger involving a loss of hope that a perceived injustice or other moral wrong, one that violated or that continues to violate one's moral expectations, will be sufficiently acknowledged and addressed.[2] The emotion can also be a prudentially rational, fitting, and morally appropriate response.

But the claim that bitterness can be legitimately *endorsed*, in these ways, may give us pause in light of the inherent harms and risks of the emotion. Bitterness is thought to be psychologically and emotionally painful to bear, and it can negatively interfere with our relationships and behavior. (A quick Google search reveals some striking anonymous quotes about bitterness: "Bitterness is a small crack in the windshield of your relationships," "Bitterness and love can't live together in the same heart," and "Bitterness has no place in a marriage" are just a few.) I do not deny that bitterness can be harmful to the agent who bears it, and people might have good prudential reasons for working to overcome the emotion for themselves and for their relationships. But focusing only on the harms and risks of bitterness can distract from its moral, epistemic, and political value, namely, its role as a

---

[1] One fairly recent non-feminist contribution to understanding bitterness is Brudholm (2008): 26–30, 44–46, 135, and 155–158. He too cites Lynne McFall.

[2] Might one be "born into bitterness," or never have had hope at all? I take it that this is a real possibility given the tragic conditions into which some people are born, conditions in which hope might never be fostered, cultivated, or supported. But I think that more common is the experience of having hope and then losing it: of starting out as hopeful (perhaps even naively hopeful, as in the case of many children), coming to learn about and see more clearly the extent of oppression and other forms of injustice in the world, then losing hopes that one had before. So I understand bitterness as, paradigmatically, a form of unresolved anger involving a loss of hope even though it might also manifest for some people as a form of learned, hopeless anger.

"moral reminder" about a past or persistent injustice, indicating that there is still moral and political work left to do in the difficult process of repair. One might, however, still worry that bitterness is damaging because it leads to despair and inaction. I show that people who are embittered may still be motivated to persist in their moral and political struggles even without hope that their effort will be successful.

What Is Bitterness?

Bitterness is an emotion that manifests in a wide range of contexts. One can be bitter about such things as their father's mistreatment of them in childhood, being denied the opportunity to go to college due to a lack of financial means, or the loss of a loved one in a mass shooting. Like other forms of anger, we experience bitterness at times when we see an action, event, or set of circumstances as wrong or unjust—either in the past or ones that are continuing. As we will see, what distinguishes bitterness from other forms of anger is its relation to hope.

I am particularly interested in instances of bitterness that respond to injustices targeting members of whole social groups, bitterness that results from people's lived experiences under oppression. James Baldwin (1955) testifies to his father's and his own bitterness in his "Notes of a Native Son," which sheds light on the experience and effects of the emotion in people's lives. Reflecting on his father's life and death, Baldwin writes:

> He had lived and died in an intolerable bitterness of spirit and it frightened me, as we drove him to the graveyard through those unquiet, ruined streets, to see how powerful and overflowing this bitterness could be and to realize that this bitterness was now mine.
>
> When he died I had been away from home for a little over a year. In that year I had had time to become aware of the meaning of all my father's bitter warnings. . . . I had discovered the weight of white people in the world. I saw that this had been for my ancestors and now would be for me an awful thing to live with and that the bitterness which had helped to kill my father could also kill me. (90)

Baldwin's bitterness evolved from his lived experiences under racial oppression. While living and working in New Jersey, he came to understand the bitter messages his father communicated to him about white people. Through the culmination of daily experiences of injustice—being denied service at restaurants, bars, and bowling alleys; being refused places to live; getting fired; and so on—racism began to its toll. Baldwin became embittered.

Baldwin was well aware of the harms of bitterness to his father's and his own wellbeing, relationships, and behavior. He describes walking down the street and feeling as though everyone was against him, walking toward him, and white. Baldwin (1955) says, "I wanted to do something to crush these white faces, which were crushing me" (97). As he walked, he came across a restaurant that he knew would not serve Black people, angrily entered, and took a seat. When the server approached him, he remembers hating her "for her white face, and for her great, astounded, white eyes" (98). And when the server explained that the restaurant "did not serve Negroes," Baldwin picked up the mug full of water on the table and hurled it at the woman. He was forced to run from the restaurant, and he describes a realization he made in that moment:

> I could not get over two facts, both equally difficult for the imagination to grasp, and one was that I could have been murdered. But the other was that I had been ready to commit murder. I saw nothing very clearly but I did see this: that my life, my real life, was in danger, and not from anything other people might do but from the hatred I carried in my own heart. (99)

Baldwin understood that, for his own good, he had to overcome his negative emotions. He concludes his essay by reflecting on the lessons he had learned about bitterness, about hate, and what he saw as necessary in his own life going forward. Interestingly, Baldwin does not advocate for hope as an alternative to negative emotions, but "acceptance, totally without rancor, of life as it is, and men as they are" and struggling against injustice "free of hatred and despair" (115).

Baldwin is likely right that living without bitterness is a better state of affairs than bearing it. But it does not follow from the recognition that bitterness is undesirable that the emotion is inappropriate or absent of any value, even for the agent who bears it. Part of what makes "Notes of a Native Son" so insightful is the way in which bitterness taints the narrative, shedding darkness on what it is like to live under racial oppression. Bitterness is, in this narrative, part of Baldwin's moral perception. It focuses his attention on the bleak realities of persistent racism that Black people in America face.

McFall (1991) takes up the challenge of developing an account of bitterness as a moral emotion to make sense of experiences like Baldwin's. She defines bitterness as a refusal to forgive and forget injustices[3] that have disappointed one's important hopes. To be bitter, on her view, is "to recite one's angry litany of loss, long past the time others may care to listen" (146). Bitterness can be either active, manifesting in vocal and vengeful forms, or passive, experienced more as deep sorrow. It can also be partial and object-directed, as when it is about losing one's job due to discrimination, or characteristic of a person, as when bitterness results from a pattern of discrimination and ends up encompassing how one perceives important aspects of one's life.

McFall argues that bitterness can be rationally and morally appropriate— particularly, on her view, when it responds to avoidable moral harms brought about by human agency. (She does not separate these different ways of evaluating the emotion.) As we will see, McFall's account of how instances of bitterness can be evaluated reveals much about her understanding of the nature of the emotion, and where she goes astray. So the question of what bitterness is overlaps with the question of how the emotion can be evaluated. On McFall's view, since bitterness is about the disappointment of hopes, the question of what makes bitterness rationally and morally appropriate is a question about whether the hope disappointed was "legitimate."

McFall argues that hopes that are extremely unlikely to be realized (either statistically or specific to the case in question) cannot be legitimate. To use her example, while the hope to escape may be legitimate for an escape artist in challenging situations, my hope to escape may be illegitimate if it is highly unlikely that I will succeed. We cannot, in other words, rationally hope for things that are highly unlikely to obtain. It is notable, however, that McFall does not explain in what sense it is irrational to hope for highly unlikely outcomes. On the view I have been defending, it might be epistemically and prudentially rational for me to hope to escape, even when the odds are against me. I might rationally believe that escaping is possible but highly unlikely (and so I am epistemically rational), and my hope to escape might enable me to search for potential escape routes, which may increase my chances of success (and so I am prudentially rational too). However, it might not be fitting for me to strongly hope to escape, if my strong hope represents the

---

[3] In her use of the language of "injustice" I take McFall to be orienting her discussion of bitterness around injustice rather than suggesting that bitterness can only be about injustice (and not moral wrongdoing more generally).

possibility of escaping in a too favorable light, given the evidence available. I come back to these different evaluative dimensions of bitterness later on.

McFall also adds a further condition for what makes a hope "legitimate" and thus what it is rational to hope for. Beyond the requirement that the outcomes for which we hope must be reasonably likely to obtain, McFall argues that legitimate hopes are ones that have "been raised by one person in another through an explicit statement of intention" (149). Though she does not say much about this condition, McFall provides an example of sexual betrayal that clarifies how the two conditions work together in practice. She argues that in the case of sexual betrayal the moral harm done is the disappointment of the hope for sexual fidelity. So in considering whether an instance of bitterness in response to sexual betrayal is appropriate, we ask whether the hope of fidelity is a legitimate hope in that instance. McFall argues:

> On the assumption that sexual fidelity is possible . . . and assuming one's lover is not exceptionally gifted in respect of waywardness, and one's vows or other communications contained an explicit statement of intention to be "true," the lover who was betrayed had her legitimate, important hope of fidelity disappointed, and so partial, passive bitterness is justified. (150)

There is, it seems, something required on the part of those in whom we invest hopes for our hopes to be rationally and morally appropriate on McFall's view. I cannot rationally hope that a romantic partner will remain sexually faithful to me unless my partner has either expressed or implied an intention to remain sexually faithful.[4]

It is a striking consequence of McFall's view that it renders the bitterness of members of oppressed groups irrational and morally inappropriate. But if the relevant question in assessing bitterness is whether the hope it is based in is legitimate (and if we accept McFall's account of how to evaluate hope), then the bitterness of individuals who belong to privileged groups will be more rationally and morally appropriate than the bitterness of members of oppressed groups, since these differential positions come to bear on the opportunities and entitlements that we have. Campbell (1994), calling attention to

---

[4] What we know about the likelihood of a hope's being realized and (where relevant) a person's intentions to realize the hope also matter, on McFall's view. If the information available to me suggests that it is likely that my partner will remain sexually faithful, then even if it is in fact unlikely that my partner will remain sexually faithful (e.g., because he has convincingly lied), my hope is legitimate.

this concern, asks: "What can a woman of Color in america legitimately hope for?" (52). She quotes Audre Lorde (2007), who points out that the anger of women of color responds to being silenced, unchosen, and hated and having their perceived "lack of humanness" taken for granted. Since these women know that many of their important hopes are not likely to be realized, their bitterness would be irrational and morally inappropriate on McFall's account. Her view unintentionally rules out the possibility of appropriate bitterness for exactly those individuals who have good reasons for having the emotion, if anyone does.[5]

It is important to note that even if McFall's view is incorrect, her error in understanding has not interfered with feminist philosophers' use of her essay as inspiration for uncovering important insights about the emotion. As Campbell (1994) makes clear, the label "bitterness" is used politically to dismiss disadvantaged members of society, functioning to shift the focus away from unjust social and political circumstances toward individuals' supposedly pathological emotional states. But I worry that while these feminist insights correctly point to a political danger of using the term "bitterness," they do not help to understand why bitterness comes about, the experience of bitterness, and its effects on the characters of individuals who bear it. Bitterness is, after all, not just a political charge but also a felt emotion.[6] And it is an emotion that has been noted by some members of oppressed groups, like Baldwin, as a consequence of their experiences living under oppression. Like other forms of anger, bitterness manifests as what Alison M. Jaggar (1989) calls an "outlaw emotion," contributing to the experiences and perceptions of members of oppressed groups who find themselves resisting, emotionally, the unjust conditions in which they exist (166). Correcting our understanding of bitterness is important for having an accurate understanding of some members of oppressed groups' experiences as well as how it is harmful and/or helpful to their moral perception and agency.

[5] This is also not a consequence that all philosophers who cite McFall notice. For example, Kathryn Norlock (2009) suggests that in the case of two South African women's bitterness in response to a white police officer's murder of their husbands, we should extend McFall's argument to characterize their bitterness as appropriate, since otherwise we would be letting the officer "off the moral hook" (89). But McFall's account cannot be extended to track our moral evaluation of this case, because the women's hopes were not likely to be realized. And it is the likelihood of realization that makes a hope legitimate and thus the bitterness based in it rational and justified on McFall's view.

[6] Meyers (2004) similarly points out that while charges of what she calls "rancorous emotional attitudes," including hypersensitivity, paranoia, anger, and bitterness, are often fabricated for political purposes, sometimes ascriptions of these emotional attitudes are warranted. She writes: "Despite an element of hyperbole embedded in these ascriptions, they are not always distortions arising from patriarchal conventions of interpretation" (147).

Fortunately, the problem that the bitterness of members of oppressed groups will get counted as rationally and morally inappropriate is a consequence for McFall's understanding of the nature and evaluative content of bitterness, not a problem inherent in the emotion. One way to proceed would be to accept McFall's understanding of the nature of bitterness, reject her account of how hope can be evaluated, and provide a new evaluative framework for hope so that the hopes of members of oppressed groups will get categorized as legitimate. The framework I offered in chapter 2 might be of help. I argued that understanding the value of hope requires attending to a range of evaluative questions, including whether the hope is epistemically and prudentially rational, whether it is fitting, and whether it is morally appropriate. But there are deeper problems with McFall's understanding of the nature of bitterness that lead to a more fruitful line of inquiry, one that sheds light on the evaluative dimensions of the emotion too. I want to argue that McFall's view does not accurately characterize the relevance of hope to bitterness, and I offer a new understanding of the emotion to correct this problem. Doing so not only corrects an important error in the feminist philosophical literature on the interesting emotion of bitterness. It will also help us to see the importance of theorizing the phenomenon of losing hope more generally to moral, social, and political life.

Let us return to the case of sexual betrayal, in which McFall argues that the harm done is the disappointment of one's hope for sexual fidelity. Notice, though, that when I enter into an exclusive romantic relationship, I don't merely hope for sexual fidelity; I morally expect it. (Moral expectations, recall, are expectations we hold of others to adhere to the moral norms we endorse whether or not we predictively expect, or anticipate, that they will do so.) Similarly, I don't merely hope for justice and equality. I have a moral expectation that others will act in accordance with the demands of justice and equality. That these are moral expectations, not merely hopes, can be seen in how we respond when others act contrary to sexual fidelity, justice, and equality. For example, if my partner in an exclusive romantic relationship cheats, I may become resentful. My resentment expresses my perception that I have been wronged, not just that my partner has disappointed my hope that they would be sexually faithful.

This alternative description better explains how bitterness is a form of anger. Campbell (1994) argues that an expression of bitterness was at one time "intended anger," where the recounting of injury and the failure of others to listen combine to form the emotion. Walker (2006) suggests that "without at least the acknowledgement by others of serious wrong and the need for repair, or without a clear demonstration of concern for suffering and loss of victims, victims and the families of victims fall prey to bitterness and despair" (108). Anger is thus prior to (but also part of) bitterness. We become angry about a perceived moral wrong or injustice, and when it is not met with an appropriate reparative response, bitterness can ensue.[7]

Walker (2006) also points out that in bitterness "one insists on what is right but with a sense of futility and alienation" (108). "Futility" in this sentence is important. Bitterness in the psychological literature has been described as a mixture of anger and hopelessness. For example, Hansjörg Znoj (2011) explains that "bitterness or embitterment can be seen as the product of a personal story of perceived injustice. The emotional quality is characterized by resignation (hopelessness) and anger" (10). Beate Schrank and Astrid Grant Hay (2011) similarly point out that the psychological impact of the perceived injustice involves dimensions of hopelessness about goals, relationships, one's sense of control, and expectations about the future. And this is unsurprising. If bitterness responds to a perceived wrong or injustice and if those who we think have wronged us and others fail to make amends, we may lose hope that they will ever acknowledge and address the injustice and meet our moral expectations in the future.

The connection between moral expectation and hope is complex. Legitimate moral expectations are fixed by moral reasons in the sense that even when it is extremely unlikely that they will be met, moral expectations continue to make demands on moral agents. For example, individuals who experience persistent injustice may lose hope that the injustice will ever end, while the legitimacy of their moral expectation for justice and the further moral expectation that injustice will be addressed are unaffected by the likelihood of those expectations being met.[8] In bitterness, we begin to lose hope that others will act in accordance with the moral expectations we continue to endorse.

---

[7] I tend to think of the classic angry response as something like "I can't *believe* she would do that! As if she thinks she can treat me that way!," whereas the bitter response is something like "Of course she behaved horribly. What else did you think might happen? She has shown her true colors."

[8] Babbitt (1997) calls attention to the fact that the bitterness of members of oppressed groups often responds to an absence of something to which they are morally entitled. She argues that the hopes of members of oppressed groups should be considered "rational" in the sense that they aim at ends that are morally appropriate (self-respect, dignity, and autonomy) even though they were not likely to be realized.

The present analysis suggests that philosophers' understanding of bitterness falls short in significant ways. Bitterness is not primarily about the disappointment of important hopes but about violations of moral expectations. It is typically a residual emotion we experience when a perceived wrong has not been put to rest through some kind of repair. Bitterness involves anger, but it is, to varying degrees, hopeless anger. In bitterness, we remain committed to the moral expectations that others have violated, and at the same time, begin to lose hope that they will attend to the harms about which we're angry and abide by our moral expectations in the future.

Consequently, to call individuals bitter as moral condemnation when the emotion is responding to real instances of injustice is to dismiss individuals who may be expressing legitimate moral expectations.[9] This is consistent with Campbell's (1994) insight that calling someone bitter shifts attention away from interpreters' failures to listen and act toward the individual's emotional states such that the charge of bitterness itself becomes a reason or excuse for not listening. She argues that we are "better off in blocking the criticism than internalizing this description of our attitude and trying to defend our bitterness" for this reason (52). But the question of whether one has prudential reasons for resisting being called "bitter" and resisting the emotion itself is separate from whether bitterness is an appropriate response. And when one comes to recognize that one bears the emotion, being able to identify that it is fitting and morally *appropriate*, and thus to resist the charge of "craziness" and that accompanies the charge of bitterness, may be the most empowering possibility available in non-ideal circumstances.

There is also an increasing political danger of the expression of bitterness in social and political contexts. One only needs to pay a visit to men's rights activism websites, browse the #WhiteLivesMatter Twitter feed, or read comments sections of news articles to see that members of privileged groups bear their own bitterness. One extreme example is that of Elliot Rodger, who killed six people and injured fourteen others at Alpha Phi, a sorority of the University of California, Santa Barbara, in 2014. In his manifesto, Rodgers describes his hopes and losses of hope throughout his life, fixating on his hopes for sex and beautiful women. Over time, these hopes were left unrealized. Rodger (2014) writes, "As time progressed, I realized how hopeless everything in my life was. The chance that I will ever rise to power [as a dictator]

---

[9] It is like Frye's carburetor case in which the woman's anger was met with the response "Crazy bitch."

and right the wrongs of the world were extremely slim. . . . My hatred for
people who have sex festered inside me like a plague. I frequently went on
walks to brood over how hopeless and unfair everything was" (57).

Rodger saw others' sexual lives as an injustice done to him, by both women
and the men whom they found more attractive. But in approaching college,
with a new haircut and clothing, Rodger regained hope. He continues:

> I then started to feel something that has been lost to me for a long
> time: Hope. Without hope, I just couldn't go on any longer. I needed to feel
> hope. Hope for the future, hope for a better life. Upon feeling this, I realized
> that it is perhaps possible for me to have the things I desire; to have a great
> social life again, to have a girlfriend, to have sex, to have all the pleasures I've
> desperately craved for so long. . . . And so began a period of great yearning.
> A great chase, so to speak. I will chase after a hope that I built for myself,
> only to have that shattered every time. (59)

Rodger's hope that he would have a "beautiful girlfriend" and his desired life
(one with a lot of sex) quickly faded and was replaced by hatred and rage
(66). (This pattern of renewed hope and struggles with despair, hatred, and
rage continues for quite a while in the very long manifesto.) He interprets
women's not having sex with him as a serious injustice, speaking of deserving
women, as though he has a moral claim to them somehow. He writes that he
had to "fight back against the cruelty of women," for there was no other hope
(124), and he would "punish all females for the crime of depriving [him] of
sex" (132). Rodger ended up believing that all women are evil beasts who
"are not capable of having morals or thinking rationally" and who should
have no rights at all (136). As Kate Manne (2018) argues in her analysis of
Rodger's misogyny, his "sexual desire for the women of Alpha Phi—and his
desire that they desire him in turn—played a crucial role in spawning his
resentment" (50). Misogyny, as Manne points out, is "less a matter of beliefs
than desires—desires and other similar states of mind that ask the world be
kept or brought in line with a patriarchal order" (69).

Rodger's bitterness, evolving from his rage and the loss of his misogynistic
hopes, was of the very worst kind: a deeply morally inappropriate bitterness
that became so infectious that he came to fantasize about the annihilation
of all women. So although Campbell is right that members of oppressed
groups may be more likely to be called bitter as a form of dismissal, they are
not the only ones who experience and express the emotion. And without an

evaluative framework for bitterness, we are left without conceptual resources for making sense of, and responding to, the most harmful instances of the emotion. It is thus possible and politically urgent to engage with the question of how to evaluate bitterness.

Evaluating Bitterness

We might begin by evaluating bitterness for rationality, similarly to other emotions. But feminist philosophers have raised concerns about rational assessments when it comes to the emotion of bitterness in particular. As Campbell (1994) explains:

> My concern, phrased in a general way, is that calculating rationality may put responsibility on the individual for her attitudes or actions without offering ways of assessing that individual's situation against the political options of others. If, as I believe to be the case, assessments of rationality are connected most deeply to questions of intelligible agency, what is not within my power to affect may not provide a rational ground for my actions or responses. (51)

This passage seems to suggest two concerns. First, evaluating whether bitterness is rational involves focusing on the mental states of the person who is accused of bitterness while failing to attend to the importance of their political situation in comparison to others. Second, talk of rationality may not make sense in such contexts because bitterness seems unconnected to what the person is capable of doing and affecting.[10]

Sylvia Burrow (2005), quoting this passage, responds to Campbell's second concern. She points out that we can evaluate emotions by noticing that "rationality" can be a function of the appropriateness of a response to some situation. She thus disagrees with Campbell that questions about rationality are restricted to questions about intelligible agency and points out that it is the very nature of some emotions that they respond to events over which we do not have control. But like Campbell, Burrow notes her hesitation with doing

---

[10] It is somewhat unclear to me how Campbell is using the language of "rationality." The first concern seems to be about the harms of focusing on whether emotions are rational. The second concern seems to be about the relationship between bitterness and rational action.

any kind of evaluative work when it comes to the emotion of bitterness. She states:

> If we are in the company of persons we consider capable of giving uptake to our emotions, it would be legitimate to expect them to do so. We might wish to add a moral force to this expectation as well, and claim that others should give uptake to legitimate instances of bitterness. But I hesitate to take this approach, because we cannot always expect others to care about our losses of hope or, in fact, any other feature of our lives. (30)

Burrow's hesitation reflects her agreement with McFall that bitterness is about the disappointment of important hopes. If we can't legitimately expect others to care about our "losses of hope," then bitterness might always be out of place. Or, at least, there may not be good reasons for expressing bitterness in the absence of compelling reasons for others to give our bitterness uptake. But I have argued that bitterness responds primarily to perceived violations of moral expectations, not disappointed hopes. If this is right, then when there is in fact an injustice or other moral wrong that has not been adequately addressed (not just a perceived one), there *are* compelling moral reasons for others to give uptake to bitterness. Moral violations generate a demand for repair, such as an apology, punishment, and efforts toward reconciliation, where the appropriate reparative response depends on the context in question. So although Burrow is right that we cannot demand that all people care about our losses of non-moral hopes (e.g., I can't demand that a stranger care about helping me realize my fitness hopes), we can certainly morally expect certain moral behavior from others.

In response to Campbell's first concern, I suggest that evaluating the bitterness of members of oppressed groups can help to call attention to the person's political situation rather than dismiss or distract from it. When bitterness responds to a perceived injustice that remains insufficiently addressed, then bitterness *calls attention to the perceived injustice*. It expresses that the injustice, if there is one, has not received a sufficient reparative response. Evaluating bitterness thus consists in asking whether there is an injustice that requires attention and action. It is a way of engaging with the reasons behind the person's emotional experience, reasons that, in political contexts, express how she construes her political circumstances against those of others.

So it is not uniquely problematic, as some philosophers have proposed, to offer an evaluative framework for bitterness once we understand more precisely the nature of the emotion. And I suggest that bitterness can be evaluated in a manner similar to other forms of anger. Recall that anger is strategically or prudentially rational when it serves one's rational ends, and so too in the case of bitterness. (Although one might worry that bitterness is always self-destructive, we will see later on how it is consistent with, and perhaps even contributes to, effective political action.) Anger is fitting when it correctly represents an action, event, or set of circumstances as wrong or unjust (e.g., racism) to a degree warranted by the severity of the wrong or injustice. The emotion is properly directed when it is directed (if at all) toward the agent(s) responsible for the injustice (e.g., white supremacists). The emotion is morally appropriate when it reveals that the agent is properly oriented toward the good.

Let's begin by considering when bitterness is fitting. Since bitterness is a form of anger, the emotion is fitting at least in part when it correctly represents an action, event, or set of circumstances as wrong or unjust to a degree warranted by the severity of the wrong or injustice. I might be resentful about being punished for a crime and become embittered about my sentencing. But if I committed the crime and my resentment incorrectly represents the decided punishment as unjust, then my resentment and resultant bitterness about the sentencing would be unfitting in terms of their shape. My resentment and bitterness would be unfitting because no moral wrong was done to me. If, in contrast, the decided punishment was only slightly unfair, and if I experience strong resentment and resultant bitterness, my emotions would be unfitting in terms of their size. They would be too strong given the severity of the injustice.

In the previous chapter, I discussed the example of white men who respond to the claim that they have "white male privilege" with unfitting resentment because they incorrectly perceive the discourse about white male privilege as an injustice done to them. And we can imagine these white men's resentment evolving into bitterness when other people fail to affirm their views and when progress toward gender and racial justice continues. But since these men's bitterness continues to incorrectly represent beneficial social justice efforts as unjust, their bitterness, too, is unfitting. They incorrectly perceive social justice efforts as wrong.

Importantly, by evaluating the bitterness of members of privileged groups, such as white men's bitterness in response to the discourse about white male privilege, another way in which bitterness is used politically becomes apparent. Members of privileged groups sometimes express bitterness to articulate moral progress as unacknowledged injustices done to them, which in turn helps to keep members of oppressed groups in their subordinated place. Bitter expressions such as "*Of course* a woman got the job, yet again" are ways in which the moral language used by members of privileged groups works to maintain their privilege at the expense of others. Like other forms of anger, their bitterness might thus be strategically rational, serving to protect white male privilege. But the emotion is unfitting because no moral wrong was done.[11]

But what makes bitterness, rather than another form of anger, a fitting response? For bitterness to be fitting, the emotion must also correctly represent in an unfavorable light the possibility of repair. In bitterness, we perceive an event or situation not only as wrong or unjust (as in other forms of anger) but as without much hope for repair. I argued in chapter 3 that anger often indicates the presence of hope(s) for repair, where hope is not part of the content of the emotion but exists in the backgrounds of our minds, influencing how our anger is felt and expressed.[12] But whereas other forms of anger indicate the presence of hope, bitterness involves a loss or absence of hope— where the loss or absence of hope is part of the content of the emotion. Bitterness is a complex emotion that results from not just the coexistence of anger and varying degrees of hopelessness but the interaction of anger with varying degrees of hopelessness. Consequently, the question of whether bitterness is fitting depends upon whether the emotion correctly represents its object as wrong or unjust and whether it correctly represents the wrong or injustice as without hope for repair.[13]

One thing to notice is that bitterness is sometimes unfitting even when anger *is* fitting, such as when my I am bitter about a friend's sexist comment and write off the possibility that he might apologize and do better in the future. It is fitting to see his action as wrong (as in anger), but it may be unfitting to be without hope for an apology and his change in behavior (as in bitterness). And when wrongdoers do apologize and display remorse for their wrongful acts, and—where relevant—the broader community responds with efforts to toward repair, the moral expectation that harms will be addressed

---

[11] Their bitterness is also morally inappropriate. White men thus have a moral responsibility to work to overcome their bitterness about the discourse of white male privilege, despite its being potentially instrumental to their aims.

[12] This subtle point about the relationship between anger and hope makes sense of why people can be not bitter but "just angry"—such as when a person might lash out in anger and where hopes for repair seem irrelevant to their emotional experience.

[13] I say more about how this complexity is relevant to moral assessments of bitterness later on.

has been met. In these cases, bitterness is unfitting because the emotion now incorrectly represents the action or event as without hope for repair. It might be most appropriate for the victim to forgive or move on.[14] What constitutes a sufficient reparative response (and who needs to give it) depends upon the nature and severity of the wrong, who is responsible, and the harm caused to individuals and groups, among many other things. But what is necessary for the hope for repair to be realized is that the injustice is acknowledged as injustice and that genuine efforts toward repair have been taken.

It is, unfortunately, often the case that the injustices about which people become embittered are in an important sense irreparable. When Black families lose a loved one to police violence, when victims of human trafficking are traumatized by rape, when an Indigenous or undocumented parent has a child taken away from them—in all of these cases, there is irreparable damage. Individuals who are bitter about these injustices often rightly judge that repair with respect to these harms is impossible. In these cases, the embittered person might lose hope not (or not only) for repair but also for their own life: a loss of hope that one can live on in any normal sort of way in the aftermath of trauma. In these cases, one might not only say things like "They will never apologize or display remorse" or "Things will never change" but also "They have unjustly destroyed my life, my future." Bitterness, in these cases, is a response to the injustice and also the irreparable damage it caused. It might, even if regrettably, always be fitting to live with bitterness for some people, though they might have good prudential reasons to work to overcome their bitterness for themselves and their relationships.

But what might make bitterness morally appropriate? I have argued that emotions are morally appropriate when they reveal that the agent is properly oriented toward the good. Because bitterness is a complex emotion involving both anger and the loss of moral hopes, both the anger and the moral hopes lost must reveal that the agent is properly oriented toward the good for bitterness to be fully morally appropriate. Suppose, to take a rather extreme example, that a pair of Black perpetrators sexually assault and murder a white female victim and that the perpetrators' life histories were shaped by racism,

---

[14] Some people might even forgive in the absence of efforts toward repair. Cheshire Calhoun (1992) explores this possibility through a defense of what she calls "aspirational forgiveness," or forgiveness of culpable wrongdoing for which there remain moral reasons for resentment. In aspirational forgiveness, we do not excuse or justify the wrongdoer's behavior but strive to make biographical sense of why the wrongdoer (as a morally flawed human being, like all of us) behaved immorally. We also do not let go of the judgment that the wrongdoer is culpable, but we do stop resentfully demanding uptake. Bitterness is thus not the only potential emotional response to a loss of hope for repair.

poverty, and conflict. We can imagine that the victim's loved ones would be intensely angry about this horrific injustice. The loved ones' anger is a fitting and morally appropriate response, correctly representing the perpetrators' actions as morally atrocious and revealing that they are strongly against the injustice. But suppose that in expressing anger the victim's sister reveals a morally inappropriate hope for what *she* sees as repair. She expresses the hope that the perpetrators receive the death penalty. They are monsters, the sister insists, that prey on white women and deserve to be killed.[15]

If the perpetrators do not receive the death penalty for their crimes, the sister might become embittered. Now, as I mentioned above, it might actually be fitting for family members in this situation to be bitter indefinitely, since it is one in which there is irreparable damage. But since, in this case, the sister's bitterness is a response to a thwarted morally inappropriate hope, the emotion is only partially fitting, and, consequently, the moral status of the emotion is mixed. The emotion reveals that the sister is against injustice (i.e., sexual assault and murder), as well as the irreparable damage it caused. But her bitterness also reveals that she is *for* a different kind of injustice: that is, the racist, revengeful killing of Black lives.[16]

The moral status of bitterness can also be compromised when bitterness is misdirected (as we saw in the case of anger). For example, the father of the victim in the case above might direct his bitterness inward, blaming himself for failing to prevent what happened to his daughter. His bitterness is fitting because it is about the serious wrong, as well as the irreparable damage it caused. He maintains, in his angry expressions, that he is bitter about the fact that his daughter was sexually assaulted and murdered, correctly representing the perpetrators' actions as unjust. But instead of directing his emotion only toward the perpetrators and toward the systemic injustices that shaped their experiences, opportunities, and actions (including racism, poverty, and sexist socialization), the father ultimately blames himself. Although it is morally appropriate for the father to be bitter about the injustice, it is morally inappropriate to blame himself for failing to prevent his daughter's

[15] See Audrey Yap (2017) for reasons to reject the characterization of men who commit sexual assault as moral monsters.

[16] There is a dark history that informs how racism would plausibly factor into a case like this one. As Kimberlé Crenshaw (1989) explains, historically in America "lynching was considered an effective remedy for a Black man's rape of a white woman. Since rape of a white woman by a Black man was 'a crime more horrible than death,' the only way to assuage society's rage and to make the woman whole again was to brutally murder the Black man" (158). See Michael Cholbi and Alex Madva (2018) for a persuasive defense of the Black Lives Matter movement's call to eliminate the death penalty.

sexual assault and murder. It reveals, for example, that he holds incorrect moral beliefs about what can be reasonably morally expected of fathers like himself.

As these cases show, our emotional responses to injustices and the trag-edies they create are extremely complex, and it is thus easy to see how our bitterness might get things right in some ways and wrong in others. Even perfectly morally appropriate bitterness can become misdirected over time. The emotion can become infectious, affecting how individuals perceive all other people and events such that they come to see the negative in everything (like Rodger's infectious bitterness, though his emotion was never appro-priate). In a political context, women's bitterness about sexist oppression may cause them to eventually lose hope in all men whom they have good reasons to believe are trustworthy allies. Or, in a personal (and political) context, a woman in an abusive relationship might come to have misdirected bitterness in response to ongoing domestic violence. Her bitterness is a fitting and mor-ally appropriate response to her circumstances, correctly representing the domestic violence as unjust and the possibility that her partner will change in an unfavorable light given the evidence (a morally appropriate hope for repair). But suppose that, over time, she begins to lash out at her own family, blaming them for not liking her partner and insisting that if only they had accepted him, he wouldn't be a hopeless abuser. The woman's bitterness still correctly represents domestic abuse as a serious injustice, and it still correctly represents her partner as without hope for changing and making amends. It is thus a fitting and, at least in part, morally appropriate response to her situa-tion. But her bitterness has become *misdirected*. It is the woman's partner, not her family members, who is the correct target for her bitterness (even if, as is often the case, she has good prudential reasons not to express bitterness to-ward him at all). And it is not morally appropriate to direct bitterness toward her family, however understandable and excusable her doing so may be.

It is thus very common and understandable for our emotions to evolve over time as we face new experiences, stressors, and other life circumstances—even if they evolve in self-destructive and somewhat morally inappropriate ways. The changing nature of our emotional experiences thus presents a challenge for evaluating emotions with the passing of time. As we live on, our emotional lives are affected by new experiences that may enhance, distort, or diminish how we think and feel about injustices done to us. For example, the passing of time in conjunction with new morally good experiences such as improved social and political conditions might make possible the rebuilding of hope even when repair for the original injustice might not be possible or forthcoming. If the same wrong is not done to me again, and if I see improvements in how my own community responds to injustices like the one that I experienced, I might have good reasons to be hopeful that the wrong will not be repeated.

Martin Luther King Jr. (1998), in describing his encounters with some white folks at Morehouse College who were committed to racial justice, describes the diminishing of his resentment that accompanied meeting white people whom he learned he could count on to stand by his moral and political aims. King explains:

> The wholesome relations we had at the Intercollegiate Council convinced me that we had many white persons as allies, particularly among the younger generation. I had been ready to resent the whole white race, but as I got to see more white people, my resentment was softened, and a spirit of cooperation took its place. (14)

The same diminishing can happen with bitterness. Even when injustice persists and sufficient efforts toward repair have not been taken, positive encounters with others who endorse and abide by our moral expectations can instill our hope that moral and political change will come.[17] On the other hand, the passing of time in conjunction with new, morally bad experiences such as worse social and political conditions may exacerbate bitterness. If similar injustices are repeated or systemic injustice continues, I may lose even more hope that perpetrators, those complicit in injustice, and my moral community will ever affirm my claims to moral entitlement. My exacerbated bitterness may be a fitting and morally appropriate response to the ongoing injustice, as I acquire more reasons to be unhopeful about the possibility of repair, even if the emotion's severity would not have been fitting or morally appropriate before.

---

[17] Although bitterness tends to be quite personal, and so one might wonder whether these other experiences really would diminish the emotion, I think matters are more complex. With the passing of time, we can become capable of reframing our experiences. For example, we might come to think: "What happened to me was never made right (and maybe it is impossible that it could be made right); and though my emotion is about my own experience, it is also about the presence of injustice more generally. So, if I can find reasons to hope that things are getting better and that others will not have to experience what I did, then I might be able to make peace with the past." I wonder whether those who have suffered serious injustice who then become advocates for a cause sometimes experience healing (of trauma, anger, and bitterness) in part because they have reframed their experiences in this sort of way.

These possibilities show that it is possible to do some evaluative work in understanding bitterness as it changes, distorts, diminishes, or exacerbates over time. But they also show just how messy the emotions can be and become. The natural diminishing of bitterness further complicates our evaluations. Sometimes, bitterness does not diminish as an understandable response to new experiences but because time has distanced us so far from the event that it no longer bears as much meaning in our lives. The idea that "time heals all wounds" sometimes resonates with our experiences. How we perceive, interpret, and attach meaning to events may change as we live on.[18] I see the complex and changing nature of our emotional experiences as an inevitable challenge for evaluating bitterness, but it is a challenge that is shared with all emotions insofar as they inevitably depend upon our continued interactions with the world.

The Value of Moral Bitterness: Moral, Epistemic, Political

There are at least three further challenges for a defense of bitterness. First, even when bitterness is a morally appropriate response, we often urge people to overcome the emotion because it is psychologically and emotionally painful to bear (i.e., for their own wellbeing and for the moral reason of self-respect). Second, we worry that bitterness will lead to epistemic irrationality, such as when bitterness about a particular person's wrongful action leads one to make negative inferences about people more generally when such inferences are unwarranted. Third, we tend to think that adopting other attitudes and traits would be more effective in one's moral and political struggles. These apparent moral, epistemic, and political problems with bitterness can be taken together as an objection that bitterness is not a valuable emotion. While not denying these risks, I want to argue that morally appropriate bitterness (hereafter, bitterness) is valuable for moral, epistemic, and political reasons. The ways in which bitterness is valuable cannot be easily pulled apart from each other but work together in earning

---

[18] Walker (2006), drawing upon Jean Améry's *At the Mind's Limits: Contemplations by a Survivor on Auschwitz and Its Realities*, discusses this point as well. She states: "Time . . . might 'heal' wounds of wrongdoing for societies as a whole and for a new generation by allowing the vividness of horrors to wane. Even wronged individuals who have not been shattered beyond healing may sometimes find it possible to 'let it go.' Time . . . can cause a shared social concern that wrong must be addressed to fade" (141).

bitterness an important (even if regrettable and undesirable) role in our lives.[19]

I take bitterness to be morally valuable, beyond what it reveals about agents' moral characters, because of its role as a "moral reminder" that marks a past event or present situation as a context in which injustice has occurred or is continuing. As McFall (1991) argues, bitterness "bears witness" to important moral truths (155). Individuals not directly or personally connected to injustices more easily forget that they have occurred, or, because of their privileged social locations, they are unable to see injustice as injustice and dismiss it. In bitterness, individuals remind other people and the broader community of violations that stand in its past and present as unfinished moral business, violations that continue to require attention and action. The emotion refuses to allow injustices and the harms they cause to be forgotten and communicates that repairing or constructing good moral and political relations will not take place until harms are adequately acknowledged and addressed.

Here, I think, is where Campbell's insights into how the charge of bitterness is used politically to dismiss the oppressed connect with her more recent work on memory. She anticipates this connection in her "Being Dismissed" in claiming that "the accusation of bitterness not only refuses to grant authority to judgments of wrongdoing but also refuses to grant authority to what counts for others as significant memory" (Campbell 1994, 53). In a chapter entitled "Remembering for the Future" from her 2014 book *Our Faithfulness to the Past*, Campbell (2014) explains that one of the aims of the Canadian Truth and Reconciliation Commission is for non-Indigenous Canadians to come to remember the past in ways that stop suppressing and ignoring the history and legacy of the Indian residential schools (136). She points out that non-Indigenous Canadians have "collectively refused" to hear the memory of Indigenous Canadians. One way to refuse to listen is to call Indigenous Canadians bitter as moral condemnation, demanding that they move on from the past. As Campbell (1994) notes, years before,

---

[19] There is a further all-things-considered practical question of whether a person *should* be embittered. Any overall normative judgment about whether an agent should (all things considered) have an emotion ought, on my view, only be answered in considering concrete cases in which we know who the moral agents are and what their particular circumstances are. And notably, objections to bitterness do not often target the overall normative judgment that some person should be embittered; it is rare that we hear anyone say this. The objection to bitterness is most often voiced as an objection to the notion that bitterness has any value at all; that's why "You're so bitter" sounds like, and is meant to be, a normative and not merely descriptive claim about the person's emotional state. *That* objection is the view my arguments here target.

in "Being Dismissed": "The accusation of bitterness may further undermine the struggle for group memory by failing again to provide the uptake that leaves the recounting of incidents established as public record" (53). In the Canadian context, Campbell suggests that renewing their relationships with Indigenous Canadians requires that settlers keep the history and legacy of the residential schools alive in their memories. Through memory activities such as honoring, witnessing, testifying to the past, and offering apologies, settler Canadians can begin to reconstruct their connections to the past and reshape their present relationships for the future.

In political contexts, remembering is crucial to responding to the bitterness of members of historically disadvantaged groups. The emotion does not call upon privileged members of society to undo the past or the harms caused by injustice (which is an impossible task) but to listen to the accounts of those affected by historical and ongoing injustices, to work toward eliminating them, and to act in ways that will not repeat the injustices in the future.[20] If, for example, non-Indigenous Canadians respond to the anger and bitterness of Indigenous Canadians with listening and openness to re-remembering their collective history from a perspective that acknowledges the fact of injustice, and if wrongdoers commit to abiding by shared moral expectations from now on, forgiveness might become possible.[21] Understanding bitterness as a moral reminder makes sense of the fact that it is the responsibility of others to listen and to act: perpetrators, the community, and institutions that continue to support colonial practices and policies. This is important moral and political work even if bitterness is ill equipped in motivating Indigenous Canadians to engage in active protest against their oppression.

Ta-Nehisi Coates's (2015a) ground-breaking book *Between the World and Me* offers another insightful illustration of the value of bitterness as a moral reminder. Coates, writing to his son, offers a narrative that is absent of hope about racism against Black people in America, urging his son to remember the dark realities of slavery. Coates reminds readers that Black people were "born into chains" for over 250 years and that many never experienced freedom. Coates states:

[20] As Walker (2006) argues, "Repair is in the history we make and make sure is told," and this is an intergenerational process (144).

[21] As Pamela Hieronymi (2001) argues: "With forgiveness, the offended agrees to bear in her own person the cost of the wrongdoing and to incorporate the injury into her own life" (551). People who are embittered may never, and justifiably, make the emotional transition from bitterness to forgiveness—especially when the damage runs so deep that the "cost" of the wrong has shattered one's hope for one's own life and future. But it may be possible to do so.

You must struggle to truly remember this past in all its nuance, error, and humanity. You must resist the common urge toward the comforting narrative of divine law, toward fairy tales that imply some irreplaceable justice. The enslaved were not bricks in your road, and their lives were not chapters in your redemptive history. . . . Enslavement was not destined to end, and it is wrong to claim our present circumstance—no matter how improved—as the redemption for the lives of people who never asked for the posthumous, untouchable glory of dying for their children. (71)

I read Coates as urging his son to resist interpreting history in a hopeful way, to not opt for hope for its benefits to wellbeing ("comfort") at the expense of truth. Elsewhere, Coates describes hope as "an overrated force in human history" (Coates 2015b). I also read Coates's *Between the World and Me* as deeply embittered, taking inspiration from James Baldwin and Derrick Bell to shed light on the bleak realities that Black people in America face today. Coates's bitter narrative is an important moral reminder of the reality of racial injustice, in both the past and present.

But while Coates's book has been met with widespread praise, it has also been met with criticism, including uncharitable criticism. In an article entitled "The Toxic World-View of Ta-Nehisi Coates," Rich Lowry (2015) questions the extent to which Coates's descriptions of race relations map onto the truth. In addition to the language of "toxic," Lowry describes Coates's narrative as "profoundly silly at times," and he suggests that Coates reads racism into some of the examples he uses throughout the book (Lowry 2015). For example, Lowry argues that Coates's narrative of a white woman's pushing his child—an event that Coates perceived as racist, leading to his anger and then conflict with the woman—is an instance where Coates misinterpreted a situation as racist. Lowry suggests that it is plausible that the white woman was simply a "jerk" and that race had nothing to do with the incident. Lowry reminds us that "white people are rude to other white people all the time, especially in New York City" (Lowry 2015). Coates, according to Lowry, erases distinctions and rejects complexities in his writing, which results in an inaccurate portrayal of race and racism in America.

Lowry's claims, and his use of the language of toxicity, can be interpreted as objections to the notion that bitterness is epistemically valuable. Instead of enabling the people who bear bitterness to grasp the truth, bitterness about racism infects the ways in which people see others, causing them to read racism into white people's actions when such assumptions are mistaken.

But it is important that Lowry is white and that he is not best positioned to interpret what is really going on in interactions involving race. Scholars of race and feminist theory have shown persuasively that members of privileged groups occupy positions of epistemic disadvantage from which they are unable to see or refuse to recognize the existence of oppression in many contexts. Coates even anticipates the kind of critique that Lowry makes in *Between the World and Me*. He states: "Part of what I know is that there is the burden of living among Dreamers, and there is the extra burden of your country telling you that the Dream is just, noble, and real, and you are crazy for seeing the corruption and smelling the sulfur" (Coates 2015a, 106). The claim that Coates's worldview is "toxic" sounds much like the critique of "craziness" that often accompanies the charge of bitterness and is yet another example of the ways in which language can be used politically (toxic, crazy, bitter) to dismiss oppressed peoples' experiences and perceptions.[22]

But even if one accepts that bitterness can be epistemically valuable and that living without hope more generally can be epistemically valuable, one might worry that bitterness is counterproductive, or prudentially irrational, because it leads to despair. Lowry criticizes Coates's book as "nihilistic because there is no positive program to leaven the despair and the call for perpetual struggle" (Lowry 2015). I do not read Coates as living in despair—or even in the complete absence of all hope.[23] But he does call for perpetual struggle. Struggle is necessary because injustice persists, even if one is without hope that one's efforts will be successful. Coates can be read as inspiring not nihilism, despair, or defeat but—as Baldwin advocated—ongoing

---

[22] Although Lowry's criticisms help to illuminate how charges of bitterness and toxicity are used to dismiss the perspectives of members of oppressed groups, there are more charitable criticisms of Coates that are certainly worth taking seriously. Chris Lebron (2015), for example, takes issue with what he sees as some bad reasons for cynicism in Coates's writing, including Coates's use of a natural disaster metaphor in describing white supremacy—a metaphor that implies that racism is naturally determined rather than sustained by responsible agents of white supremacy. Melvin L. Rogers (2015) similarly objects to Coates's narrative that implies, incorrectly, that Black people are "helpless agents of physical laws." And Myisha Cherry (2015) finds Coates's perspective incomplete, without resources to give Black people a guide for how they can survive and thrive. All of these perspectives are critical of Coates in a constructive rather than dismissive way and helpfully urge us to think about whether Coates's perspective on race and racism is ultimately right or beneficial for racial justice.

[23] Evidence that Coates may not have lost all hope entirely can be found elsewhere. For example, Coates (2015b) says of white supremacy: "The point is not that White supremacy won't ever diminish, nor that it won't ever change form. The point is that it will always be with us in some form, and the best one can reasonably hope for is that it will shrink in impact." Coates may be deeply pessimistic and bitter, but his hope for shrinking injustice (rather than its elimination) shows that he is not living in complete despair. And as mentioned earlier, Coates's perspective shifted at least temporarily to become more hopeful as he witnessed the outpouring of solidarity against racial injustice in response to the murder of George Floyd.

struggle despite the importance of accepting that injustice is, in Baldwin's terms, "commonplace." It is a kind of struggle in the absence of hope that one's efforts to resist injustice will amount to any sort of substantive change.

Loss of Hope and Agency

But what does it look like for a moral agent to continue on in her moral and political struggles in the absence of hope that her efforts will be successful? The loss of hope that perpetrators will ever acknowledge and address our moral claims may involve, at the same time, a loss of hope that one's own agency will make a difference to our moral and political struggles. This apparent deficiency is particularly worrisome for injustices that are alive and well today. If, for example, individuals who are subjected to racism have become embittered, they may no longer believe that their own actions against racism will be effective. There seems to be no point in continuing to demand that perpetrators of and those complicit in oppression acknowledge their attitudes and actions as wrong and change their ways when they have shown, time and time again, that they will not do so. Without hope, one might worry, moral motivation is lost.

But bearing bitterness can actually be consistent with moral motivation and positive political action. Lisa Tessman (2009) offers insights into this possibility through her work on pessimism without hope. Tessman argues that individuals living under oppressive conditions who have become pessimistic about their circumstances can still find ways to go on politically. The reason is that some pessimists sustain other virtues that enable them to actively resist oppression even when they know that their moral and political aims will likely not be achieved. Pessimists' self-respect, integrity, and "sense of a 'claim' on the sort of flourishing that is unattainable under conditions of oppression" guard against the concern that they will give up on their morally praiseworthy ends (Tessman 2009, 14–15). Tessman draws upon Derrick Bell's testimony of his interaction with Biona MacDonald, a Black civil rights activist, to illustrate what struggling against oppression in the absence of hope looks like. Bell (1992a) explains:

> I realized that Mrs. MacDonald didn't say she risked everything because she hoped or expected to win out over the whites who, as she well knew, held all the economic and political power, and the guns as well. Rather,

she recognized that—powerless as she was—she had and intended to use courage and determination as a weapon to, in her words, "harass white folks." (xi–xii)

This example suggests that pessimism is consistent with other moral values and traits that motivate people to act against injustice even in the absence of hope that the injustice will end. Tessman and Bell nicely attend to the complexity of moral characters and how questions about moral motivation cannot be answered without considering the various beliefs, traits, values, and emotions of individuals that motivate or deter them from action only when taken together. Similarly, by focusing solely on the risk that bitterness can lead to despair and inaction, it is easy to miss seeing the ways in which bitterness can be deeply connected to our moral convictions and other moral values and traits. If I believe that I, someone else, or certain social groups have been wronged, if I have the courage to stand up for what I think is right, and if I am determined to do so even in the face of dismissal, resistance, and penalties, I may be motivated to continue on in my struggles against oppression with bitterness and without hope that my efforts will be successful. And since bitterness can help people see clearly where there are no longer reasons for hope, bitterness might even be prudentially rational for some agents in resisting oppression.

In fact, Bell himself exemplifies the moral agent who is motivated to continue struggling against racial injustice with bitterness and in the absence of hope.[24] Bell made many important contributions to legal theory and critical race theory throughout his scholarly career. But the one I want to focus on is his "racial realism" thesis, defended in his 1992 *Faces at the Bottom of the Well: The Permanence of Racism* (from which the quote about Biona MacDonald above is a part), and a 1992 article entitled "Racial Realism" in the *Connecticut Law Review*. In *Faces at the Bottom of the Well*, Bell (1992a) states the thesis in the following way:

---

[24] Bell identifies himself as embittered in a number of places throughout his writing. In his description of a fictional encounter with a bitter and pessimistic Black taxi driver, Bell (1992a) says: "Your bitterness mirrors my own when I think about all the school systems I helped desegregate back in the 1960s, sure that I was guaranteeing thousands of black children a quality, desegregated education. It took a long time to recognize that the school officials—when they finally complied with desegregation court orders—were creating separate educational programs for black children within schools that were integrated in name only" (18–19). Bell also describes himself as bitter in the second sentence of "White Superiority in America: Its Legacy, Its Economic Costs" (Delgado and Stefancic 2005, 27).

I want to set forth this proposition, which will be easier to reject than re-
fute: Black people will never gain full equality in this country. Even those
herculean efforts we hail as successful will produce no more than tempo-
rary "peaks of progress," short-lived victories that slide into irrelevance as
racial patterns adapt in ways that maintain white dominance. This is a hard-
to-accept fact that all history verifies. We must acknowledge it, not as a sign
of submission, but as an act of ultimate defiance. (12)

The very same quotation appears in the 1992 "Racial Realism" article, but the
last sentence is different. It reads:

We must acknowledge it and move on to adopt policies based in what
I call: "Racial Realism." This mind-set or philosophy requires us to acknowledge the permanence of our subordinate status. That acknowledgment enables us to avoid despair, and frees us to imagine and implement
racial strategies that can bring fulfillment and even triumph. (Bell 1992b,
373–374)

I come back to the connection Bell makes between avoiding despair, fulfillment, and triumph in chapter 5. But what is important for now is that
although Bell is clearly without hope for racial justice in America, he nevertheless believes in the necessity of struggle and the importance of stubborn
resistance to oppression. The value of lacking hope in this context arises from
the epistemic risks of having hope identified in chapter 2, namely, that certain
hopes—such as the hope that one is (or will soon be) living in a "post-racial
society"—distract from the kinds of actions and policies that are necessary
for circumstances to improve.

Bell also believed in the necessity of struggle not only without hope that
his efforts would be successful but also with the fear that such efforts would
make things worse. He writes:

While implementing Racial Realism we must simultaneously acknowledge
that our actions are not likely to lead to transcendent change and, despite
our best efforts, may be of more help to the system we despise than to the
victims of that system we are trying to help.[25] (Bell 1992b, 378)

---

[25] For example, Bell acknowledged after the fact that his protest against Harvard Law School's decision to not hire a woman of color may have ultimately been harmful. Bell had not consulted with the

Bell's racial realism thesis combined with how he lived his everyday life demonstrates what it looks like to be motivated in one's moral and political struggles in the absence of hope that one's efforts will be successful. Even while bearing bitterness and lacking hope more generally, Bell was a political activist who throughout his lifetime demonstrated an active commitment to racial justice despite believing that racism is permanent. For example, Bell resigned from his position as dean of the University of Oregon School of Law in protest of the school's decision to not hire an Asian American female professor (Delgado and Stefancic 2005, 10).[26] As a visiting professor at Stanford Law School, he encouraged students to protest the racist actions and decisions of Stanford law faculty,[27] actions and decisions for which the dean (Dean John Ely) eventually apologized but did so by urging Bell to forget (12). Bell responded not by letting the instance of racism slide but by publishing a lengthy column calling out Stanford's racism in "The Price and Pain of Racial Remedies" in the *Stanford Lawyer* and mailing letters detailing what had happened to deans at law schools across the nation. He did so in an attempt to encourage them to discuss the matter at faculty meetings so as to avoid similar cases in the future (12). In another case, during his time at Harvard, Bell—persuaded by the argument made by women students of color that Black men and white women could not understand the unique experiences of women of color in the law profession—assisted a group of students in urging Harvard Law to hire its first woman professor of color. When Harvard failed to hire a Black woman from a top school in 1989–1990, Bell took an unpaid leave of absence in protest and refused to return "until Harvard Law School hired its first woman of color" (13).

Bell's acceptance of the permanence of racism coupled with his continued struggles against racial injustice demonstrate that bitterness, and a loss of

candidate in advance, and the "publicity and backlash" that ensued because of his protest may have cost her the position (G. Taylor 2005, 442).

[26] The school had ranked the Asian American woman as third in over a hundred candidates for a teaching position, but when the top two candidates declined, the search committee reopened the search instead of hiring the Asian American woman (Delgado and Stefancic 2005, 10).

[27] Bell was teaching constitutional law with an emphasis on the ways in which the framers of the Constitution "were men of wealth, with investments in land, slaves, manufacturing, and shipping" and that the document was thus constructed to serve their interests (Delgado and Stefancic 2005, 11). Students complained to faculty that Bell was teaching them constitutional law "in a strange and unconventional way" (11). When two other faculty allowed Bell's students to sit in on their classes instead, attendance in Bell's class diminished. Bell was also invited by a student group to speak on race as part of a lecture series, but he found out from Black students that it was actually organized by a faculty member with the aim of remedying Bell's perceived weaknesses as a professor. Black students argued that the lecture series was racist and protested in solidarity with Bell.

hope more generally, is compatible with moral motivation and political action. But we might wonder, further, whether bitterness and a loss of hope for racial justice (or other forms of injustice) are compatible with any sort of hope. I think that, in many contexts, bitterness is compatible with having hope. The emotion is not necessarily global in the way that a bitter disposition would be, a disposition that would taint individuals' perceptions of all people and events in the world. It is consistent with finding and cultivating new hopes, such as the hope that one's actions alongside other members of oppressed groups and those standing in solidarity will make short-lived progress or, at least, prevent injustice from getting worse.

Concluding Thoughts

I have argued that bitterness is a kind of unresolved anger that ruminates about a moral wrong or injustice without much hope for acknowledgment and repair. Correcting our understanding of bitterness invites an important shift in our evaluative language. It is not individuals' responsibility to defend the rationality of their disappointed hopes to show that their bitterness is appropriate, as some feminist philosophers have thought. Bitterness can be fitting and morally appropriate, particularly when bitterness responds to a legitimate injustice that has not (and likely will not) receive an appropriate reparative response. The emotion reveals that the agent cares about, and orients their attention toward, injustices that have not been put to rest through repair. And though it may ultimately be better for moral agents who bear bitterness to challenge and overcome it for their wellbeing and relationships, focusing on the harmfulness of the emotion and the personal responsibilities of the individuals who bear it can distract from the individual and collective responsibilities of others. When bitterness is caused by unresolved social and political injustices, the emotion serves as a moral reminder that there is still moral and often political work left to do in the difficult process of repair.

Although bitterness is valuable in these ways, the emotion can still have detrimental effects on agency. Becoming embittered and losing hope can harm agents' motivation to act in pursuit of their important moral and political goals. Sometimes, when people lose hope that their anger will receive uptake and that injustices will be addressed, they resign themselves to the unjust conditions in which they live. This is indeed a risk of becoming embittered and losing hope. But we have seen that it is not a necessary consequence.

Beyond hope, other traits and attitudes such as courage, integrity, and determination provide sources of motivation that enable individuals to act against
injustice in the absence of hope that their efforts will be successful. And bitterness, in orienting our attention toward those injustices and toward the
people, groups, and institutions in whom there are good reasons to have lost
hope, may even help direct individual and collective efforts in pursuing the
most effective strategies in struggle.

But one might wonder where bitterness and an absence of hope leave
those of us who find hope to be intrinsically valuable in our lives, for those of
us who assess first-personally that we need hope to go on. As Myisha Cherry
(2015) argues, knowledge, understanding, and struggle are not enough. And
in response to Coates's *Between the World and Me*, she writes that "consciousness makes us aware of the fact that we need more than itself to help us survive and thrive in the struggle." So what else?

5

Hope, Faith, and Solidarity

The previous chapter charted the value of bitterness, and losing hope more generally, to moral and political life. It revealed that losing hope—particularly, the hopes we invest in individuals and institutions in positions of power—can inspire new ways of responding to oppression and advancing moral and political ends. We can see these responses in the lives of activists like Derrick Bell, but also in social movements: the women's liberation movement, the civil rights movement, Idle No More, Black Lives Matter, NoDAPL, Me Too, Extinction Rebellion, and many others that have risen up to resist various forms of oppression. Marches, flash mobs, vigils, fundraisers, boycotts, and highway blockings are just a few examples of collective actions undertaken by people who are committed to building a more just world.

In the previous chapter, we began to see what resistance without hope looks like. Derrick Bell, for instance, believed that racism is permanent, and thus he did not have hope for racial justice. Yet Bell spent his life and career struggling against racism. Bell teaches us that it is not necessary to have hope in order to be motivated to resist oppression. But one important fact about Bell that I have not yet mentioned is that he had religious faith. Bell (2002) says of himself, "In hard times, my Christian faith provides reassurance that is unseen but no less real. It never fails to give me the fortitude I need when opposing injustice" (76).

It would be a mistake to ignore the role of faith in Bell's life and the lives of so many others who are remarkably capable of continuing to fight for what they believe is morally right and just, with or without hope that their efforts will be successful. Many prominent activists have appealed to faith as fundamental to their pursuits (often in relation to hope). This chapter develops an analysis of hope, faith, and solidarity in struggles against oppression.

I begin by introducing faith into the discussion. I distinguish between three forms of faith—spiritual faith, faith in humanity, and moral faith—any or all of which help to support moral agency in the face of seemingly insurmountable barriers and dwindling possibilities. Supported by faith (sometimes, but not always, with hope for the ends toward which they are striving) and

Hope Under Oppression. Katie Stockdale, Oxford University Press. © Oxford University Press 2021.
DOI: 10.1093/oso/9780197563564.003.0006

sustained by other traits and attitudes such as courage and determination, people come together in what I think of as moral-political solidarity: that is, solidarity based in a shared moral vision carried out through political action. Through solidarity, individuals share in a collective intention of the solidarity group to pursue a form of justice. And when they come together in collective action settings, a form of collective hope can emerge. The object of collective hope is, very broadly, justice as a guiding ideal. Sometimes, our hopes for justice manifest as utopian hopes whose realization would radically transform our world such that a moral ideal, the object of hope, is attained. Other times, they are modest hopes whose realization would make progress toward justice, or even just help to mitigate it. I argue that both utopian hope and modest hope are ways in which individuals and collectives can hope well for justice.

Faith

Faith is a remarkably complex phenomenon, earning much attention in the philosophy of religion and epistemology. Unlike trust, it is typically considered to be an attitude that is "not normally subject to definitive proof or refutation by any specifiable finite set of experiences" (Adams 1995, 86). We often (rightly, I think) remark that trust must be earned. People, groups, and institutions earn our moral trust by providing evidence that they have the integrity to act on shared moral standards. But we don't commonly talk of earning faith in the same way. Faith in the Christian God is not earned by God proving his existence and worthiness. And asking God to prove himself prior to cultivating faith in him does not even make sense. Such a demand seems contrary to the very nature of what it means to have faith.

There are two kinds of faith in the above description, and understanding them will be helpful in locating the role of faith in moral and political life. First, there is faith that God exists, or *propositional* faith. Second, there is faith *in* God—that is, *attitudinal* faith (Audi 2008, 92). The notion of propositional faith captures the common thought that since faith embodies more confidence than hope, when faith that p is lost, we can still hope that p. For example, women might lose faith that sexist oppression will someday end before losing hope that sexist oppression will someday end. In other words, it makes sense to say, "I no longer have faith that sexist oppression will end, but I still have some hope." But this description does not fully capture experiences of faith and hope, since it is possible for women to lose hope that sexist oppression will end while still having some kind of faith. The faith they sustain is not faith that sexist oppression will end (i.e., it is not propositional faith). The relevant kind of faith sustained does not share the same object as hope. It is faith *in* someone or something—that is, attitudinal faith. For example, even if a person has lost hope that sexist oppression will end, her faith in God might permit her to find meaning in the state of the world: if one acts morally in this world, one will find oneself in heaven where there is no injustice of any kind.

But how, exactly, can we understand the role of different manifestations of faith in the pursuit of justice? I take it that a plausible account of the faith that arises in this context ought to account for the mechanism by which faith enables agents to persist in the face of obstacles, setbacks, and failures that might otherwise cause them to abandon their efforts. And I suggest that Lara Buchak's (2012; 2017) account of faith, what she calls the "risky commitment" account, is a good starting point for understanding the nature of faith in agents' practical pursuits. But as we will see, it needs to be supplemented with an account of *intrinsic faith*. Intrinsic faith, I argue, is a deep belief in the intrinsic value of one's actions or way of life. Both forms of faith are at work, though in different ways, in sustaining agents in the pursuit of justice.

Let's begin by considering Buchak's account of faith. Buchak understands faith as a commitment to take on risks on the basis of a proposition's being true without searching for further evidence (Buchak 2012; Buchak 2017). And we can see this faith at work through many acts of faith. For example, a person may perform an act of faith when they lay down their weapon, an action that expresses the faith that the other person will put down their weapon too (Buchak 2012). We might imagine, more specifically, a police officer who puts down her gun in the face of a hostage taker who is holding an innocent person at gunpoint. Without certainty that the hostage taker will put down their weapon, and without running through the evidence for and against the likelihood of the hostage taker laying down their weapon any further, the officer commits to acting on the proposition that the hostage taker will put down their weapon if only they are treated like a human being. In response to bystanders who might inquire how the officer knew that the hostage taker would put down their weapon, she would likely reply, "I didn't. I took a leap of faith." Similarly, faith in God on Buchak's view is a commitment to act on the basis of God's existence and goodness without searching for further evidence (i.e., evidence that God exists and is good). Expressing such faith might involve attending church, saying prayers, and behaving how one imagines God would want one to behave.

Faith, on this view, is risky, in the sense that it involves taking risks on the basis of a proposition's being true without searching for further evidence, and sometimes even declining to consider counterevidence (e.g., that the hostage taker won't lay down their weapon, or that God doesn't actually exist or isn't good). And this risk element of faith can help us to see how faith sometimes operates in struggles against oppression. This is because people who act on faith in the pursuit of justice are operating in a non-ideal world full of injustice, where there are significant risks to acting, where acting will be most effective if done now (as opposed to later, when more evidence comes in), and where their commitments to justice are unwavering. Commitments, recall, are active, sustained intentions to pursue a project or end—ones that are resistant to reconsideration or revision (Calhoun 2009). When I commit to a practical pursuit (as Calhoun argues), I am willing to take on greater obstacles, setbacks, and failures than when I merely desire an end. For example, I might desire justice but lack hope that justice will ever be attained, seeing in an unfavorable light the possibility of justice, given the past and current state of the world. But if I am committed to justice, I reason that obstacles, setbacks, and failures must be very severe for me to give up on my commitment. And faith is even stronger. For in "risky commitment" faith, one does not search for further evidence and may even decline to examine additional evidence that comes in (Buchak 2017).[1]

So whereas an agent who is committed to the possibility of attaining justice without faith might eventually give up her pursuit in the face of persistent obstacles, setbacks, and failures, an agent who has faith—especially strong faith—will not.[2] By considering new counterevidence that threatens the truth of p (e.g., that a form of justice will be attained) as relevant to whether

[1] One might worry that such faith is irrational. Buchak (2012) argues that faith can be both epistemically and practically rational. On her view, people who have faith that p often have properly evaluated the evidence that p, and such evidence can even lead them to develop faith. Faith is also practically rational (or prudentially rational), on Buchak's view, when acting on faith is in one's rational self-interest. She gives the example of a prospective monk who most prefers to live the life of a monk, if God exists. In this case, continuing to search for proof of God's existence would cancel out that option entirely. Thus, Buchak argues that the prospective monk has good reasons for deciding to forgo the search for further evidence and committing to live a life of a monk, given the costs of searching for and waiting on the evidence.
   I leave open how, exactly, we should understand the value of faith. (I am not convinced that faith is an emotion that is sufficiently similar to hope, anger, and bitterness for us to evaluate it in the same way.) But we should not read people of faith as irrational simply in virtue of their faith.
[2] Unless, of course, they have a "crisis of faith."

one should remain committed to acting on the basis of p, and by questioning one's acceptance of p in light of new information, one displays a lack of faith. Instead, the agent of faith focuses on the possibility that new evidence might be misleading and continues to accept p (e.g., that a form of justice will be attained) and to act on its basis. And since faith is a form of commitment (which, as Calhoun demonstrated, allows agents to continue on in their practical pursuits in the face of obstacles, setbacks, and failures), and since it requires forgoing the search for further evidence and sometimes declining to examine new counterevidence, "risky commitment" faith can enable resilience. As Buchak explains, "Faith allows us to adhere to an act over time—to complete a risky long-term project—in a way that is decoupled from future evidence that the project will fail or isn't worth it. *Faith keeps us from being blown about by the changing winds of evidence*" (Buchak 2017, 123).

It seems to me undeniable that some of us do give up the search for evidence, and sometimes decline to consider new evidence, acting instead on faith in the pursuit of justice in the way that Buchak describes. For example, a human rights advocate might have faith in humanity that is supported by the many acts of human kindness she has witnessed (even if she has lost all hope that the most horrific human rights violations will end in her lifetime). Her faith in humanity is a commitment to acting on the basis of the goodness of humanity, focusing on examples of humanity's goodness and the human potential for goodness, and even declining to consider new evidence to the contrary. But as we will see, activists who appeal to faith as fundamental to their pursuits do not always forgo the search for, or decline to consider, new evidence that arises. The evidence is right in front of them, yet they continue on. Drawing upon testimony of social justice scholars and activists, I defend a non-epistemic form of faith to make sense of this phenomenon, what I call *intrinsic* faith. Whereas epistemic faith is a commitment to act on the basis of p's being true while forgoing the search for further evidence, intrinsic faith is a deep belief in the intrinsic value of one's pursuit and a commitment to acting on that basis. Intrinsic faith enables resilience not by changing the way the agent of faith relates to evidence but by rendering evidence irrelevant to one's actions.

Intrinsic faith is an alternative to despair when all hope is lost or out of reach. And I am not talking about despair in the narrow sense of despairing about some particular outcome, such as when I despair that I will be taken as seriously as my male colleagues. I am talking about a kind of all-encompassing despair that damages moral agency. This despair is also not quite the opposite of "basal hope" in Calhoun's (2018) sense of the term: hope that is about taking an interest in the future generally or globally rather than taking an interest in particular outcomes. I can have all-encompassing despair about sexist oppression while taking an interest in the future generally or globally, pursuing other ends compatible with living under sexist oppression and forming hopes about attaining those ends: that I am awarded tenure, that the pandemic will end, and so on. But my all-encompassing despair about sexist oppression might prevent me from engaging in activities directed toward eliminating it. Despair has damaged my moral agency.

I think we can get a better grasp of all-encompassing despair by thinking about what despair looks like in contrast to hope, and this will be helpful to see where faith comes in. I have been talking about hope as an attitude that consists in seeing in a favorable light the possibility that a desired outcome obtains. Despair, then, consists in desire, belief, and seeing in a wholly unfavorable light the possibility that a desired outcome obtains. And though we often waver between hope and despair (depending on our mood, etc.), despair can be absolute, involving resignation or giving up altogether on the possibility of attaining a desired outcome, along with feelings of helplessness, dread, and defeat. In cases where people are struggling with hope but are prevented from despair, I think they are prevented from despair of this kind. In moments in which all hope seems lost or out of reach, some other attitude—in many cases intrinsic faith—emerges and prevents them from all-encompassing despair and its characteristic feelings.

I want to understand three distinct but intricately related forms of faith in the struggle for justice: spiritual faith, faith in humanity, and moral faith. Sometimes, these forms of faith manifest as epistemic faith, enabling agents to forgo the search for, or even decline to consider, evidence that might threaten the efficacy of their actions. But other times, and I think more powerfully, they manifest as intrinsic faith. While facing the evidence in clear view, agents of faith deeply believe in the intrinsic value of their actions and are committed to acting on this basis, seeing the evidence as irrelevant to whether they continue on. Faith is thus part of the story of what brings people together in solidarity against oppression. Exploring it will help us to better understand what prevents people from falling into despair when hope is threatened or lost, and how hope remerges from the ground up—through struggle and collective action.

Spiritual Faith

Have you ever taken a hard look at those pictures from the sit-ins in the '60s, a hard, serious look? Have you ever looked at the faces? The faces are neither angry, nor sad, nor joyous. They betray almost no emotion. They look out past their tormentors, past us, and focus on something way beyond anything known to me. I think they are fastened to their god, a god whom I cannot know and in whom I do not believe. But, god or not, the armor is all over them, and it is real.

Ta-Nehisi Coates

In this passage from *Between the World and Me*, Coates (2015a) identifies the powerful role of spiritual faith in struggles against racial oppression. The activists' armor, in the photos Coates is referring to, is Black activists' resilience to injustices under the severe conditions of oppression in which they live. Coates suspects that these Black activists' resilience flows from their faith in the Christian God, and there are testimonies that support this reading. For example, Martin Luther King Jr. (1998), in recounting white people's resistance to the Montgomery bus boycott, notes that he "began to have doubts about the ability of the Negro community to continue the struggle" (73). After yet another racist incident involving a phone call threat, King recounts being "ready to give up" (77). He tells us:

With my head in my hands, I bowed over the kitchen table and prayed aloud. The words I spoke to God that midnight are still vivid in my memory. "Lord, I'm down here trying to do what's right. I think I'm right. I am here taking a stand for what I believe is right. But Lord, I must confess that I'm weak now, I'm faltering. I'm losing my courage. Now, I am afraid." (77)

King recalls hearing an inner voice speaking to him: "Martin Luther, stand up for righteousness. Stand up for justice. Stand up for truth. And lo, I will be with you. Even until the end of the world" (78). King interpreted the voice as Jesus urging him to continue on in his struggle, and in that moment, he regained strength. He writes: "Almost at once my fears began to go. My uncertainty disappeared. I was ready to face anything" (78).

Not every reader will believe that Jesus was in fact talking to King in that moment, or that there really is a god that hears our prayers. It is, however, undeniable that King's spiritual faith is what gave him the inspiration, assurance, and strength he needed to find the courage to continue fighting for justice—in this moment and in many others like it.[3] As Cornel West (2018) argues, King (along with W. E. B. Du Bois) embodies "spiritual forti-tude (courage and greatness and character) or sheer existential resilience of remembrance, reverence, and resistance"—even when considering new ev-idence might have enabled nihilism and despair (517). The phone call King recounts was yet another setback, but his faith reminded him that despite what might occur, God supported his pursuit of racial justice.

King's faith, in the moment, might not have manifested as faith that ra-cial justice will be attained. It does not share the same object, or end, toward which he was striving. King's faith was, instead, spiritual: that is, faith *in* God. King might have had epistemic faith in God, or a commitment to act on the basis of God's existence and goodness without searching for further evidence (i.e., evidence that God exists and is good). But King's epistemic faith in God did not, by itself, sustain him. As Paul Taylor (2018) argues, the significance of the inner voice in this example indicates that King's spiritual faith was importantly existential. It was about King's connection to something larger than himself, a connection that is somehow embodied in the divine (56). For Taylor, existential faith is not "cognitively or epistemically deep"; rather, the depth of faith comes from the "rich feeling of experiences" (57).

Three days later, during a meeting at the First Baptist Church, King found out that his home had been bombed, and he credits his religious experience as what gave him the strength to face it. King urged people to go home and adhere to nonviolence "with the faith that what we are doing is right, and with the even greater faith that God is with us in the struggle" (79).

Taylor's insights help us to see the existential nature of King's spiritual faith that "God is with us," but I think that intrinsic faith helps us to see "the faith

---

[3] There is a worry that spiritual faith (such as Christian faith) protects, or supports, vices. I think this is often true, but I agree with Anne Jeffrey (2017) that it is not necessarily so. Jeffrey, working within a virtue-theoretic Christian framework, argues that genuine faith is regulated by other virtues to guard against such things as self-deception, bigotry, and intolerance. When Christians have the virtues of love and hope (not hope for this or that outcome, but hope in God), these traits enable pa-tience, acceptance, and tolerance of religious diversity and life paths with which Christians disagree, modeling God's patient acceptance. There are many examples of people with Christian faith that sup-port Jeffrey's argument (e.g., those affiliated with Christian LGBTQ+ organizations).

But one issue to keep in mind is that some Christians do have incorrect moral beliefs (e.g., the belief that being queer or trans is morally wrong) that damage their ability to love. See, for example, Dawne Moon and Theresa W. Tobin (2018) on the ways in which some Christians harshly shame LGBTQ+ Christians but frame their toxic shaming practices as acts of Christian love. There is much more to be said about what virtues are required to prevent Christian faith from supporting vices. But I leave these issues aside to focus on spiritual faith that is not damaged in this way.

that what we are doing is right." In other words, King's spiritual faith in God permitted him to see meaning and value in the struggle for racial justice— not only as something that God was with him through but as something that God wanted him to do and was worth doing, despite whatever evidence in the world might threaten the efficacy of his actions.[4] King's continued actions on the basis of his spiritual faith in God was thus not primarily about evidence, evidence for either the existence of God or the attainability of racial justice. Existential and intrinsic faith—or a deep belief in the intrinsic value of his pursuit of racial justice—was King's armor, much like the armor of faith that Coates reads into Black activists in their collective actions against racial segregation.

Khan-Cullors (2018) similarly testifies to the role of her own spiritual faith in racial justice activism. In her powerful memoir *When They Call You a Terrorist*, Khan-Cullors describes how she coped with her Black mentally ill brother being repeatedly arrested and sent to prison, the absence of mental health supports available to him (in and outside of prison), the abuse to which he was subjected by law enforcement, and the damages these injustices caused to her and her family's wellbeing. Khan-Cullors (2018) writes: "We lived alongside the steady buzz of anxiety. I turned ever more toward spirit, toward that which I could not see but could feel at all times, in order to manage my emotions. This is to say I prayed often and surrounded myself more closely with the family I'd created. . . . They sustained me" (112).

Khan-Cullors's brother was charged with terrorism after a fender bender with a white woman in which no one was hurt, placed in solitary confinement, denied his psychiatric medication, and refused his right to see family on scheduled visitation days (116–119). On his court date, Monte entered the court room strapped down to a gurney, behind a face mask, and in a psychotic break, yelling and talking to himself (as three white men laughed). Khan-Cullors testifies to experiencing shock and intense anger in witnessing this event and learning that because the arrest was Monte's third strike, he would be sentenced to life in prison (123–125). In response, she walked over to the public defender and forcefully asserted that they would be hiring a lawyer. Khan-Cullors describes this moment as requiring a "walk-on-water faith" (127). She writes:

[4] As Paul Taylor (2018) explains, "For King, one might say, God tells us how to identify the right, the good, and the virtuous" (54).

It's the faith that drove us to run without maps or compasses, money or friends, with dogs trained by demons following behind. It's the faith that sent four Black students, on February 1, 1960, Joseph McNeil, Franklin McCain, David Richmond and Ezell Blair, to sit down at a "whites-only" lunch counter at a Woolworth's in Greensboro, North Carolina, and refuse to move, risking bodily harm and their very lives. It's the faith that allowed Robert Parris Moses to keep pushing for voting rights in the deep south in 1965 despite only being able to register one Black man that first summer in Amite County, Mississippi.

The stories I learned as a small girl who read about civil rights and Black power and Black culture flowed everywhere in me and through me. The lessons I'd learned from the Strategy Center about how to organize in the face of unrelenting odds had taken full root. (Khan-Cullors 2018, 127)

Khan-Cullors's description of "walk-on-water faith" is of a faith that is sustained in the face of evidence that is in clear view—segregation, inequality, a denial of basic human rights, violence, and so on—yet is not shaken in the face of it. Her faith, though, is not Christian. Khan-Cullors identifies with the Ifa tradition, an African spiritual practice in which the Supreme Being, Olodumare, is benevolent and generous, and all living beings are interdependent (151). Khan-Cullors's faith is spiritual but also importantly existential (P. Taylor 2018), connecting her own actions to those of others, and to Olodumare. And for those of us, like Khan-Cullors, who sustain faith in something bigger than us, a god or spirit and even the spiritual interconnectedness of our lives, such faith provides an additional source of strength in the face of obstacles and setbacks. God, or spirit, is with those who have spiritual faith. They are not alone in their struggle.

Sometimes spiritual faith might manifest as epistemic faith, as when the interpersonal support that spiritual faith provides gives people the courage to stop considering the evidence counting against the efficacy of their actions. It might be less difficult to decline to consider new evidence that might threaten the efficacy of one's risky actions in the pursuit of justice with spirit, or God, by one's side. Khan-Cullors's description of turning toward spirit, surrounding herself with family, and her felt connection to other activists seems to support this reading. But the evidence for and against the efficacy of Khan-Cullors's actions seems, in an important sense, irrelevant to her pursuit of racial justice. Khan-Cullors deeply believes in the intrinsic value of Black lives, affirming and fighting for them, even while white supremacy continues.[5]

Similarly, in her memoir *We Have Always Been Here*, Samra Habib testifies to the role of Muslim faith as a source of resilience throughout her life and activism. Habib is an Ahmadi Muslim queer woman of color who grew up in Pakistan and emigrated to Canada at a young age who has endured experiences of racism, sexism, xenophobia, and homophobia throughout her life, as well as suicidal thoughts. Yet she writes: "When I felt absolutely hopeless, I would turn to Allah for guidance" (Habib 2019, 94). For Habib, her Muslim faith is her "anchor when [she] is lost at sea" (214). Through spiritual faith, Habib was able to continue on. She ultimately found her way to a supportive faith community and to social justice activism, including a photography project documenting the lives of LGBTQ+ Muslims. Her project took her to North Carolina, where she met activists committed to struggling for justice and whose work had been focused on protesting police violence against Black Americans as "an extension of their Muslim faith" (208). These activists were fearful about how at the time the recent election of Donald J. Trump as president would exacerbate Islamophobia, homophobia, transphobia, white supremacy, hate crimes, voter suppression, Muslim registries, and deportations. But in the face of all of these serious challenges, Habib observes the "group's resilience. They insisted on fighting back, *no matter what*" (208, emphasis added). As Sufia, one of her subjects, explained, her Muslim identity is importantly political but in its "purest form . . . simply a way of life" (209). These activists' faith is thus spiritual as well as intrinsic, manifesting as a deep belief in the intrinsic value of their actions and ways of life.

Spiritual faith can also be a bedrock for hope. It is something that people turn to for assurance, for comfort, and to inspire hope when they need it the most. This is how I read the story of Plenty Coups (his Crow name was Alaxchiiaahush, or "Many Achievements") who was chief of the Crow nation in the nineteenth century (Lear 2006, 20). Plenty Coups led the nomadic hunting tribe in what is now Montana and Wyoming at a time when the threat

---

[5] Similarly, Opal Tometi, one of the other founders of Black Lives Matter, identifies herself with justice, joy, and faith, where justice is itself a spiritual practice, rather than merely a prerequisite for the pursuit of justice (Lloyd 2018b). And as Hebah Farrag (2018) explains in her discussion of Black Lives Matter, "Spiritual practices *impart meaning*, heal grief and trauma, [and] combat burn-out" (78, emphasis added). Through spiritual faith, people deeply believe that the pursuit of justice is meaningful in itself, providing them with reasons to act despite the effects of their actions on the world. They are sustained by intrinsic faith.

of white settler colonialism was exacerbated by intertribal warfare between the Crow, Sioux, Cheyenne, Arapaho, and Blackfeet people. The Crow had lost thousands of their people through war, disease, and malnutrition; and with the arrival of white European settlers, they became increasingly reliant on knives, hatchets, tools, and guns for survival (Lear 2006, 23). Jonathan Lear (2006) explores the threat to cultural devastation that the Crow endured during this time. Beyond the real threat of genocide, even if the Crow were to survive, their ways of life were coming to an end. As the Crow were forced to move onto reservations, they were no longer capable of participating in traditional Crow ways of life: they could not count coups or plant coup sticks (activities that were the hallmarks of Crow courage);[6] they could not hunt buffalo; they could not participate in the Sun Dance.[7] And they were ultimately forced to transform their culture if it were to survive (Lear 2006).[8]

Lear argues that Plenty Coups confronted the cultural devastation of the Crow people with "radical hope." He tells us: "What makes . . . hope radical is that it is directed toward a future goodness that transcends the current ability to understand what it is. Radical hope anticipates a good for which those who have the hope as yet lack the appropriate concepts with which to understand it" (Lear 2006, 103).[9] Plenty Coups' radical hope was inspired by a dream-vision at the age of nine. Dream-visions, according to the Crow, reveal in enigmatic ways "an order in the universe . . . typically hidden from conscious life" (67). Plenty Coups prayed to God, Ah-badt-dadt-deah, and had a dream-vision in which buffalo were replaced by cows and Plenty Coups was urged to listen and learn from others. The dream was interpreted by Yellow Bear, a wise

[6] "Counting coups" was a term used to describe a number of courageous actions on the part of Crow warriors: striking an armed enemy with one's coup stick, taking the enemy's weapons will he is still alive, stealing a horse from the enemy's camp, and so on (Lear 2006, 19). Planting a coup stick was a practice whereby a Crow warrior would plant a coup stick in the ground, marking a boundary between the tribes that the enemy ought not to cross and signaling that he would not retreat or leave the stick but would fight to protect his people (13–14).

[7] The Sun Dance is a prayer for revenge in the context of battle (Lear 2006, 36).

[8] As Walker (2018) points out, Lear's simplistic characterization of the "Crow way of life" and the language of cultural devastation without genocide is problematic. Walker writes: "Lear's image of a culture that vanishes without a trace uncomfortably echoes the persisting trope of the 'vanishing' Indian so deeply and purposefully ingrained in the imaginations of other Americans" (231). So it's worth reading Lear's historical and cultural claims with caution, despite the clear philosophical significance of this book.

[9] Radical hope, as Lear understands it, might also be at work in people's responses to the threat of climate change to their cultures and nations. For example, Claire Anterea, co-coordinator of the Kiribati Climate Action Network, said: "I feel hopeless in one way that our people are suffering, but I also have the hope that they will try to find a way to adapt" (Bowers 2017). Perhaps Anterea's hope is radical, in the sense that hope in the face of climate change (for the people of Kiribati, whose islands are at risk of becoming uninhabitable) is hope for an unimaginable future good beyond what she and others have the conceptual resources to grasp.

Crow man, to mean that white settler colonizers would take over the country, that Plenty Coups was the one who was tasked with listening and learning from them, and that the Crow must ally with the white men if they were to survive (72–73). Lear suggests that Plenty Coups might have realized, in part due to the content of his dream, that traditional Crow ways of life were coming to end and that there was nothing the Crow could do to change that reality (Lear 2006). And though Lear does not interpret this realization as a loss of hope, I think it is clearly a loss of hope. The Crow people no longer perceived in a favorable light the possibility of preserving traditional Crow ways of life, an outcome that they very much desired. Instead, they perceived the possibility of cultural preservation in any traditional sense unfavorably, feeling as though their efforts were more productively channeled into survival.

But Plenty Coups had faith in Ah-badt-dadt-deah and in his dream-vision. If Lear's description of Plenty Coups' moral psychology is accurate, spiritual faith in Ah-badt-dadt-deah played a distinctive role in the formation of his radical hope for the Crow's collective future. Without his dream-vision, Plenty Coups may not have found reasons to hope that survival and flourishing was possible for his people. Indeed, Lear (2006) suggests that Plenty Coups' "specifically religious beliefs were crucially important to him. . . . They gave him the sustenance with which he could hold on to this core commitment [to the unimaginable future good] through the storm" (121–122). Martin (2014), citing Lear, argues that radical hope as Lear conceives of it is itself a form of faith. Because hope for an unimaginable outcome is hope for an outcome whose nature and goodness transcends one's own ability to understand it, the radical hoper can (rationally, on Martin's view) adopt an attitude of faith, or "meta-confidence . . . that nothing she experiences will give her reason to abandon her hope" (116). For Martin, people of faith are resilient in the face of what look like setbacks and failures because they do not construe these events as evidence against the object of faith—in the case of Plenty Coups, that an unimaginable future good would emerge. Such hopes are "immune to empirical disappointment" (Martin 2014, 101). Martin thus identifies a further form of faith that sustains agents in their practical pursuits.

What all of these narratives teach us is that spiritual faith can sustain people in desperate circumstances, enabling them to continue striving for what they believe is morally right and just in a world that so often disappoints our moral hopes. There are, of course, important risks that come with having spiritual faith quite like the risks of hope. In offering people strength and support in the face of setbacks and failures, spiritual faith might make some people prone to wishfully hoping badly. If God has a plan, I can take comfort in my faith that things will be okay, that whatever happens does so "for a reason," and those who suffer in this world will—at least—be at peace in the next. It is because of these risks that Karl Marx (1970) declared religion to be "the sigh of the oppressed creature, the heart of the heartless world and the soul of soulless conditions. It is the opium of the people" (131). Faith, like hope, can lead to epistemic irrationality. I see this risk as more of a problem for epistemic faith than it is for intrinsic faith, since people of intrinsic faith have faith in the value of acting for its own sake while keeping the evidence in full view. And despite these potential risks of at least some forms of spiritual faith, spiritual faith is beneficial for many people in struggling against oppression.

Of course, not all of us have spiritual faith to sustain us. Some people cannot turn to a god or spiritual worldview for inspiration, assurance, comfort, or hope. If atheists need faith, they must find it in something else. And often, people do testify to having a kind of faith—faith in humanity—as what keeps them going. With or without spiritual faith, faith in humanity does seem to contribute to positive action.

Faith in Humanity

There is not much discussion of faith in humanity in the philosophical literature. One notable exception is Ryan Preston-Roedder's account of faith in humanity as a moral virtue. According to Preston-Roedder (2013), people who have faith in humanity have faith in people's decency. Faith in humanity is not "a vague sense that 'people are generally pretty good,'" or that "people are capable of living together in peace, given favorable conditions" (666). It is, on Preston-Roedder's view, faith in the decency of those people with whom one comes into contact in one's own life, or the particular people about whom one is deliberating. It is a disposition to evaluate others' actions, intentions, or characters by giving them the benefit of the doubt, trusting that they will act decently or at least that right action is attainable for them in the face of evidence to the contrary (666).[10] And those with the moral virtue of faith in

[10] Valerie Tiberius (2008) similarly defends the virtue of what she calls "realistic optimism" about human nature. The realistic optimist is committed (by way of their realism) to the truth and discovering the truth, including the truth about human beings. But through their optimism, they see human beings as always capable of improvement, and they are disposed to make positive generalizations about human potential for goodness and to act on this basis

humanity do not only judge that people do or can live "morally decent lives" (668). They are also committed to that possibility, demonstrating this commitment through their own actions too. For example, people who have faith in humanity actively encourage other people to act well, and they act in ways that set a good example for others.

Preston-Roedder turns to Mohandas Gandhi as an example of someone who possessed the moral virtue of faith in humanity. Throughout Gandhi's campaign for the civil rights of Indian immigrants in South Africa, he and other activists used nonviolent resistance in an attempt to convince white South Africans of the fact of injustice, demonstrating faith in white South Africans' ability to recognize and ultimately end their oppression (Preston-Roedder 2013, 672). Preston-Roedder points out that Gandhi also demonstrated faith in the Indians who joined him in his campaign: faith in their ability to endure the consequences of their activism, including insults, imprisonment, injury, and the possibility of death, and to succeed in their pursuits. I would add that it is possible, and common, to have faith in humanity generally: to have faith in the goodness of human nature, from which faith in particular human beings derives. As Gandhi (2002) himself writes: "You must not lose faith in humanity. If a few drops are dirty, the ocean does not become dirty" (317). When we look at the ocean or humanity collectively, rather than focusing on its constituent members, *that* is often the object of faith.

I take Preston-Roedder (2013) to be talking primarily about faith in humanity in the epistemic sense, focusing on Gandhi's advice that we should treat as an "article of faith" that there is no one who cannot be "converted by love" (664). And Gandhi was clearly willing to act on the basis of his faith in humanity, taking on great risks, in his pursuits. But it's not clear that his faith in humanity enabled him to decline to consider counterevidence about what particular human beings were in fact like, and what they were likely to do. Gandhi's faith in humanity was importantly intrinsic. We can see how Gandhi's faith in humanity manifested as intrinsic faith through his commitment to *satyagraha* ("holding on to truth," "Love-force," or "Soul-force"), which requires *ahimsa*, or nonviolence, as well as virtues such as love, compassion, and forgiveness (Gandhi 2001, 6; Godrej 2006).[11] As Farah Godrej (2006) explains, *ahimsa* is "the willingness to treat all beings as one's self, a

---

[11] Human beings' inability to grasp the Absolute Truth generates a moral constraint on our actions, on Gandhi's view. Since we are incapable of full knowledge, we are not ourselves competent to punish other human beings (Godrej 2006).

complete absence of ill-will, and goodwill toward all life"—and not just for its instrumental value (295). It is a "way of life" through which one comes closer to union with Absolute Truth (or God) (296).[12] Although practicing nonviolence and relational virtues such as love, compassion, and forgiveness might be instrumentally valuable to the pursuit of justice, Gandhi deeply believed in the intrinsic value of relating to other human beings through *ahimsa* and in their capacity to be satyagrahis too.[13] People who have faith in humanity are thus committed to demonstrating the goodness of humanity in their own actions not only as a means to an end but because they deeply believe in the intrinsic value of relating to others with love, kindness, and other virtues.

The Brazilian philosopher and educator Paulo Freire (2005) even defends the necessity of faith in humanity to dialogue, that is, the process through which people name and transform the world. And because dialogue is essential to liberation of the oppressed, faith in humanity is essential to liberation. Freire writes:

> Dialogue requires an intense faith in humankind, faith in their power to make and remake, to create and re-create, faith in their vocation to be more fully human (which is not the privilege of an elite, but the birthright of all). Faith in people is an *a priori* requirement for dialogue; the "dialogical man" believes in others even before he meets them face to face. . . . He is convinced that the power to create and transform, even when thwarted in concrete situations, tends to be reborn. (91)

Freire's faith in humanity initially fits well with Buchak's account of faith as a commitment to taking risks on the basis of humanity's goodness before assessing the evidence (i.e., "before he meets them face to face").

---

[12] See also Karuna Mantena (2018), who points out that, for Gandhi, "nonviolence encompassed an entire philosophy of living" (89). Gandhi's faith in humanity was also intricately connected to his spiritual faith, or faith in God, where he understood God to be Absolute Truth in which human beings can participate through their endless striving for perfection (Godrej 2006).

[13] As Iain Atack (2012) explains, principled proponents of nonviolence such as Gandhi (and King) "are committed to the use of nonviolent methods because they assign it intrinsic value or significance" (10). He distinguishes between principled and pragmatic proponents of nonviolence to show that the former believe in the intrinsic value of their actions, while the latter believe that nonviolence is a means to an end. See also Mantena (2018) for discussion of this distinction in relation to Gandhi and King. Mantena points out that the strict contrast between these approaches to nonviolence can be misleading, since "the philosophy of nonviolence was not just the motivational grounds for adopting a tactic; it provided the reasoning for why and how nonviolent techniques would be politically effective" (85). But, of course, actions and practices can be both intrinsically and instrumentally valuable.

When we enter into dialogue with others as an act of faith, we risk that they might disappoint us. This act of faith is essential if we are to name and transform the world for the better. But Freire's faith in humanity is also importantly intrinsic, once we combine these insights to his understanding of humanity and morality. To be human, on Freire's view, is to engage in praxis, that is, to reflect and act in concert with others. And this praxis requires faith in humanity, as well as love, humility, trust, and hope. For Freire, praxis is itself a moral ideal, and humanization comes from realizing this capacity (Roberts 1998, 107). Freire apparently exemplified his faith in humanity throughout his own life too. His widow, Nita Freire, explains that "he taught himself consistency, humbleness, tolerance, generosity, compassion, and the ability to authentically listen and love" (quoted in Kirylo and Boyd 2017, 59). Educator and activist Shirley Steinberg similarly characterizes Freire as someone "imbued with a radical love that blended spiritual and social commitment as a way of life" (Kirylo and Boyd 2017, 59). Such faith in humanity does not require either assessing or forgoing the search for evidence about whether other people will act morally, when one acts on faith in humanity. It is a constitutive part what it means to be a human being.[14]

It is not necessary to agree with Gandhi's and Freire's strong endorsements of faith in humanity to see its role in supporting moral and political action. Such faith enables people to interact with others through dialogue, trust, and bonds of solidarity and through demonstrating humanity's goodness in one's own actions too. Faith in humanity is risky, in the sense that acting on faith in humanity can dispose one to exploitation and harm (Preston-Roedder 2018). People who have faith in humanity are willing to take on those risks, sometimes by committing to act on the basis of humanity's goodness while forgoing the search for further evidence (e.g., in acts of epistemic faith that other people will reciprocate and treat one with goodwill). But those who have faith in humanity often deeply believe that treating others well is intrinsically valuable, regardless of who they are or what they might do. In other words, if I have intrinsic faith in humanity, nothing people do can make me

---

[14] Both Gandhi's and Freire's faith in humanity are bound up with their spiritual faith (and, as we will see, there are connections between spiritual and moral faith as well). So there is much more to say about the nature of their faith, the relationship between forms of faith, and how they might support one another. I am focused more modestly on showing the importance of different manifestations of faith in the pursuit of justice.

see other human beings as worthy of hatred and violence and unworthy of compassion and love.[15]

Faith in humanity can also be restored or strengthened through witnessing other human beings treat one another well or perform acts of kindness, even while many others are failing. bell hooks (2003), for example, describes the significance of witnessing white feminists engage in anti-racist actions to her own faith. She writes:

> Often I am asked to explain why I could, can, and do critique the racism of white women within the feminist movement and in our society as a whole and yet maintain deep bonds of solidarity, care, and love with individual white women. My explanation is rooted in the recognition and praise of the individual anti-racist white women I encountered and encounter in feminist movement who are utterly and steadfastly committed to eradicating racism, to racial justice. As comrades in struggle, the presence and actions of these individual white women renew my faith in the power of white people to resist racism. I feel this especially during times when I am discouraged about the more widespread white female passive acceptance of racism. (59)[16]

There are many examples of people declaring that their faith in humanity has been renewed or restored by witnessing others' actions. Such examples are diverse, but all of them are moments that display acts of human goodness, however big or small. In a hospital in Mohali, India, a Hindu family and a Muslim family came together to help each other through a paired kidney exchange. Sujeet Kumar (a Hindu man) donated his kidney to Abdul Aziz (a Muslim man); and Aziz's wife, Shazia, donated her kidney to Kumar's wife, Devi (*Times of India* 2019). The *Times of India* (2019) writes: "At a time when communal disharmony has become a norm in many parts of the world, a hospital in Mohali just resurrected faith in humanity." In Toronto, Canada, a group of neighbors came together to build a wheelchair ramp for their

---

[15] This doesn't mean, at least on my view, that faith in humanity is inconsistent with tough love, where loving others is compatible with anger.

[16] In an interview with George Yancy in which she again talks about her solidarity with white women, hooks (2015) explains, "I believe wholeheartedly that the only way out of domination is love." But she sees love as compatible with anger (even rage) about white supremacy. hooks describes meeting the Buddhist monk Thich Nhat Hanh and expressing her anger about racism and sexism, to which he advised hooks to hold on to her anger and "use it as a compost for your garden." Anger, for hooks, is a compost: it is energy that can be recycled for good.

ninety-five-year-old neighbor. In witnessing her neighbors' act and the local Home Depot's donation of materials, Cathy Marro said that "it was a nice, beautiful experience. It honestly restored my faith in humanity" (Dunham 2019). In 2012, Buzzfeed published an article titled "21 Pictures That Will Restore Your Faith in Humanity," including photos of Christians in Chicago at a pride parade wearing T-shirts that read "I'm sorry" (to apologize for the Church's homophobia), two Norwegian men rescuing a sheep from the ocean, and a man giving his shoes to a homeless girl in Rio de Janeiro, Brazil (Shepherd 2012). There are countless stories like these ones.

What is going on when we witness a morally praiseworthy act and feel as though our faith in humanity has been restored? One the one hand, we acquire evidence in favor of humanity's goodness and thus reasons to support our epistemic faith. But these moments are also extremely affectively complex, through which we experience what Jonathan Haidt (2000) refers to as *moral elevation*, or the "warm, uplifting feeling that people experience when they see unexpected acts of human goodness, kindness, and compassion" (1).[17] Haidt and his colleagues (Haidt 2000) found that experiences of moral elevation cause people to see humanity in a more optimistic light, to want to connect with others, and to be better people (3). He writes: "A common theme in most of the narratives [of moral elevation] is a social focus—a desire to be with, love, and help other people" (Haidt 2000, 3).[18] Through moral elevation, people's cognitive structures are altered at the surface, promoting positive thinking and prosocial behavior (Haidt 2000).

Moral elevation thus enables us to bounce back from negative thinking about human nature, renewing or strengthening our faith in humanity. As Haidt (2003) explains: "Powerful moments of elevation sometimes seem to push a mental 'reset button,' wiping out feelings of cynicism and replacing them with feelings of hope, love, and optimism, and a sense of moral inspiration" (8). I suspect that these mental states are not so easily pulled apart from one another, such that we could investigate the role of each state on its own terms in inspiring people to act morally. But what these cases show is that seeing the goodness of humanity in practice can restore or strengthen our epistemic faith in humanity (since such cases are new evidence of humanity's

[17] Jill Suttie (2018) makes this connection between faith in humanity and moral elevation as well.
[18] Haidt (2003) notes that it does not appear that moral elevation is unique to Western cultures. He conducted a series of interviews in Orissa, India, in 1997 in which participants reported the same sorts of warm feelings upon witnessing an act of human goodness that Western participants reported. Haidt's student Yuki Amano conducted similar interviews in Japan in 1998 in which she observed similar patterns among Japanese participants from diverse backgrounds.

goodness). Witnessing others act morally can also remind us of our intrinsic faith in humanity, that is, our deep belief in the intrinsic value of treating others as we witness the kind person do—through love, compassion, and other virtues.

And whereas hope is often vulnerable to evidence, faith in humanity can be sustained even in the absence of hope. If one has epistemic faith in humanity in the sustained rather than momentary sense (it is possible to have the latter but not the former, as I do), one is committed to taking risks on humanity's goodness while forgoing the search for further evidence. Other times, faith in humanity is intrinsic faith, or a deep belief in the intrinsic value of virtues such as love and compassion toward others. And this sustained faith in humanity can serve as a bedrock for hope. Despite how people are behaving right now (e.g., despite the human rights violations, corruption, and human-caused suffering across the world), turning to faith in humanity and reminding oneself of one's commitment to the goodness of humanity and to relating to other human beings as such (perhaps seeking out moments of moral elevation) can inspire a new hope that the dark moment will pass, and that things will get better.

Faith in humanity, along with spiritual faith, is closely related to moral faith. As I show next, it is possible to have moral faith without either spiritual faith or faith in humanity. And even a very minimal kind of moral faith can prevent people from falling into despair.

Moral Faith

Robert Merrihew Adams defends a well-known account of moral faith. He argues that moral faith is a "a stance in relation to goodness and duty, and in relation to possibilities of human action, thought, and feeling and their larger context in human life and the universe" (Adams 1995, 76). Faith in the possibilities of human action, thought, and feeling sounds much like faith in humanity described previously. But Adams's understanding of moral faith as a stance in relation to goodness and duty is distinct. It is faith in morality itself, a faith that can take many forms. For example, he argues that we can have moral faith that our moral convictions are true (i.e., propositional faith), since we know that we live in a world in which there is more than one reasonable moral perspective to take, and there is a sense in which "we could be wrong" (77).

Moral faith thus sometimes manifests as epistemic faith, as when we commit to acting on the basis of the truth of our moral beliefs and to taking risks on their basis while forgoing the search for further evidence that our moral beliefs are true.[19] We also have faith that the moral life is itself worth living, either because living morally is good for other people or because it is "good for the world"— that one's devotion to justice will not be futile in the end (Adams 1995, 80).

Moral faith can also manifest as epistemic faith that our moral ends will someday be attained (a faith that, arguably, neither Bell nor Coates has). Adams (1995) credits Kant for his articulation of moral faith in the actual attainability of moral good (83). Annette Baier (1980), inspired by Kant, explores the potential for a kind of secular moral faith, where such faith is "in the human community and its evolving procedures—in the prospects for many-handed cognitive ambitions and moral hopes" (293). People with secular moral faith have faith in the attainability of a just society despite the profound injustice of the actual society in which they live. And acting on such faith can give rise to hope. As Baier (1980) explains, people who act to promote justice are, by their actions, ruling out one ground on which it might be feared impossible (146).

But moral faith can also be intrinsic, as when one has faith that living a moral life is intrinsically valuable despite the effects one's moral actions have on the world (Adams 1995, 80). Both Bell and Coates seem to have intrinsic moral faith. In the epilogue "Beyond Despair" to his *Faces at the Bottom of the Well: The Permanence of Racism*, Bell defends a kind of hope that emerges from faith in the oppressed combined with moral faith in the intrinsic value of living a moral life. Bell (1992a) reminds us that slaves and freed Black people knew that there was no escape or way out of their oppression given the "social consensus that they were 'a brutish sort of people'" (197). Despite this knowledge, Black people engaged themselves "to carve out a humanity. To defy the murder of self-hood. Their lives were brutally shackled, certainly—but *not without meaning despite being imprisoned*" (198).[20] Bell defends struggling against racial oppression despite his belief in the permanence of racism because there is meaning in the struggle itself. Drawing upon psychiatrist Irvin Yalom's definition of meaningfulness as "a by-product of engagement and commitment," Bell argues that slaves made something out of nothing—with

---

[19] Adams argues, consistently with Buchak, that moral faith involves "being disposed to act on the assumption" that the moral claim is true (88).

[20] Perhaps moral faith also helped sustain King, who, as West (2018) points out, saw in the end that "there is no guarantee of ultimate victory or grounds for progress" (517).

imagination, will, strength, humility, and courage (198). Continued action, for Bell, is both futile and necessary. And he means morally necessary, because of the "unalterable conviction that something must be done" (199).[21]

Coates cites Bell as inspiration in articulating his own defense of the intrinsic value of living a moral life of struggle, though Coates does not have spiritual faith. Coates (2015a), in rejecting a narrative of moral progress, says:

> Perhaps struggle is all we have because the god of history is an atheist, and nothing about his world is meant to be. So you must wake up every morning knowing that no promise is unbreakable, least of all the promise of waking up at all. This is not despair. These are preferences of the universe itself: verbs over nouns, actions over states, struggle over hope. (71)

There are many instances throughout *Between the World and Me* where Coates describes the intrinsic value of living a moral life of struggle, and he emphasizes that struggle assures not victory but "an honorable and sane life" (96–97). This is a manifestation of intrinsic moral faith, a faith that seems to help Coates from falling into despair. People with moral faith thus do not need to see their actions produce their intended effects to find value and meaning in acting morally. Because they deeply believe in the value of living a moral life for its own sake (and committed to taking on risks on this basis), the state of the world is irrelevant to whether they will act on their moral beliefs and cultivate and practice moral virtues.

Perhaps intrinsic moral faith helps to make sense of climate scientists and activists like Kate Marvel (2018), who defends courage rather than hope in the face of climate change. Although she used to have "hope in science," Marvel is now convinced that the climate crisis cannot be reversed. She does not, however, advocate for despair in response to what we have lost and what we will continue to lose, but courage to face the inevitable and the "resolve to do well without the assurance of a happy ending." In her "Home is Always Worth It," climate activist and writer Mary Annaïse Heglar (2019a) critiques both despair and hope in the face of climate change. Nihilism and despair, she cautions, are only afforded to the most privileged among us (often, in her experience, white men), who have the option of retreating into complacency, who can declare without much consequence to their lives that we have

---

[21] See Zeus Leonardo and Angela P. Harris (2013) for further discussion of Bell's commitments that lend support to this reading of his intrinsic faith.

failed. Yet the narrative of hope, which Heglar explains is an imperative for many in the climate community, can betray honesty about the severity of the problems we face. Heglar, in contrast, advocates for continued action "because it's worth it. Because we're worth it." She writes:

> I've never seen a perfect world. I never will. But, I know that a world warmed by 2 degrees Celsius is far preferable to one warmed by 3 degrees, or 6. And I'm willing to fight for it, with everything I have, because it *is* everything I have. I don't need a guarantee of success before I risk everything to save the things, the people, the places that I love. . . . We don't get to give up.

I don't know how much hope, if any, Heglar has. But it seems clear that she has intrinsic moral faith: a faith that our lives are worth living and worth fighting for, even if our actions "salvage just one blade of grass." Heglar deeply believes in the value in struggling against climate injustice as an expression of love for our home (Heglar 2019a) and out of our "debt" (or moral duty) to future and previous generations (Heglar 2019b), regardless of the difference these actions ultimately make in the end.

Moral faith, along with spiritual faith and faith in humanity, helps us to continue striving for what we believe is right and just in a world that so often fails to meet our moral expectations and realize our hopes. It prevents us from falling into all-encompassing despair even when hope is lost or out of our reach. Turning to spirit, to our common humanity, and feeling pulled by the intrinsic importance and meaningfulness of morality despite all of the bad in the world are strategies, or natural ways, in which we resist all-encompassing despair. These forms of faith also support our collective actions in pursuit of justice. And, as we will see, a distinctive form of hope emerges when individuals come together in solidarity against injustice and oppression.

Solidarity and Emerging Hope

> In these moments of rupture, people find themselves members of a "we" that did not until then exist, at least not as an entity with agency and identity and potency; new possibilities suddenly emerge, or that old dream of a just society reemerges—and—at least for a little while—shines.
>
> Rebecca Solnit

There is emerging interest in the concept of solidarity in the philosophical literature—most notably in moral, social, and political philosophy and in bioethics. In an increasingly complex and global world, philosophers have begun to recognize that the concepts and commitments most familiar to us—such as individual rights and autonomy—are incapable of generating adequate moral guidelines for how we should live (Sherwin 2012). In shifting focus away from the individual toward the collective, the concept of solidarity challenges us to think about not just how I should live and act but how we should live and act together. Thus solidarity, some philosophers have argued, holds promise for helping us to understand our moral obligations in addressing threats that target whole social groups—indeed, in the case of global threats such as climate change, the whole planet—and to build a better world (Jennings and Dawson 2015; Doan and Sherwin 2016; Kolers 2016; Sherwin and Stockdale 2017).

Scholars have distinguished between many different kinds of solidarity including feminist solidarity, Black solidarity, and other forms of race-based solidarity (Mohanty 2003; Shelby 2005; Blum 2007; Scholz 2009; hooks 2015). I want to focus on what I think of as *moral-political solidarity*, namely, solidarity based in a shared moral vision carried out through political action. Within moral-political solidarity, there will certainly be what Sally Scholz (2008) refers to as social solidarity: solidarity based on common experiences and identities, such as women's common experience of sexism in a patriarchal society. This form of solidarity brings people together based on their shared sense of identity that includes "cultural forms, practices, or ways of life" (Young 1990, 43). There is, for example, social solidarity among women, Black people, and Indigenous people who find themselves in solidarity with others based on their shared social location. But it is not only members of an oppressed social group who share a moral vision for the elimination of the relevant form of oppression and who undertake political actions to eliminate it. People from many different backgrounds voluntarily join in solidarity with others against sexism, racism, colonialism, and other forms of oppression. I want to understand the relationship between hope and this form of moral-political solidarity as it brings people together across difference, united not always by shared experiences or identities but by their sense of what has to be done together in the pursuit of justice. And moral-political solidarity can give rise to collective hope.

Scholz (2008) explores the role of hope in solidarity in her *Political Solidarity*, arguing quite strongly that "hope is the only necessary feeling for political solidarity" (81). She says:

> Political solidarity is primarily a movement of social change. . . . Hope means that they believe the future can be better than the present. The moral sentiment of hope motivates activity within solidarity because it fosters the desire for the final ends or goals . . . of political solidarity. (Scholz 2008, 81–82)

It is not exactly clear how hope might be necessary for solidarity. One interpretation is that hope is necessary for moral motivation to join in solidarity. As Scholz suggests, "Without it [hope] there would be no reason to act collectively" (82). It is certainly right that hope can motivate people to come together in solidarity against injustice. But it is also the case that the beginnings of a solidarity movement are evidence not of hope for some participants but rather of its loss or absence. The emergence of solidarity and corresponding resistance efforts can sometimes reveal a loss or absence of hope that traditional means of realizing moral and political goals—such as government and law enforcement—will pull through. As journalist and activist Sarah Jaffe (2018) writes in the context of the Me Too movement: "Perhaps one of the deepest assumptions of the Me Too movement is that the society we live in provides us no real options for justice. The court system does not work for survivors and HR is a tool of the boss. The tools we need do not exist yet, so we must build from the ground up." So hope in the court system, for example, is lost. Yet it seems that social movements like Me Too can themselves create or restore hope for those of us who might otherwise find ourselves in despair. Hope can, in other words, be produced by solidarity.

The hope borne of solidarity begins with the recognition that there exist other people who are committed to standing by oneself against injustice. There are many examples of this kind of hope from testimony of members of oppressed groups and those standing with them in solidarity against injustice. Rita Wong, Canadian writer and environmental activist, recounts finding hope through participating in the Healing Walk in Alberta's Tar Sands. She says:

> On my own, I think I would have shrunk down into despair or numbed myself because I felt incapable of addressing the huge, overwhelming scale of the

destruction. Yet, on this walk, the sick feeling co-exists with a quietly hopeful one, invoked by the efforts of my co-walkers, as well as the many people we know who cannot make the journey to Fort McMurray, the epicentre of tar sands extraction in Northern Alberta, but who ask us to carry their wishes and prayers for the healing of the land with us. (Truth and Reconciliation Commission 2015, 103)

Wong's testimony of the "overwhelming scale of destruction" captures the threat to hope that Indigenous and environmental activists face as they challenge powerful institutions to fight for Indigenous lands and waters, and for the health of the whole planet. But her testimony also embodies a renewed hope that arose through solidarity. Wong found hope as she joined her co-walkers, who share her moral vision for a healthy planet on which Indigenous lands and waters are protected from environmental damage and stand with her in opposition to the people and institutions standing in the way of this shared vision. Similarly, Patrisse Khan-Cullors explains that Black Lives Matter seeks to "provide hope and inspiration for collective action to build collective power to achieve collective transformation, rooted in grief and rage but pointed towards vision and dreams" (Solnit 2016, xiv).

These examples suggest that there is a way to collectively recover hope for those of us who might be struggling to find hope on our own. As Victoria McGeer (2004) suggests, "Recovering hope depends on discovering some new way of relating to others, specifically a way that recognizes the interdependence of the self and other in generating the best confidence for keeping hope alive" (McGeer 2004, 122). Perhaps the hope that is generated through solidarity manifests at times as an existential or basal emotion—a felt sense of hope without an object (Ratcliffe 2013; Calhoun 2018). But I think that the hope borne of solidarity is often a renewed or strengthened hope *for* some form of justice. It is a kind of collective hope for justice.

Collective Hope

What exactly does it mean for hope to be collective?[22] I begin with the intuition that there seems to be something fundamentally different between, for

---

[22] There is some empirical literature that explores the nature of collective hope in solidarity movements. See, for example, Sasha Courville and Nicola Piper (2004), who characterize hope and collective hope solely in terms of desire. My approach to collective hope draws upon the characterization of hope advanced in this book.

example, hoping for one's own happiness alongside others who share in the hope for happiness and hoping for justice for women as part of the Me Too movement alongside others who share in the hope for justice for women. In the happiness case, it would seem odd to construe the hope as a collective hope even though most of us, as a group of human beings, hope for happiness. The hope of the Me Too movement is different. It seems to belong not to each individual who hopes for justice for women but to the group: women and allies who participate in the hope of the movement.

There are at least two routes to take in order to make sense of the hope of the Me Too movement. The first is to argue that the hope is an aggregate of and reducible to the hopes of individuals, and the second is to argue that there is a kind of hope—collective hope—that is appropriately ascribed to the movement, or to the solidarity group.[23] I argue that collective hope emerges alongside a collective intention of the solidarity group, namely, an intention to pursue the form of justice that inspires the movement. As we will see, the reductivist about collective hope faces the challenge of capturing the phenomenology of collective hope—a felt experience of hope that is quite different from the phenomenology of individual hopes.

Let us briefly revisit the nature of hope. Hope involves seeing or perceiving in a favorable light the possibility that a desired outcome one believes to be possible but not certain obtains. I suggest that hope becomes collective when:

1. The hope is shared by at least some others.
2. The favorable perception of the possibility that the desired outcome might obtain, and corresponding hopeful feelings, is caused (or is strengthened) by activity in a collective action setting.
3. The reciprocal hopeful expressions of individual group members result in an emotional atmosphere of hope that extends across the group.

The first condition is relatively straightforward: in order to have collective hope, or any genuinely collective emotion, the emotion must be experienced by more than one person. (I say more about what it means to "share" a hope below.) The second condition captures the causal and dependency relations between the group and the hope: the hope is caused or strengthened

---

[23] I use "solidarity group," "movement," and "collective" interchangeably to include members of the relevant oppressed group and their allies. I acknowledge that there is much more to say about who is a member of these collectives and who counts as an "ally."

by a collective action setting and depends upon collective activity for its existence. For example, a woman might have very little hope about women's equality and rights, and she might participate in a protest out of anger and a strong sense of justice despite believing that the protest won't be effective. But joining a group of women and allies coming together at a march, perhaps to take action on sexual violence against women and to promote women's reproductive rights, might cause the woman to feel a sense of hope for women's equality and rights, seeing the possibility of gender justice in a more favorable light in that moment than she otherwise would.

The second and third conditions capture the difference between hoping for one's own happiness alongside others who also hope for their own happiness and hoping for justice for women as part of a solidarity movement. In the former case, I see in a favorable light the possibility of achieving my own happiness. Although other people (e.g., my loved ones) might also see the possibility of my attaining happiness favorably, there is no group formed around the goal of achieving my happiness.[24] When I hope for justice for women alongside others in a collective action setting, in contrast, the hope belongs to the group whose goal is to achieve justice for women and whose members intend to pursue the outcome as a group. The hope is part of a collective rather than multiple individuals who happen to share the same hope.

But understanding how hope emerges at the level of a collective requires a deeper understanding of the collective itself. Philosophers interested in collective activity have explored the ways in which collectives might have beliefs, intentions, actions, and emotions of their own. I want to suggest that collective hope emerges from the collective intentions and actions of the solidarity group. Borrowing from Margaret Gilbert: "A population P has a collective intention to do A if and only if members of P are *jointly committed* to intending *as a body* to do A" (Gilbert 2002, 125; 2014).[25] Joint commitments cannot be broken down into each individual's personal decision to pursue A. Such commitments arise from individuals together determining what they

[24] There might be cases in which a group *is* formed around the goal of achieving my happiness or wellbeing. For example, people in psychiatric facilities often have a team of healthcare providers assigned to their case: physicians, psychologists, social workers, nurses, and so on. Since the team of healthcare providers makes up a group of people formed around a common goal—namely, improving the patient's wellbeing—they might share in a collective hope to improve the patient's wellbeing. My focus is collective hope in social and political contexts, but there are other potential cases of collective hope that are interesting and important too.

[25] There are many competing accounts of collective intention, and I do not have the space to consider all of them. My strategy is to illustrate how insights from a persuasive and influential account of collective intention helps us to make sense a kind of hope that arises through solidarity.

intend, as a group, to do. Consequently, I might be jointly committed to intending to do *A* as part of a body without any sort of personal commitment to intending to do *A*. I might, for example, be jointly committed to intending to pursue justice for women as part of the Me Too movement even if I have no personal commitment to doing so on my own. (Perhaps I judge that such an intention would be futile.)

Social movements have their own goals and intentions, which direct the activities of the collective.[26] And it is not difficult to find out about the goals, intentions, and actions of social movements at work. This information is readily available on official websites and social media pages through "missions" and "vision statements." On the Me Too movement website, we find that the Me Too vision is, broadly, justice for women with respect to holding perpetrators of sexual violence accountable for their actions. Within this broad goal of the solidarity movement, the focus is primarily on helping survivors (especially young women of color from low-income communities). As the movement has grown, this vision has broadened: "What started as a grassroots work has expanded to reach a global community of survivors from all walks of life" (Me Too 2018). The vision states:

> Our goal is also to reframe and expand the global conversation around sexual violence to speak to the needs of a broader spectrum of survivors. Young people, queer, trans, and disabled folks, Black women and girls, and all communities of color. We want perpetrators to be held accountable, and we want strategies implemented to sustain long term, systemic change. . . . We want to uplift radical community healing as a social justice issue and are committed to disrupting all systems that allow sexual violence to flourish. (Me Too 2018)

These goals and priorities belong to the group itself, not any one individual desiring, intending, or acting alone. Although Tarana Burke as an individual founded the Me Too movement in 2006, and thus her personal intention to pursue social justice with respect to sexual violence against women has certainly helped to shape the movement, Me Too is essentially a collective endeavor. It is a product of multiple individuals coming together

---

[26] As bell hooks (2015) explains, "To experience solidarity, we must have a community of interests, shared beliefs and goals around which to unite, to build Sisterhood. . . . Solidarity requires sustained, ongoing commitment" (67).

and negotiating the movement's goals, intentions, and priorities and how the group will pursue its ends.

But the joint commitment to intend to pursue justice for women as part of the Me Too movement will not necessarily secure the outcome. It is quite possible that the collective actions of the group will fail. Thus, individuals who are jointly committed to intending to pursue justice for women as part of the collective might form the hope that their efforts will be successful. Of course, they might hope in the standard individual sense (as when a bystander hopes that the Me Too movement succeeds in its aims) or as a member of the group (as when I form the group-based hope as a woman that the Me Too movement succeeds in its aims). But they might also hope in the collective sense: desiring justice for women, believing that success in securing the outcome is possible but not certain, and coming to see the possibility of achieving justice for women in a favorable (or more favorable) light, with new or strengthened hopeful feelings, through participating in the collective actions of the solidarity group. Importantly, too, one might not have an individual hope or a group-based hope yet share in the collective hope. A male ally might not be hopeful about achieving justice for women on his own. And I might not be hopeful (as a woman) that justice for women will come. But when the ally and I jointly commit alongside others to pursue justice for women as part of the movement and show up in a collective action setting, we might find ourselves sharing in the collective hope for positive change.[27]

But what, exactly, does it mean to share in a collective hope? I suggest that the difference between sharing in a collective hope (rather than having the same individual hopes as other people) lies in the phenomenology of individual as opposed to collective hopes.[28] In the individual case, hope is an affective state that feels like something for the individual. And the affective character of collective hope episodes—how, exactly, collective hope feels at various moments in time—will be different from individual hope. In other

---

[27] Gilbert (2014) discusses another way in which her theory of collective intention might make sense of collective emotions. She argues that collective emotions are emotions to which group members are jointly committed. I think this view requires too strong of an endorsement of one's emotion. I might not be committed to hope, though in jointly committing to an end and participating alongside others in a collective action setting, I might find myself swept up in a collective hope that we will succeed. Collective hope is a perceptual and affective state that is appropriately ascribed to groups. It is not a joint commitment to experiencing the emotion itself.

[28] I imagine that two individuals sharing a hope might also have a distinct phenomenological character. For example, pair figure skaters' hope that they (together) will win nationals might have a distinct phenomenological experience in comparison to a solo skater's hope that they win nationals. I set these interesting cases aside to focus on hopes borne of solidarity in social and political contexts.

words, seeing in a favorable light the possibility that *our* (those of us here, in this moment) desired end might be attained feels differently from seeing in a favorable light the possibility that *my* desired end might be attained.

New research in the philosophy of mind supports this hypothesis. Joel Krueger (2014), for example, discusses the possibility of what he calls environmentally extended emotions: emotions that are extended beyond an agent's body in such a way that the emotion is constituted by factors external to the agent. Krueger discusses the case of environmentally extended emotions through music. Emotions become environmentally extended through music in the sense that the listener "integrates with musical dynamics in a reciprocal, mutually-modulatory way"; or, in other words, that what the listener hears determines how he responds by way of the emotions, and those responses shape what the listener hears, which then informs further responses (Krueger 2014, 544). Krueger argues that emotions might become *collectively* environmentally extended when they are shared by two or more individuals. As he puts it: "The emotion is something that emerges over time as a group-level trait; it extends across the various individuals making up the group" (536). Krueger uses the example of a funeral and how the subdued nature of funeral music combined with the presence of other people grieving results in a collective experience of grief that shapes the character of grief for individuals. The dynamic results in an "emotional convergence" between them. When others react (for example, when they cry), one feels one's own responses align with the emotional responses of others nearby.

Emotional convergence between individuals is what results in a sharing of hope. So collective hope, unlike individual hope, requires contact and emotional convergence between individuals who are jointly committed to intending to pursue an outcome together. As Dario Páez and Bernard Rimé (2014) explain, individuals' gestures, movements, speech, and so on result in "an atmosphere of emotion and fervor" that transforms individual emotional feelings into shared emotional feelings (Páez and Rimé 2014, 207). These shared emotional feelings, along with the experience of being in community with other group members, combine in such a way that "participants evolve to a sense of group membership" and "experience the 'we' in place of the 'I'" (207). For example, in listening to a feminist activist's speech in a room full of supporters, the speech (including the content of words spoken, tone, and volume of voice) as well as the presence of others passionately listening (their facial expressions, verbal responses, and body language) shapes how individuals perceive and feel, including by way of their emotions. They come to see in a favorable light the possibility of the desired outcome's obtaining, often more intensely than they otherwise would, with new or strengthened feelings of hopefulness. Their hopeful expressions (e.g., smiling, nodding, cheering) then feed back into the group, enhancing the hopeful feelings of others. The result is emotional convergence, a shared feeling of hope, which transforms the sense that "I am hoping" into the sense that "we are hoping together." Individuals become aware of a hope that stretches beyond all of them, a hope in which each person can share, but which belongs to the "we" that has formed in this moment.

This is not to say that how collective hope feels is equivalent among members of the collective. The collective "we" notably includes people who occupy different social locations that affect how they emotionally experience the world, and consequently how they hope. For example, Black women, Indigenous women, other women of color, and white women may collectively hope for gender justice, yet how they experience collective hope in response to an Indigenous woman's powerful call to action at a rally will likely vary. Hope is relational, even at the collective level. This is consistent with the existence of a collective hope for gender justice in which all participants who are jointly committed to gender justice can participate. Just like each person's actions as part of a collective action depend upon who they are in relation to others and to the cause, so too each participant's emotional experience as part of a collective hope depends upon who they are in relation to others and to the cause.

These reflections suggest that there are good reasons to think that a form of collective hope emerges in social movements when individuals come together in solidarity. I suspect that what is "collective" about collective hope, or what is not easily reducible to the hopes of individuals, is the phenomenological character of collective hope. Although it is felt and experienced by individuals, the hope extends beyond them in and through the group, resulting in an emotional atmosphere of hope that belongs to the group itself.[29] Research in philosophy and the social sciences on "emotional convergence" and "emotional atmosphere" helps to illustrate how collective hope emerges, paving the way for developing new and insightful ways of understanding collective emotional phenomena in solidarity movements. But

---

[29] As Bennett Helm (2014) suggests, "The idea is not that the group itself has a mind and mental states in exactly the same way as individuals do; rather, it is that there is a phenomenon at the level of the group that can properly be understood to be an emotional phenomenon and that is irreducible to the states of mind of the individual group members" (47).

there remains much room for debate about how to best characterize collective hope. My aim has been quite modest: to provide a starting point for theorizing one form of collective hope in the pursuit of justice.

But what is the object of collective hope? Solnit suggests that the "old dream of a just society" emerges in these moments of rupture, moments in which individuals find themselves as part of a "we" through which new possibilities emerge. The emergence of collective hope borne of solidarity thus raises the question of how we might hope well for justice. For some of us, our hopes for justice are modest, as we hope for small victories that will improve the world for the better, however slightly, and however long those improvements last. For others, their hopes for justice are ambitious. Some people even sustain hope for justice itself. I want to suggest that these two ways of hoping for justice, what I call modest hope and utopian hope, are ways in which we can individually and collectively hope well for justice.

Hoping Well for Justice

When we hope for racial justice, the elimination of sexist oppression, and a world in which all people have the income and resources they need to live a good life, we are hoping for outcomes that would contribute to the collective project of achieving that dream of a just society: a state in which there would be no more moral work left to do but to maintain the end we have reached. The utopian hope for complete justice is thus a hope whose realization would radically transform the world such that a moral ideal of complete justice (hereafter, justice), the object of hope, is obtained. Although I wish to remain neutral about what theory of justice is correct, if any, I understand the utopian hope for justice as a hope to achieve the moral ideal of justice.[30]

As Luc Bovens (1999) aptly puts it in his discussion of the value of individuals' hopes, it is "notoriously difficult to make sense of utopian hopes" (674n4). The difficulty is that for some people the utopian hope for justice

---

[30] We might reasonably rule out clearly misguided and harmful utopian hopes, such as the hope that "America will be made great again" where "greatness" seems to refer to a history of colonialism, racism, sexism, homophobia, transphobia, and other forms of oppression envisioned in some sort of utopian American future. We might also rule out utopian hopes that are unrealistic, such as the utopian hope to live in a world of only altruists (see Howard 2018, 7). I limit my focus to utopian hopes for justice where the conception of justice envisioned does not clearly miss the mark, about both what is just and what is possible. I don't suppose most agents who hope for justice have a well-worked-out theory of justice either, though they might still testify to having the hope for justice nonetheless. And I take their expressions of hope to be genuine.

functions as a guiding ideal that directs their more modest hopes, but it is itself not really a hope. In other words, some agents appeal to the moral ideal of "justice" to form hopes the realization of which would constitute progress toward the ideal, even if they do not hope that we will ever reach the ideal in reality. For example, one might hope to prevent a pipeline from being built that will be detrimental to Indigenous lands, waters, and health; and the hope to prevent the pipeline from being built is part of the hope for environmental justice. The hope for environmental justice is, then, part of the hope for justice. But not everyone who has the first hope has the second; and not everyone who has the first and second hopes has the third. It is possible to hope to prevent a pipeline from being built while having no hope that environmental justice, and (by implication) justice, will ever be attained.

We can see these different hopes for justice at work in collective action settings too. Some people might show up at a rally for environmental justice inspired by the approval for a pipeline to be built, participating in the collective intention to prevent the construction of the pipeline to protect Indigenous lands, waters, and health. We can imagine some participants attending the rally out of a sense of duty, even if they have no hope that collective efforts to prevent the pipeline from being built will succeed. Others might participate out of the modest hope that activists might prevent this one pipeline from being built, without hope that environmental justice will ever be attained. But even these participants who are unhopeful about the possibility of environmental justice itself, as individuals, might find themselves sharing in a collective hope for environmental justice. As they listen to powerful and inspiring speeches from Indigenous Water Protectors, read signs that say "We Demand Environmental Justice!," and witness the hopeful verbal and behavioral expressions of others, they might find themselves swept up in the collective hope for environmental justice, perhaps even seeing in a favorable light the possibility of justice itself.

But what lessons can we draw from these collective experiences of hope? When the collective diffuses and we retreat to our homes and everyday lives, which of the above hopes should we sustain and pursue? Feminist scholar and activist Rebecca Solnit defends hoping only for small victories, not justice as a moral ideal. As she says: "This is Earth. It will never be heaven. There will always be cruelty, always be violence, always be destruction. . . . We cannot eliminate all devastation for all time, but we can reduce it, outlaw it, undermine its sources and foundations: these are victories. A better world, yes; a perfect world, never" (Solnit 2016, 78). Although the dream of a just society emerges at various moments, we can only reasonably hope to achieve small victories, without judging that the realization of these hopes for small victories would constitute a step closer to realizing some moral ideal of justice in our not-yet-foreseeable collective future.

Similarly, Kathryn Norlock (2019) suggests that evil and suffering will never be eliminated and argues that "there is no reason to believe that the future will be one in which evils cease to be" (11). Although human beings are capable of changing for the better, their ability to do so is outmatched by the seriousness of the problems facing humanity. We are also essentially imperfect, according to Norlock. So the utopian hope for justice, which require us to believe that achieving a moral ideal is possible, is not justified. It entails a mistaken understanding of what it means to be human. But this unhopeful stance toward the possibility of attaining justice itself is nevertheless compatible with forming and pursuing more modest hopes, hopes that are even guided by the moral ideal Norlock believes is impossible to attain. We can, she points out, engage in efforts aimed at constructing just institutions even if "our efforts may be inadequate, or undone, or not sustained after we die" (15). And Norlock rejects the charge that she is advocating for a Sisyphean existence, for moral agents to continue rolling a ball up a hill only to have it tumble back down, over and over, for eternity. On Norlock's view, there is no hill, and "directional metaphors" are bound up with our wishful thinking that moral progress has an endpoint that we can reach if we just continue on in our moral and political struggles (16). We ought to, instead, just do our best, reveling in other goods of life including activism, recreation, and loving relationships as we navigate the necessarily imperfect world we share.

I share these feminist scholars' unhopeful stance toward the possibility of achieving complete justice someday in the future. I suspect many others will share this perspective, unable to see in a favorable light the possibility of obtaining justice in the future, even slightly, and unable to feel hopeful anticipation in thinking about a future state of the world that is just. Like Solnit and Norlock, such people might not feel pulled by the need to hope for justice itself; they might, instead, be motivated to pursue justice by pursuing the mitigation of injustice. And I think that this is one way of hoping well for justice. But I want to make room for utopian hopers: those who really do believe in moral progress and who continue to hope that we might someday succeed in living in a just world. Utopian hopers, too, can hope for justice well.

Utopian hopers desire justice, believe that justice is possible but not certain, see in a favorable light the possibility of attaining justice (perhaps pointing to moral improvements and advancements toward the ideal), and feel hopeful about the possibility of achieving justice in the future. The cynics among us might be inclined to reject the idea that the utopian hope for justice can be a reasonable hope to have: they might judge that the moral ideal is nowhere within reach, and hoping for justice itself can be a distraction from the concrete, real-world actions we need to take to mitigate injustice in the here and now. But importantly, it might be morally valuable for people to form hopes related to their moral projects, even when those projects are wildly ambitious, perhaps even doomed to fail. An agent's strong hope that sexist oppression will be eliminated in one's lifetime might be a morally praiseworthy attitude because of what it reveals about the agent's moral character, even if it is unfitting to hope for this outcome given the evidence available. The agent might hope well by preserving the hope that sexist oppression will end, just not in our lifetime. This revised hope is an example of what Michael Milona (2018) calls *patient hope*: a hope for an outcome in the very distant future, one that orients attention and action toward what one can do to make incremental progress toward the hoped-for end.

The revised hope, the hope that sexist oppression will someday end, might then be part of the hope for justice, and we can run the same argument to defend the hope for justice. Interestingly, too, it is difficult to criticize the hope for justice as a moral ideal. It is certainly fitting to see justice as desirable and the possibility that justice might someday be attained in a favorable light, given the vagueness of the "someday" represented in the hope. It even seems fitting to be strongly hopeful about the possibility that all forms of oppression will eventually end and that justice "will someday prevail." When agents have this hope, the "someday" referred to is so far into the future that it is barely even foreseeable—a faint, abstract future that is indeterminate. The utopian hope for justice is vague, open, and inarticulate; and this is precisely what makes criticizing it so difficult. It reaches for a moral ideal that we have never seen obtained before, and it might, then, be bound up with faith. For example, in hoping that justice "will someday prevail," one might have faith in humanity and appeal to one's faith as justification for continuing to hope.

We might, for example, have epistemic faith in humanity in Rawls's sense of the term. To say that human nature is good, for Rawls (1999), "is to say that citizens who grow up under reasonable and just institutions . . . will affirm those institutions and act to make sure their social world endures" (7). And reflection on the contingency of historical evils and the goodness of human nature demonstrates that "we must not allow these great evils of the past and present to undermine our hope for the future" (22). Rawls thus believes that a future just society is a realistic possibility for which we can reasonably hope. And in arguing that a just society "could and may exist," he notices that justice is physically possible (i.e., consistent with the natural order of how human beings are and how they might be) as well as possible for our future world—a world in which historical and current injustices continue to affect us (Howard 2019, 6). Inspired by Kant, Rawls's hope for justice rests on a kind of faith beyond what we see in the world right now, faith that vindicates the hope for justice.

One might faithfully hope well by recognizing that one's utopian hope is not (right now) within reach and form hopes toward the moral ideal that are more clearly in view. The agent might shift the target of the utopian not-yet-graspable hope to more concrete, realistic outcomes the obtaining of which would make progress toward justice. For example, one might hope for gender justice as part of one's hope for justice by forming the less ambitious hopes for equal pay for equal work and increased government and public support of people's reproductive rights. Or one might find oneself sharing in a collective hope for gender justice while remaining mindful about the obstacles we must collectively encounter before this hope can be realized.

Rawls seems to think that reasonable people are required to maintain the utopian hope for a just future, since doing so guards against feelings of futility and diminished moral motivation. But the claim that hope is required for moral motivation is too strong. We have seen that people can be motivated to continue on in their moral and political struggles without hope that their efforts will be successful. And as Solnit and Norlock teach us, people can also hope well for justice by hoping only for small victories that diminish harm and improve people's lives in the here and now while remaining hopeless about the possibility of attaining justice as a moral ideal.

I see both Rawls on the one hand and Solnit and Norlock on the other as taking two different but equally permissible stances toward the future. As long as the agent who hopes only for small victories does not lose her commitment and motivation to continue striving to attain her moral ends, she is justified in forming and pursuing her modest hopes while remaining hopeless about the possibility of achieving justice as a moral ideal. And as long as the agent who hopes that justice "will someday prevail" has, as Rawls does, rational beliefs about the magnitude and severity of evil, suffering, and injustice in the world right now, they are justified in their ambitious hope. What is important is that the object of hope, or the guiding ideal—the elimination of all forms of injustice in the world—structures and guides individual and collective action, and that we do not lose sight of where we have been, how things are now, and where we need to go.

Concluding Thoughts

This chapter has explored the relationship between hope, faith, and solidarity in collective struggles against oppression. Or, at least, it has scratched the surface of the relationship between three very complex phenomena that work together in motivating moral agents to pursue a more just world. Even when all hope seems out of reach based on the evidence before us, faith can prevent us from falling into all-encompassing despair. Sometimes, agents might have epistemic faith that justice might actually be attained in the distant future, committing to act on this basis while forgoing the search for further evidence. But I have argued that intrinsic faith, or faith in the intrinsic value of one's actions in the pursuit of justice, can powerfully sustain agents in struggle. Through spiritual faith, faith in humanity, and moral faith, agents come to deeply believe in the intrinsic value of what they are doing independently of the efficacy of their actions in securing their moral and political ends. Faith can even serve as a bedrock for the renewal, restoration, or strengthening of hope when hope might otherwise be lost.

Sustained by faith, people come together in what I have called moral-political solidarity: solidarity based in a shared moral vision carried out through political action. Sometimes, moral-political solidarity is identity-based, bringing people together with common experiences of oppression such as Black solidarity and women's solidarity. But other times, solidarity movements unite people from diverse backgrounds who come together in collective actions based on their shared moral vision for change. And through solidarity in collective action settings, a form of collective hope can emerge. The object of the collective hope borne of solidarity is justice. Whether people are hoping for justice by hoping for small victories which might be short-lived or hoping ambitiously for justice as a moral ideal, modest hope and utopian hope are ways in which we can hope well for justice.

Conclusion

Hope Looking Forward

My task in this book has been to illuminate what hope looks like in conditions of oppression. We are living in a time when these oppressions are being exacerbated both locally and globally. Individuals and governments have been turning their backs on refugees, Indigenous people, immigrants, women, transgender people, religious minorities, and other groups considered to be a threat, in some way, to individual and national self-interest. At the same time, a global pandemic has spread across the world, killing hundreds of thousands of people, and the real threat of climate change looms large. Unsurprisingly, people who are worse off are disproportionately affected, while the privileged are often able to ignore, neglect, and even deny these harms. From the lens of moral and political progress, it seems that the world is moving backward, and even in new and terrifying directions.

So where is hope in this story? Politicians call for hope; corporations and nonprofit organizations brand themselves with it; and we tend to encourage one another to "never give up hope." Philosophers writing on hope in recent years have been interested in the question of what, exactly, hope is. And this is a helpful starting point for finding it. I have argued that hope is a way of seeing in a favorable light the possibility that a desired outcome obtains. But I have also argued that we do not need a perfect theory of the nature of hope to understand how hope is formed, maintained, and lost in the lives of real human beings who find themselves forming, struggling with, and losing hope. By setting aside the debate about the constitutive features of hope to focus on human differences in our hopes, including social, economic, and political differences, we have gained a richer understanding of how hope operates in real human lives. Attending explicitly to the ways in which patterns of privilege and oppression—based on gender, race, immigration status, ethnicity, and the like—structure these differences reveals that the character, objects, and strength of our hopes are significantly affected by our differential positions. Privilege bolsters opportunities for

Hope Under Oppression. Katie Stockdale, Oxford University Press. © Oxford University Press 2021.
DOI: 10.1093/oso/9780197563564.003.0007

hope by expanding the space of possibility in our lives, while oppression is a threat to hope.

I have argued that oppression can damage not only people's hopes for this or that outcome but also their very capacities for cultivating and sustaining hope. At the same time, individuals and institutions in positions of power can exploit the hopes of people in powerless positions. Hope is promised, manufactured, sold, and bought into in political, corporate, and health care contexts. Exploring more deeply how the language of hope is coopted by privileged members of society in ways that reinforce oppression is crucial if we are to adequately understand the potential risks and harms of hope in moral, social, and political life. This book is thus a starting point for a broader, and much needed, ethics and politics of hope.

Seeing hope through the lens of oppression has implications for theorizing not only the nature of hope but the value and risks of hope as well. For example, although hope might often be good for members of oppressed groups to cultivate in resisting oppression for prudential reasons, hope is itself threatened by oppression (and hope can even be used as a tool of oppression). Those of us who might be tempted to advocate for the idea that people *should* hope, or that there might be an imperative to keep one's hopes alive, must wrestle with the challenge of prescribing hope to people who— through no fault of their own—cannot hope, or who quite reasonably see no reasons for hope. I have argued that there are reasons to be skeptical that hope really is what we most need in all cases, and I have defended a nuanced evaluative framework through which hope can be evaluated along multiple dimensions: epistemic and prudential (or strategic) rationality, but also fittingness and morality. There is, most importantly, a moral constraint on emotions, including hope. When we find ourselves with morally inappropriate hopes, we have sufficient reason to overcome or revise them. There is room to explore further what happens when we *don't* overcome our morally inappropriate emotions: how their presence might corrupt other aspects of our moral characters. Morally inappropriate emotions may not only reveal that the agent is not properly oriented, in important ways, toward the good. These emotions might also reinforce themselves, leading to other immoral attitudes and vices.

I have also shown that, beyond familiar rational assessments, hope can be assessed as a fitting or unfitting emotional response. Hope is fitting when the agent correctly represents a hoped-for outcome as favorable to a degree that is warranted by the context in question. And there might be good prudential reasons for sustaining strong hope even when one's hope is unfitting given the low odds of success (as in the case of cancer patients' hopes for a cure). Other times, the (epistemic and prudential) risks of hope might override its benefits to individual wellbeing. There is no perfect formula for determining the value of hope. The practical question of what, exactly, a person should feel is a matter of wise judgment that varies between contexts and who the moral agents hoping are. And in social and political contexts, it is often apt to shift our normative assessment to the level of society, attending to the role of power, privilege, and oppression in bringing about, shaping, or damaging peoples' hopes. Understanding these influences on hope is essential if we are to move beyond theorizing the rationality of individual hopes toward the value and risks of hope in an unjust social world.

The focus of this book has been largely on the nature and value of individuals' attitudes of hope, particular episodes of hope and their capacities for forming and pursuing those hopes. Although I have not said much about the potential virtue of hope, the analysis I offer might help to inform virtue-theoretic approaches to hope, which are making a comeback in the philosophical literature. If hope is not just an attitude or state of mind but also a virtue, a number of questions emerge. Given that the capacity for hope is threatened and often damaged by oppression, who can access the virtue of hope? How might the virtue of hope look different as it is cultivated and practiced by people who occupy different social locations? Virtue-theoretic approaches often proceed similarly to discussions about the nature of hope as an attitude, beginning with the "What is hope?" question in the abstract followed by an account of how such an attitude might manifest as a virtue. This book suggests that we need to think seriously about the effects of privilege and oppression on the potential virtue of hope as well.

But theorizing hope on its own fails to capture its role in our emotional lives as a whole. I have shown that there is an important relationship between hope and anger—an emotion that is commonly experienced and defended in response to injustice and oppression. On the one hand, anger often responds to thwarted hopes. We invest our hopes in other people, groups, and institutions to abide by our moral expectations, and when they fail to meet those expectations, we tend to experience anger. But on the other hand, anger often implies, or is accompanied by, the formation of new hopes: the hope that wrongdoers apologize and display remorse, the hope that the criminal justice system does right by victims of injustice, the hope that relationships can be repaired for the future, and so on. In disagreement with Nussbaum

(2016), anger does not always or necessarily involve a wish (or hope) for payback, but rather a broad range of outcomes for which angry people might hope. It might be worth exploring further whether vindictive hopes, hopes that are for payback, can ever be morally appropriate.

But as we have seen, the anger of members of oppressed groups is not commonly met with reparative uptake, and the hopes which accompany their anger responses tend to remain unrealized. In these cases, anger often interacts with varying degrees of hopelessness to evolve into bitterness. Philosophers theorizing the emotion of bitterness have followed Lynne McFall (1991) in arguing that bitterness is about the disappointment of hopes. But this view rests on a mistaken understanding of the relationship between hope, moral expectation, and anger. I have argued that bitterness is not primarily about the disappointment of hopes but about violations of moral expectations. More specifically, bitterness is paradigmatically a form of anger involving a loss of hope that a perceived injustice or other moral wrong—one that violated one's moral expectations—will be sufficiently acknowledged and addressed. Or, in cases where bitterness is in part a response to irreparable damage, the emotion involves a loss of hope for one's own life. There is a further and interesting question of whether individuals can be "born into bitterness," that is, whether they can learn to be hopelessly angry without first experiencing anger alongside hope for a better life and world. Perhaps this is a topic for psychologists interested in the formation of hope in childhood to pursue, and one about which philosophical insights about hope can inform.

Bitterness in everyday life is commonly thought to be an inherently inappropriate and destructive emotion, as is evidenced by quotes on the internet like "Bitterness is its own prison" and "Bitterness and love can't live together in the same heart." That's why calling someone "bitter" carries with it an accusation that one should not be that way—that one should not be bitter. But despite its unfortunate reputation, I have argued that bitterness, just like other forms of anger, can be a fitting, morally appropriate response, and even prudentially rational response. Bitterness is fitting when it correctly represents an action, event, or set of circumstances as both wrong or unjust and without hope for repair. It is morally appropriate to the extent that the emotion reveals that the agent is properly oriented toward the good. And though bitterness involves a loss of hope, it does not necessarily lead to despair and inaction. Agents can be motivated to continue on in their moral and political struggles without hope that their efforts will be successful. And since the emotion can contribute to political action through its role in moral perception, bitterness can even be prudentially rational for some agents. We can see losses of hope and continued resistance in the lives of Derrick Bell, Ta-Nehisi Coates, and other activists who take part in social movements to resist ongoing and wide-reaching moral failures.

But thinking about how, exactly, moral agents persist without hope that their efforts will be successful led me to theorize faith. In reading Derrick Bell, it became clear that Bell was pessimistic and unhopeful, yet his spiritual faith kept him going. And Ta-Nehisi Coates, despite not having any kind of spiritual faith, seems supported by moral faith that living a moral life is intrinsically valuable. But there are different ways in which these forms of faith can manifest. As Buchak (2012; 2017) argues, faith can manifest as a commitment to take risks on the basis of a proposition's being true while forgoing the search for further evidence or even declining to consider further evidence. Other times, as I have argued, faith is intrinsic, enabling agents to commit to a pursuit because of their deep belief in the intrinsic value of the pursuit itself. Such faith can flow from faith in a supernatural entity or felt spiritual connection (spiritual faith), faith in other human beings or humanity at large (faith in humanity), and faith in one's moral convictions and in the intrinsic value of morality (moral faith). I have argued that faith enables resilience to the conditions in which people find themselves and can serve as a bedrock for the renewal or strengthening of hope when all hope is lost or out of reach.

One question that comes to mind is the kind of despair that faith helps to prevent in these contexts. It is not despair of this or that outcome but an absolute, all-encompassing despair that prevents the formation of particular hopes or taints them. If I despair, for example, that sexist oppression will ever end, then when I hope for an outcome related to the elimination of sexist oppression—for example, that this particular perpetrator of sexual violence will be brought to justice—my hope might be tainted by despairing thoughts. "What will his going to prison really do in the grand scheme of things? Most perpetrators get off free, or nearly free. And women will never escape systematic violence." There is very little discussion in analytic philosophy about the nature of despair, perhaps because despair is commonly thought to be the opposite of hope. But this kind of all-encompassing despair is illuminating. Agents with despair might have insightful moral perceptions (as in agents with bitterness) but damaged moral agencies, lacking faith, hope, and other attitudes and emotions that might otherwise propel them forward. I have only gestured at the potential relationship between despair, moral perception, and agency. But the topic is worth exploring further—especially in contexts of oppression in which individuals' capacities for hope can be damaged, and to which despair is an understandable response.

But with faith and, perhaps other attitudes and emotions that prevent moral agents from falling into despair, individuals often come together in what I call moral-political solidarity, or solidarity based in a shared moral vision carried out through political action. I have argued that through solidarity a new form of hope emerges—a collective hope borne of solidarity. Hope is collective when it is shared by at least some others, when the perception in a favorable light of the possibility that the hoped-for outcome will occur results from (or is strengthened by) group activity within a collective action setting, and when the reciprocal hopeful expressions of group members result in an emotional atmosphere of hope that stretches across the group. I suspect that the challenge for the reductivist about collective hope will be to capture the phenomenology of collective hope experiences: both "emotional convergence" and "emotional atmosphere." Cutting-edge research in the social sciences, along with insights in the philosophy of mind and emotions, hold promise for advancing new ways of thinking about collective hope.

The object of collective hope borne of solidarity is justice as a guiding ideal—often a particular form of social justice attached to the "vision" of a social movement. Members of a solidarity group jointly commit to pursuing a form of justice together. And seeing that success in securing their goals is possible but not certain, they often find themselves hoping—individually and collectively—that they will succeed. I have argued that whether one is ultimately hoping for complete justice ("utopian hope") or hoping only for small victories that might fade away as injustices take new shapes and forms ("modest hope"), both of these ways in which people hope for justice can be ways of hoping well for justice. What is important is that we do not lose sight of where we have been, where we are now, and where we need to go.

I started this book by explaining how I arrived at the subject of hope to begin with. Engaging with feminist approaches to moral, social, and political philosophy and seeing more clearly the nature and scope of oppression caused me to struggle with hope in my personal and political life. My own hopes have not changed much. I still look to the future with fear and doubt that humankind will ever escape the problems we face. Like many people, I often find myself overwhelmed about the persistent, widespread, and increasingly significant injustices affecting so many lives on this planet (and threats to the planet itself). I even sometimes retreat into despair, pulling away from the news and social media and taking space from the moral and political tragedies occurring around the world. I know that many others share this experience of moral exhaustion and defeat. I now wonder how privilege might allow people the time and space to sit with their despair, and how that position of privilege might even exacerbate despair. Having the time and resources to learn about historical and contemporary tragedies, to write about them, and to debate their implications at professional conferences and other venues might encourage the imagination of future possibilities which lead to a kind of despair of the privileged.[1] Such despair might even be particularly dangerous, since it accompanies those who have the option of being complacent and for whom complacency is already a temptation. Philosophers thus need to sort out not only what it means to despair of an outcome (or to be in despair) but how despair might manifest differently in the lives of those who are privileged from the lives of those who are oppressed.

But perhaps people who find themselves in despair can learn from scholars and activists, especially those who live under oppression, about how to resist giving up on living a moral life in a world that seems hostile to the realization of our moral hopes. Bell, Coates, Norlock, and Solnit teach us that it is possible and essential to struggle against oppression even without hope that justice will someday, ultimately, prevail. Whether or not we are capable of forming and pursuing the utopian hope for justice, we can look to the future with the hope that solidarity efforts will continue, that more and more people will find the motivation and courage to resist injustice, and that we do not lose sight of the possibility of change that grounds our hopes for the future.

---

[1] I am talking about a different kind of despair of the privileged than Vincent Lloyd (2016), who speaks of white despair in terms of "white tears" about one's own misfortunes of guilt (rather than the misfortunes of the world).

References

Abrahams, Hilary. 2010. *Rebuilding Lives after Domestic Violence*. London: Jessica Kingsley.

Adams, Robert Merrihew. 1985. "Involuntary Sins." *Philosophical Review* 94 (1): 3–31.

Adams, Robert Merrihew. 1995. "Moral Faith." *Journal of Philosophy* 92 (2): 75–95.

Ahmed, Sara. 2004. *The Cultural Politics of Emotion*. New York: Routledge.

Amnesty International. 2016. "Out of Sight, Out of Mind: Gender, Indigenous Rights, and Energy Development in Northeast British Columbia, Canada." https://www.amnesty.ca/outofsight.

Assembly of First Nations. 2016. "Assembly of First Nations National Chief Calls for Immediate Action to Deal with State of Emergency in Attawapiskat First Nation." April 11, 2016. https://www.afn.ca/16-4-11-assembly-of-first-nations-national-chief-calls-for-immediate-a/.

Atack, Iain. 2012. *Nonviolence in Political Theory*. Edinburgh: Edinburgh University Press.

Audi, Robert. 2008. "Belief, Faith, and Acceptance." *International Journal for Philosophy of Religion* 63 (1–3): 87–102.

Austen, Ian. 2018. "More Remains Found Near Home Used by Suspected Canadian Serial Killer." *New York Times*, July 5, 2018. https://www.nytimes.com/2018/07/05/world/canada/bruce-mcarthur-toronto-serial-killer-.html.

Averill, James R., George Catlin, and Kyum K. Chon. 1990. *Rules of Hope: Recent Research in Psychology*. New York: Springer-Verlag.

Babbit, Susan. 1997. "Personal Integrity, Politics, and Moral Imagination." In *A Question of Values: New Canadian Perspectives in Ethics and Political Philosophy*, edited by Samantha Brennan, Tracy Isaacs, and Michael Milde, 107–134. Amsterdam: Rodopi Press.

BBC News. 2019a. "Europe and Right-Wing Nationalism: A Country-by Country Guide." November 13, 2019. https://www.bbc.com/news/world-europe-36130006.

BBC News. 2019b. "Older Women Exploited by IVF Clinics, Says Fertility Watchdog." April 22, 2019. https://www.bbc.com/news/uk-48008635.

Baier, Annette. 1980. "Secular Faith." *Canadian Journal of Philosophy* 10 (1): 131–148.

Baier, Annette. 1986. "Trust and Antitrust." *Ethics* 96 (2): 231–260.

Baier, Annette C. 2012. *Reflections on How We Live*. Oxford: Oxford University Press.

Baldwin, James. 1955. *Notes of a Native Son*. Boston: Beacon.

Bartky, Sandra Lee. 1990. *Femininity and Domination: Studies in the Phenomenology of Oppression*. New York: Routledge.

Basu, Rima. 2019. "The Wrongs of Racist Beliefs." *Philosophical Studies* 176 (9): 2497–2515.

Baum, Kathryn Blaze. 2016. "Manitoba Community Seeks Answers as Youth Suicides Soar." *Globe and Mail*, March 11, 2016. https://www.theglobeandmail.com/news/national/a-community-seeks-answers-as-youth-suicides-soar/article29199297/.

Beech, Hannah, Dharisha Bastians, and Kai Schultz. "Religious Minorities Across Asia Suffer Amid Surge in Sectarian Politics." *New York Times*, April 21, 2019. https://www.nytimes.com/2019/04/21/world/asia/sri-lanka-religion-christians.html.

Bell, Derrick. 1992a. *Faces at the Bottom of the Well: The Permanence of Racism*. New York: Basic Books.

Bell, Derrick. 1992b. "Racial Realism." *Connecticut Law Review* 24 (2): 363–379.

Bell, Derrick. 2002. *Ethical Ambition*. New York: Bloomsbury.

Bell, Macalester. 2005. "A Woman's Scorn: Toward a Feminist Defense of Contempt as a Moral Emotion." *Hypatia* 20 (4): 80–93.

Bell, Macalester. 2009. "Anger, Virtue, and Oppression." In *Feminist Ethics and Social and Political Philosophy: Theorizing the Non-Ideal*, edited by Lisa Tessman, 165–183. Dordrecht: Springer.

Bell, Macalester. 2013. "The Standing to Blame." In *Blame: Its Nature and Norms*, edited by D. Justin Coates and Neal A. Tognazzini, 263–281. New York: Oxford University Press.

Benton, Matthew A. 2019. "Epistemological Aspects of Hope." In *The Moral Psychology of Hope*, edited by Claudia Blöser and Titus Stahl, 135–151. Lanham, MD: Rowman & Littlefield.

Ben Ze'ev, Aaron. 2001. *The Subtlety of Emotions*. Cambridge, MA: MIT Press.

Blöser, Claudia. 2019. "Hope as an Irreducible Concept." *Ratio* 32 (3): 205–214.

Blöser, Claudia, Jakob Huber, and Darrel Moellendorf. 2020. "Hope in Political Philosophy." *Philosophy Compass* 15 (5): 1–9.

Blöser, Claudia, and Titus Stahl. 2017. "Fundamental Hope and Practical Identity." *Philosophical Papers* 46 (3): 345–371.

Blum, Lawrence. 2007. "Three Kinds of Race-Related Solidarity." *Journal of Social Philosophy* 38 (1): 53–72.

Bosman, Julie. 2015. "Pine Ridge Indian Reservation Struggles With Suicides Among Its Young." *New York Times*, May 1, 2015. https://www.nytimes.com/2015/05/02/us/pine-ridge-indian-reservation-struggles-with-suicides-among-young-people.html.

Bovens, Luc. 1999. "The Value of Hope." *Philosophy and Phenomenological Research* 59 (3): 667–681.

Bowers, Mike. 2017. "Waiting for the Tide to Turn: Kiribati's Fight for Survival." *Guardian*, October 23, 2017. https://www.theguardian.com/world/2017/oct/23/waiting-for-the-tide-to-turn-kiribatis-fight-for-survival.

Bowlby, John. 1973. *Attachment and Loss*, vol. 2, *Separation: Anxiety and Anger*. New York: Basic Books.

Brudholm, Thomas. 2008. *Resentment's Virtue: Jean Améry and the Refusal to Forgive*. Philadelphia: Temple University Press.

Buchak, Lara. 2012. "Can It Be Rational to Have Faith?" In *Probability in the Philosophy of Religion*, edited by Jake Chandler and Victoria S. Harrison, 225–247. Oxford: Oxford University Press.

Buchak, Lara. 2017. "Faith and Steadfastness in the Face of Counter-Evidence." *International Journal for Philosophy of Religion* 81 (1–2): 113–133.

Burrow, Sylvia. 2005. "The Political Structure of Emotion: From Dismissal to Dialogue." *Hypatia* 20 (4): 27–43.

Butler, Joseph. 1726. *Fifteen Sermons Preached at the Rolls Chapel*. London: J. and J. Knapton.

Cahn, Steven M. 2004. "The Happy Immoralist." *Journal of Social Philosophy* 35 (1): 1–1.

Calhoun, Cheshire. 2003. "Cognitive Emotions?" In *What Is an Emotion? Classic Readings in Philosophical Psychology*, edited by Cheshire Calhoun and Robert C. Solomon, 236–247. New York: Oxford University Press.

Calhoun, Cheshire. 1992. "Changing One's Heart." *Ethics* 103 (1): 76–96.

Calhoun, Cheshire. 1995. "Standing for Something." *Journal of Philosophy* 92 (5): 235–260.

Calhoun, Cheshire. 2008. "Losing One's Self." In *Practical Identity and Narrative Agency*, edited by Kim Atkins and Catriona Mackenzie, 193–211. New York: Routledge.

Calhoun, Cheshire. 2009. "What Good Is Commitment?" *Ethics* 119 (4): 613–641.

Calhoun, Cheshire. 2018. *Doing Valuable Time: The Present, the Future, and Meaningful Living*. New York: Oxford University Press.

Callina, Kristina, Nancy Snow, and Elise D. Murray. 2018. "The History of Philosophical and Psychological Perspectives on Hope: Toward Defining Hope for the Science of Positive Human Development." In *The Oxford Handbook of Hope*, edited by Matthew W. Gallagher and Shane J. Lopez, 9–25. New York: Oxford University Press.

Campbell, Sue. 1994. "Being Dismissed: The Politics of Emotional Expression." *Hypatia* 9 (3): 46–65.

Campbell, Sue. 2014. *Our Faithfulness to the Past: The Ethics and Politics of Memory*. New York: Oxford University Press.

Canadian Women's Foundation. 2015. "Everyone has a Reason to Move for Hope." May 11, 2015. https://canadianwomen.org/blog/everyone-has-reason-move-hope/.

Card, Claudia. 1988. "Gratitude and Obligation." *American Philosophical Quarterly* 25 (2): 115–127.

Card, Claudia. 1996. *The Unnatural Lottery: Character and Moral Luck*. Philadelphia: Temple University Press.

Chakravarti, Sonali. 2014. *Sing the Rage: Listening to Anger after Mass Violence*. Chicago: University of Chicago Press.

Cherry, Myisha. 2015. "The Conscious Gospel and Its Shortcomings." *Daily Nous*, August 18, 2015. http://dailynous.com/2015/08/18/philosophers-on-coates-between-world-me/.

Cherry, Myisha. 2017. "The Errors and Limitations of Our 'Anger-Evaluating' Ways." In *The Moral Psychology of Anger*, edited by Myisha Cherry and Owen Flanagan, 49–65. Lanham, MD: Rowman & Littlefield.

Cherry, Myisha. 2019. "Love, Anger, and Racial Injustice." In *The Routledge Handbook of Love in Philosophy*, edited by Adrienne M. Martin, 157–168. New York: Routledge.

Chignell, Andrew. 2013. "Rational Hope, Moral Order, and the Revolution of the Will." In *Divine Order, Human Order, and the Order of Nature*, edited by Eric Watkins, 197–218. New York: Oxford University Press.

Chignell, Andrew. 2019. *What May I Hope?* London: Routledge.

Chignell, Andrew. forthcoming. "The Focus Theory of Hope (and Despair)." *Hope*, edited by Nancy Snow. New York: Oxford University Press.

Cholbi, Michael, and Alex Madva. 2018. "Black Lives Matter and the Call for Death Penalty Abolition." *Ethics* 128 (3): 517–544.

Chudnoff, Elijah. 2012. "Presentational Phenomenology." In *Consciousness and Subjectivity*, edited by Sofia Miguens and Gerhard Preyer, 51–72. Frankfurt: Ontos Verlag.

Climate One. 2019. "Katharine Hayhoe: Why We Need to Talk about Climate Change." January 22, 2019. https://www.climateone.org/audio/katharine-hayhoe-why-we-need-talk-about-climate-change.

Coates, Ta-Nehisi. 2015a. *Between the World and Me*. New York: Penguin Random House.

Coates, Ta-Nehisi. 2015b. "Hope and the Historian." *Atlantic*, December 10, 2015. https://www.theatlantic.com/politics/archive/2015/12/hope-and-the-historian/419961/.

Coleman, Rebecca, and Debra Ferreday. 2010. "Introduction: Hope and Feminist Theory." *Journal for Cultural Research* 14 (4): 313–321.

Collins, Patricia Hill. 1999. *Black Feminist Thought: Knowledge, Consciousness, and the Politics of Empowerment.* New York: Routledge.

Cooper, Brittney. 2015. "I Could Have Been Sandra Bland: Black America's Terrifying Truth." *Salon*, July 23, 2015. https://www.salon.com/2015/07/23/black_americas_terrifying_truth_any_of_us_could_have_been_sandra_bland/

Coulthard, Glen Sean. 2014. *Red Skin, White Masks: Rejecting the Colonial Politics of Recognition.* Minneapolis: University of Minnesota Press.

Courville, Sasha, and Nicola Piper. 2004. "Harnessing Hope through NGO Activism." *Annals of the American Academy of Political and Social Science* 292 (1): 39–61.

Crawford, Neta C. 2018. "Hope, Fear, and the Formation of Specific Intention in Genocide." In *Emotions and Mass Atrocity: Philosophical and Theoretical Explorations*, edited by Thomas Brudholm and Johannes Lang, 42–63. New York: Cambridge University Press.

Crenshaw, Kimberlé. 1989. "Demarginalizing the Intersection of Race and Sex: A Black Feminist Critique of Antidiscrimination Doctrine, Feminist Theory and Antiracist Politics." *University of Chicago Legal Forum* 140:139–167.

Crenshaw, Kimberlé. 1991. "Mapping the Margins: Intersectionality, Identity Politics, and Violence against Women of Color." *Stanford Law Review* 43 (6): 1241–1299.

Cudd, Ann. 2006. *Analyzing Oppression.* New York: Oxford University Press.

D'Arms, Justin, and Daniel Jacobson. 2000. "The Moralistic Fallacy: On the 'Appropriateness' of Emotions." *Philosophy and Phenomenological Research* 61 (1): 65–90.

D'Arms, Justin, and Daniel Jacobson. 2010. "Demystifying Sensibilities: Sentimental Values and the Instability of Affect." *The Oxford Handbook of Philosophy of Emotion*, edited by Peter Goldie, 585–613. Oxford: Oxford University Press.

David, E. J. R., and Annie O. Derthick. 2014. "What Is Internalized Oppression, and So What?" In *Internalized Oppression: The Psychology of Marginalized Groups*, edited by E. J. R. David, 1–30. New York: Springer.

Dawson, Michael C. 2012. "Racial Tragedies, Political Hope, and the Tasks of American Political Science." *Perspectives on Politics* 10 (3): 669–673.

Davey, Ed. 2019. "Have Hope, Humanity Is Finding Ways to Defeat Climate Change." *Climate Home News*, April 18, 2019. https://www.climatechangenews.com/2019/04/18/hope-humanity-finding-ways-defeat-climate-change/.

Day, J. P. 1969. "Hope." *American Philosophical Quarterly* 6 (2): 89–102.

Decamme, Guillaume. 2016. "Losing Hope, Some Migrants Are Starting to Leave Europe." *Business Insider*, March 7, 2016. https://www.businessinsider.com/afp-hopeless-and-broke-some-afghan-migrants-return-from-europe-2016-3.

Deer, Ka'nhehsí:io. "Meet 5 Indigenous Youth Who Are Spreading Hope in Communities on World Suicide Prevention Day." *CBC News*, September 10, 2019. https://www.cbc.ca/news/indigenous/indigenous-youth-suicide-prevention-day-1.5275889.

Delbaere, Marjorie, and Erin Willis. 2015. "Direct-to-Consumer Advertising and the Role of Hope." *Journal of Medical Marketing* 15 (1–2): 26–38.

Delgado, Richard, and Jean Stefancic. 2005. *The Derrick Bell Reader.* New York: New York University Press.

Demille, Cecil B. 2018. "'Your Truth is the Most Powerful Tool'—Oprah's Globes Speech, in Full." *Golden Globe Awards*, January 9, 2018. https://www.goldenglobes.com/articles/your-truth-most-powerful-tool-oprahs-globes-speech-full.

Department of Health. 2013. "Aboriginal and Torres Strait Islander Suicide: Origins, Trends and Incidence." Last updated 2013. https://www1.health.gov.au/

internet/publications/publishing.nsf/Content/mental-natsisps-strat-toc~mental-natsisps-strat-1~mental-natsisps-strat-1-ab.

Doan, Michael D., and Susan Sherwin. 2016. "Relational Solidarity and Climate Change in Western Nations." In *Bioethical Insights into Values and Policy: Climate Change and Health*, edited by Cheryl C. Macpherson, 79–88. Springer Verlag.

Döring, Sabine. 2014. "What May I Hope? Why It Can Be Rational to Rely on One's Hope." *European Journal for Philosophy of Religion* 6 (3): 117–129.

Dorsett, Pat. 2010. "The Importance of Hope in Coping with Severe Acquired Disability." *Australian Social Work* 63 (1): 83–102.

Downie, Jocelyn, and Jennifer J. Llewellyn. 2012. *Being Relational: Reflections on Relational Theory and Health Law and Policy*. Vancouver: University of British Columbia Press.

Downie, R. S. 1963. "Hope." *Philosophy and Phenomenological Research* 24 (2): 248–251.

Drahos, Peter. 2004. "Trading in Public Hope." *Annals of the American Academy of Political and Social Science* 592 (1): 18–38.

Dunham, Jackie. 2019. "'Restored Faith': Neighbours Deem Wheelchair Ramp Unsafe for Senior, Build Him New One." *CTV News*, June 5, 2019. https://www.ctvnews.ca/lifestyle/restored-faith-neighbours-deem-wheelchair-ramp-unsafe-for-senior-build-him-new-one-1.4452956.

Environmental Justice Foundation. 2018. "On the Front Lines: Climate Change in Bangladesh." October 7, 2018. https://ejfoundation.org/reports/on-the-frontlines-climate-change-in-bangladesh.

Estes, Nick. 2019. *Our History Is the Future: Standing Rock versus the Dakota Access Pipeline, and the Long Tradition of Indigenous Resistance*. New York: Verso.

Farrag, Hebah. 2018. "The Spirit in Black Lives Matter: New Spiritual Community in Black Radical Organizing." *Transition* 125 (1): 76–88.

Federation of Sovereign Indigenous Nations' Mental Health Technical Working Group. 2017. "Discussion Paper Regarding Saskatchewan First Nations Suicide Prevention Strategy." September 22, 2017. https://web.archive.org/web/20180313174832/http://www.fsin.com/wp-content/uploads/2017/09/SK-FN-SPS-Discussion-Paper-FINAL.pdf.

FitzPatrick, William J. 2004. "Reasons, Value, and Particular Agents: Normative Relevance without Motivational Internalism." *Mind* 113 (450): 285–318.

Flowers, Rachel. 2015. "Refusal to Forgive: Indigenous Women's Love and Rage." *Decolonization: Indigeneity, Education, and Society* 4 (2): 32–49.

Freire, Paulo. 2005. *Pedagogy of the Oppressed*. New York: Continuum.

Fricker, Miranda. 1999. "Epistemic Oppression and Epistemic Privilege." *Canadian Journal of Philosophy* 29 (supplement): 191–210.

Frye, Marilyn. 1983. *The Politics of Reality: Essays in Feminist Theory*. New York: Crossing.

Gallagher, Matthew W. 2018. "Introduction to the Science of Hope." In *The Oxford Handbook of Hope*, edited by Matthew W. Gallagher and Shane J. Lopez, 3–7. New York: Oxford University Press.

Gandhi, M. K. 2001. *Non-Violent Resistance (Satyagraha)*. Newburyport, MA: Dover.

Gandhi, Mahatma. 2002. *The Essential Gandhi: An Anthology of His Writings on His Life, Work, and Ideas*. Edited by Louis Fischer. New York: Vintage.

Gilbert, Margaret. 2002. "Collective Guilt and Collective Guilt Feelings." *Journal of Ethics* 6 (2): 115–143.

Gilbert, Margaret. 2014. "How We Feel: Understanding Everyday Collective Emotion Ascription." In *Collective Emotions: Perspectives from Psychology, Philosophy, and Sociology*, edited by Christian von Scheve and Mikko Salmela, 17–131. New York: Oxford University Press.

Gilmore, Jonathan. 2011. "Aptness of Emotions for Fictions and Imaginings." *Pacific Philosophical Quarterly* 92 (4): 468–489.

Global Optimism. 2019. https://globaloptimism.com/.

Godrej, Farah. 2006. "Nonviolence and Gandhi's Truth: A Method for Moral and Political Arbitration." *Review of Politics* 68 (2): 287–317.

Goldie, Peter. 2004. "Emotion, Feeling, and Knowledge of the World." In *Thinking about Feeling: Contemporary Philosophers on Emotions*, edited by Robert C. Solomon, 91–106. New York: Oxford University Press.

Goldie, Peter. 2009. "Getting Feelings into Emotional Experiences in the Right Way." *Emotion Review* 1 (3): 232–239.

Gonzalez, John, Estelle Simard, Twyla Baker-Demaray, and Chase Iron Eyes. 2014. "The Internalized Oppression of North American Indigenous Peoples." In *Internalized Oppression: The Psychology of Marginalized Groups*, edited by E. J. R. David, 57–82. New York: Springer.

Greenspan, Patricia. 2000. "Emotional Strategies and Rationality." *Ethics* 110 (3): 469–487.

Gumbel, Andrew. 2018. "'They Were Laughing at Us': Immigrants Tell of Cruelty, Illness and Filth in US Detention." *Guardian*, September 12, 2018. https://www.theguardian.com/us-news/2018/sep/12/us-immigration-detention-facilities.

Habib, Samra. 2019. *We Have Always Been Here*. Toronto: Penguin Random House Canada.

Haidt, Jonathan. 2000. "The Positive Emotion of Elevation." *Prevention and Treatment* 3 (1): 1–5.

Haidt, Jonathan. 2003. "Elevation and the Positive Psychology of Morality." In *Flourishing: Positive Psychology and the Life Well-Lived*, edited by Corey M. Keyes and Jonathan Haidt, 275–289. Washington, DC: American Psychological Association.

Halperin, Eran, et al. 2011. "Anger, Hatred, and the Quest for Peace: Anger Can Be Constructive in the Absence of Hatred." *Journal of Conflict Resolution* 55 (2): 274–291.

Hampton, Jean, and Jeffrie G. Murphy. 1988. *Forgiveness and Mercy*. Cambridge: Cambridge University Press.

Harvey, Jean. 2004. "Gratitude, Obligation, and Individualism." In *Moral Psychology: Feminist Ethics and Social Theory*, edited by Peggy DesAutels and Margaret Urban Walker, 33–46. Lanham, MD: Rowman & Littlefield.

Hayes, Kelly. 2018. "Standing Rock and the Power and Determination of Indigenous America." *Pacific Standard*, September 7, 2018. https://psmag.com/magazine/standing-rock-still-rising.

Heglar, Mary Annaïse. 2019a. "Home Is Always Worth It." *Medium*, September 12, 2019. https://medium.com/@maryheglar/home-is-always-worth-it-d2821634dcd9.

Heglar, Mary Annaïse. 2019b. "Climate Change Isn't the First Existential Threat: People of Color Know All about Building Movements, Courage, and Survival." *Medium*, February 18, 2019. https://zora.medium.com/sorry-yall-but-climate-change-ain-t-the-first-existential-threat-b3c999267aa0.

Held, Virginia. 1990. "Feminist Transformations of Moral Theory." *Philosophy and Phenomenological Research* 50 (supplement): 321–344.

Helm, Bennett. 2014. "Emotional Communities of Respect." In *Collective Emotions: Perspectives from Psychology, Philosophy, and Sociology*, edited by Christian Von Scheve and Mikko Salmela, 47–60. New York: Oxford University Press.

Hieronymi, Pamela. 2001. "Articulating an Uncompromising Forgiveness." *Philosophy and Phenomenological Research* 62 (3): 529–555.

Hieronymi, Pamela. 2008. "The Reasons of Trust." *Australasian Journal of Philosophy* 86 (2): 213–236.

Hill, Douglas L., and Chris Feudtner. 2018. "Hope in the Midst of Terminal Illness." In *The Oxford Handbook of Hope*, edited by Matthew Gallagher and Shane J. Lopez, 191–206. New York: Oxford University Press.

Hirschfield, Kevin. 2019. "God's Lake First Nation Declares State of Emergency after String of Suicides." *Global News*, August 29, 2019. https://globalnews.ca/news/5833847/gods-lake-first-nation-declares-state-of-emergency-after-string-of-suicides/.

Hobbes, Thomas. 2018. *The Leviathan, Reprinted from the Edition of 1651*. Minneapolis: Learner.

hooks, bell. 1995. *Killing Rage: Ending Racism*. New York: Henry Holt.

hooks, bell. 2003. *Teaching Community: A Pedagogy of Hope*. New York: Routledge.

hooks, bell. 2015. *Feminist Theory: From Margin to Center*. New York: Routledge.

Howard, Dana S. 2019. "The Scoundrel and the Visionary: On Reasonable Hope and the Possibility of a Just Future." *Journal of Political Philosophy* 27 (3): 294–317.

Huber, Jakob. 2019. "Defying Democratic Despair: A Kantian Account of Hope in Politics." *European Journal of Political Theory* 0 (0): 1–20.

Human Rights Watch. 2009. "From Horror to Hopelessness: Kenya's Forgotten Somali Refugee Crisis." March 30, 2009. https://www.hrw.org/report/2009/03/30/horror-hopelessness/kenyas-forgotten-somali-refugee-crisis.

Human Rights Watch. 2013. "Those Who Take Us Away: Abusive Policing and Failures of Protecting Indigenous Women and Girls in Northern British Columbia." February 13, 2013. https://www.hrw.org/report/2013/02/13/those-who-take-us-away/abusive-policing-and-failures-protection-indigenous-women.

Human Rights Watch. 2017. "'All of My Body Was Pain': Sexual Violence against Rohingya Women and Girls in Burma." November 2017. https://www.hrw.org/sites/default/files/report_pdf/burma1117_web_1.pdf.

Jaffe, Sarah. 2018. "The Collective Power of #MeToo." *Dissent*, Spring 2018. https://www.dissentmagazine.org/article/collective-power-of-me-too-organizing-justice-patriarchy-class.

Jaggar, Alison M. 1989. "Love and Knowledge: Emotion in Feminist Epistemology." *Inquiry* 32 (2): 151–176.

James, Leah, et al. 2014. "The Mental Health of Syrian Refugee Children." *Forced Migration Review* 47:42–44.

Jeffrey, Anne. 2017. "Does Hope Morally Vindicate Faith?" *International Journal for Philosophy of Religion* 81 (1): 193–211.

Jennings, Bruce, and Angus Dawson. 2015. "Solidarity in the Moral Imagination of Bioethics." *Hastings Center Report* 45 (5): 31–38.

Jones, Karen. 1996. "Trust as an Affective Attitude." *Ethics* 107 (1): 4–25.

Jones, Karen. 2004. "Gender and Rationality." In *The Oxford Handbook of Rationality*, edited by Alfred R. Mele and Piers Rawling. New York: Oxford University Press.

Kadlac, Adam. 2015. "The Virtue of Hope." *Ethical Theory and Moral Practice* 18 (2): 337–354.

Kant, Immanuel. 1996. *Metaphysics of Morals*. Translated and edited by Mary Gregor. Cambridge: Cambridge University Press.

Kant, Immanuel. 1998. *Critique of Pure Reason*. Edited by Paul Guyer and Allen W. Wood. Cambridge: Cambridge University Press.

Kassam, Ashifa. 2017. "Guatemalan Women Take On Canada's Mining Giants over 'Horrific Human Rights Abuses.'" *Guardian*, December 13, 2017. https://www.theguardian.com/world/2017/dec/13/guatemala-canada-indigenous-right-canadian-mining-company.

Khaleeli, Homa. 2016. "#SayHerName: Why Kimberlé Crenshaw Is Fighting for Forgotten Women." *Guardian*, May 30, 2016. https://www.theguardian.com/lifeandstyle/2016/may/30/sayhername-why-kimberle-crenshaw-is-fighting-for-forgotten-women.

Khan-Cullors, Patrisse, and Asha Bandele. 2018. *When They Call You a Terrorist*. New York: St. Martin's.

King, Martin Luther, Jr. 1998. *The Autobiography of Martin Luther King, Jr.* Edited by Clayborne Carson. New York: Warner.

Kirylo, James D., and Drick Boyd. 2017. *Paulo Freire: His Faith, Spirituality, and Theology*. Rotterdam: Sense.

Klein, Ezra. 2020. "Why Ta-Nehisi Coates Is Hopeful." *Ezra Klein Show* (podcast). June 5, 2020. https://podcasts.apple.com/us/podcast/why-ta-nehisi-coates-is-hopeful/id1081584611?i=1000476756446.

Kolers, Avery. 2016. *A Moral Theory of Solidarity*. New York: Oxford University Press.

Kretz, Lisa. 2019. "Hope, The Environment, and Moral Imagination." *Theories of Hope: Exploring Alternative Dimensions of Human Experience*, edited by Rochelle M. Green, 155–176. London: Lexington.

Krishnamurthy, Meena. 2015. "(White) Tyranny and the Democratic Value of Distrust." *The Monist* 98 (4): 391–406. https://doi.org/10.1093/monist/onv020.

Krueger, Joel. 2014. "Varieties of Extended Emotions." *Phenomenology and the Cognitive Sciences* 13 (4): 533–555.

Kwong, Jack. 2020. "Hope and Hopefulness." *Canadian Journal of Philosophy*.

Lamb, Michael. 2016. "Aquinas and the Virtues of Hope: Theological and Democratic." *Journal of Religious Ethics* 44 (2): 300–332.

Lear, Jonathan. 2006. *Radical Hope: Ethics in the Face of Cultural Devastation*. Cambridge, MA: Harvard University Press.

Lebron, Chris. 2015. "Black Fathers, Black Sons, and the Problem of Evil." *Daily Nous*, August 18, 2015. http://dailynous.com/2015/08/18/philosophers-on-coates-between-world-me/.

Lee, Jenny Y., and Matthew W. Gallagher. 2018. "Hope and Well-Being." In *The Oxford Handbook of Hope*, edited by Matthew W. Gallagher and Shane J. Lopez, 287–298. Oxford: Oxford University Press.

Legacy of Hope Foundation. n.d. https://legacyofhope.ca/.

Leonardo, Zeus, and Angela P. Harris. 2013. "Living With Racism in Education and Society: Derrick Bell's Ethical Idealism and Political Pragmatism." *Race, Ethnicity, and Education* 16 (4): 470–488.

Little, Margaret Olivia. 1995. "Seeing and Caring: The Role of Affect in Feminist Moral Epistemology." *Hypatia* 10 (3): 117–137.

Lloyd, Genevieve. 1979. "The Man of Reason." *Metaphilosophy* 10 (1): 18–37.

Lloyd, Vincent. 2016. "For What Are Whites to Hope?" *Political Theology* 17 (2): 168–181.

Lloyd, Vincent. 2018a. "'A Moral Astigmatism': King on Hope and Illusion." *Telos* 2018 (182): 121–138.

Lloyd, Vincent. 2018b. "How Religious Is #BlackLivesMatter?" In *Humanism and the Challenge of Difference,* edited by Anthony B. Pinn, 215–237. Springer Verlag.

Long, Laura J., and Matthew W. Gallagher. 2018. "Hope and Posttraumatic Stress Disorder." In *The Oxford Handbook of Hope,* edited by Matthew W. Gallagher and Shane J. Lopez, 233–242. Oxford: Oxford University Press.

Lorde, Audre. 2007. *Sister Outsider: Essays and Speeches by Audre Lorde.* Berkeley: Crossing Press.

Lowry, Rich. 2015. "The Toxic Worldview of Ta-Nehisi Coates." *Politico,* July 22, 2015. https://www.politico.com/magazine/story/2015/07/the-toxic-world-view-of-ta-nehisi-coates-120512.

Lugones, María. 1995. "Hard to Handle Anger." In *Overcoming Racism and Sexism,* edited by Linda A. Bell and David Blumenfeld, 203–218. Lanham, MD: Rowman & Littlefield.

Mackenzie, Catriona, and Natalie Stoljar. 2000. *Relational Autonomy: Feminist Perspectives on Autonomy, Agency, and the Social Self.* New York: Oxford University Press.

MacLachlan, Alice. 2010. "Unreasonable Resentments." *Journal of Social Philosophy* 41 (4): 422–441.

Maclean's. 2015. "Justin Trudeau, For the Record: 'We Beat Fear with Hope.'" October 20, 2015. https://www.macleans.ca/politics/ottawa/justin-trudeau-for-the-record-we-beat-fear-with-hope/.

Macnamara, Coleen. 2015. "Reactive Attitudes as Communicative Entities." *Philosophy and Phenomenological Research* 90 (3): 546–569.

Manne, Kate. 2018. *Down Girl: The Logic of Misogyny.* New York: Oxford University Press.

Mantena, Karuna. 2018. "4. Showdown for Nonviolence: The Theory and Practice of Nonviolent Politics." In *To Shape a New World: Essays on the Political Philosophy of Martin Luther King, Jr,* edited by Tommie Shelby and Brandon M. Terry, 78–102. Cambridge, MA: Harvard University Press.

Martin, Adrienne M. 2008. "Hope and Exploitation." *Hastings Center Report* 38 (5): 49–55.

Martin, Adrienne M. 2014. *How We Hope: A Moral Psychology.* Princeton, NJ: Princeton University Press.

Martin, Adrienne. 2019. "Interpersonal Hope." In *The Moral Psychology of Hope,* edited by Claudia Blöser and Titus Stahl, 229–248. Lanham, MD: Rowman & Littlefield.

Marvel, Kate. 2018. "We Need Courage, Not Hope, to Face Climate Change." *On Being Project,* March 1, 2018. https://onbeing.org/blog/kate-marvel-we-need-courage-not-hope-to-face-climate-change/.

Marx, Karl. 1970. *Critique of Hegel's 'Philosophy of Right.'* Edited by Joseph O'Malley. Cambridge: Cambridge University Press.

Mastony, Colleen. 2009. "In Tough Times, Don't Lose Hope—Instead, Buy It in a Jar." *Chicago Tribune,* April 5, 2009. https://www.chicagotribune.com/news/ct-xpm-2009-04-05-0904030393-story.html.

McCormick, Miriam Schleifer. 2017. "Rational Hope." *Philosophical Explorations* 20 (sup1): 127–141.

McFall, Lynne. 1991. "What's Wrong with Bitterness?" In *Feminist Ethics,* edited by Claudia Card, 146–160. Lawrence: University Press of Kansas.

McGeer, Victoria. 2004. "The Art of Good Hope." *Annals of the American Academy of Political and Social Science* 592 (1): 100–127.

McGeer, Victoria. 2008. "Trust, Hope and Empowerment." *Australasian Journal of Philosophy* 86 (2): 237–254. https://doi.org/10.1080/00048400801886413.

McLeod, Carolyn. 2000. "Our Attitude Towards the Motivation of Those We Trust." *Southern Journal of Philosophy* 38 (3): 465–479. https://doi.org/10.1111/j.2041-6962.2000.tb00911.x.

Meirav, Ariel. 2009. "The Nature of Hope." *Ratio* 22 (2): 216–233.

Me Too. 2018. metoomvmt.org.

Meyers, Diana. 2004. *Being Yourself: Essays on Identity, Action, and Social Life*. Lanham, MD: Rowman & Littlefield.

Milona, Michael. 2018. "Finding Hope." *Canadian Journal of Philosophy* 49 (5): 710–729.

Milona, Michael. 2020. "Discovering the Virtue of Hope." *European Journal of Philosophy* 28 (3): 740–754.

Milona, Michael, and Hichem Naar. 2020. "Sentimental Perceptualism and the Challenge from Cognitive Bases." *Philosophical Studies* 177 (10): 3071–3096.

Milona, Michael, and Katie Stockdale. 2018. "A Perceptual Theory of Hope." *Ergo: An Open Access Journal of Philosophy* 5 (8): 203–222.

Mittleman, Alan. 2009. *Hope in a Democratic Age: Philosophy, Religion, and Political Theory*. Oxford: Oxford University Press.

Moellendorf, Darrel. 2006. "Hope as a Political Virtue." *Philosophical Papers* 35 (3): 413–433.

Moellendorf, Darrel. 2019. "Hope for Material Progress in the Age of the Anthropocene." In *The Moral Psychology of Hope*, edited by Claudia Blöser and Titus Stahl, 249–264. Lanham, MD: Rowman & Littlefield.

Mohanty, Chandra Talpede. 2003. *Feminism without Borders: Decolonizing Theory, Practicing Solidarity*. Durham, NC: Duke University Press.

Moon, Dawne, and Theresa Weynand Tobin. 2018. "Sunsets and Solidarity: Overcoming Sacramental Shame in Conservative Christian Churches to Forge a Queer Vision of Love and Justice." *Hypatia* 33 (3): 451–468.

Moscrop, David. 2018. "It's Time for Climate Change Defeatists to Get Out of the Way." *Maclean's*, December 6, 2018. https://www.macleans.ca/society/environment/its-time-for-climate-change-defeatists-to-get-out-of-the-way/.

Murphy, Jeffrie G. 2000. "Two Cheers for Vindictiveness." *Punishment and Society* 2 (2): 131–143.

Narayan, Uma. 1988. "Working Together across Difference: Some Considerations on Emotions and Political Practice." *Hypatia* 3 (2): 31–47.

National Inquiry into Missing and Murdered Indigenous Women and Girls. 2019. *Reclaiming Power and Place: Executive Summary of the Final Report*. https://www.mmiwg-ffada.ca/wp-content/uploads/2019/06/Executive_Summary.pdf.

Naylor, Hugh. 2014. "Report: Syria's Refugees Increasingly Denied Entry by Neighbors." *Washington Post*, November 13, 2014. https://www.washingtonpost.com/world/report-syrian-refugees-face-new-level-of-hopelessness-as-border-controls-tighten/2014/11/13/1342cecd-4157-4ec2-94da-b86d26275297_story.html.

Neu, Jerome. 2010. "An Ethics of Emotion?" In *The Oxford Handbook of Philosophy of Emotion*, edited by Peter Goldie, 501–518. Oxford: Oxford University Press.

Ngabo, Gilbert. 2018. "Pride Weekend: The Idea is to Show Strength and Support." *Star*, June 25, 2018. https://www.thestar.com/news/gta/2018/06/24/pride-weekend-the-idea-is-to-show-strength-and-support.html.

Nock, Samantha. 2014. "Anchored by Love, Fuelled by Anger: Indigenous Women's Resistance. *Rabble*, August 20, 2014. https://rabble.ca/blogs/bloggers/samantha-nock/2014/08/anchored-love-fuelled-anger-indigenous-womens-resistance.

Nolen, Stephanie. 2017. "The Lost Ones: Inside Brazil's Indigenous Suicide Crisis." *Globe and Mail*, March 3, 2017. https://www.theglobeandmail.com/news/world/canada-indigenous-suicide-crisis-in-brazil/article34199700/.

Norlock, Kathryn J. 2009. *Forgiveness from a Feminist Perspective*. Lanham, MD: Lexington.

Norlock, Kathryn J. 2019. "Perpetual Struggle." *Hypatia* 34 (1): 6–19.

Nussbaum, Martha. 2004. "Emotions as Judgments of Value and Importance." In *Thinking about Feeling: Contemporary Philosophers on Emotions*, edited by Robert C. Solomon, 183–199. New York: Oxford University Press.

Nussbaum, Martha. 2016. *Anger and Forgiveness: Resentment, Generosity, Justice*. New York: Oxford University Press.

Obama, Barack. 2006. *The Audacity of Hope: Thoughts on Reclaiming the American Dream*. New York: Crown.

Openshaw, John J., and Mark A. Travassos. 2020. "COVID-19 Outbreaks in US Immigrant Detention Centers: The Urgent Need to Adopt CDC Guidelines for Prevention and Evaluation." *Clinical Infectious Diseases* 1–2. https://doi.org/10.1093/cid/ciaa692.

Oxfam America. 2016. "Refugees in Greece Recount the Dangers of Flight and their Longing for a Better Future." June 20, 2016. https://www.oxfamamerica.org/explore/stories/refugees-in-greece-recount-the-dangers-of-flight-and-their-longing-for-a-better-future/.

Páez, Dario, and Bernard Rimé. 2014. "Collective Emotional Gatherings: Their Impact Upon Identity Fusion, Shared Beliefs, and Social Integration." In *Collective Emotions: Perspectives from Psychology, Philosophy, and Sociology*, edited by Christian Von Scheve and Mikko Salmela, 204–216. New York: Oxford University Press.

Parliament of Canada. 2016. "Request for Emergency Debate: Situation in Indigenous Communities." *House of Commons Debates* 148 (037): 2039–2157. https://www.ourcommons.ca/DocumentViewer/en/42-1/house/sitting-37/hansard.

Pettigrove, Glen. 2012. "Meekness and 'Moral' Anger." *Ethics* 122 (2): 341–370.

Pettit, Phillip. 2004. "Hope and Its Place in Mind." *Annals of the American Academy of Political and Social Science* 592 (1): 152–165. www.jstor.org/stable/4127684.

Philosophy. n.d. "Face Moisturizers and Creams." https://www.philosophy.com/skin-care/face-moisturizers.

Poupart, Lisa M. 2003. "The Familiar Face of Genocide: Internalized Oppression among American Indians." *Hypatia* 18 (2): 86–100.

Preston-Roedder, Ryan. 2013. "Faith in Humanity." *Philosophy and Phenomenological Research* 87 (3): 664–687.

Preston-Roedder, Ryan. 2018. "Three Varieties of Faith." *Philosophical Topics* 46 (1): 173–199.

Rabinowicz, Wlodek, and Toni Rønnow-Rasmussen. 2004. "The Strike of the Demon: On Fitting Pro-attitudes and Value." *Ethics* 114 (3): 391–423.

Randhawa, Selena. 2017. "'Our Society Is Broken': What Can Stop Canada's First Nations Suicide Epidemic?" *Guardian*, August 30, 2017. https://www.theguardian.com/inequality/2017/aug/30/our-society-is-broken-what-can-stop-canadas-first-nations-suicide-epidemic.

Rappleye, Hannah, et al. 2019. "Thousands of Immigrants Suffer in Solitary Confinement in U.S. Detention Centers." *NBC News*, May 21, 2019. https://www.nbcnews.com/politics/immigration/thousands-immigrants-suffer-solitary-confinement-u-s-detention-centers-n1007881.

Ratcliffe, Matthew. 2013. "What Is It to Lose Hope?" *Phenomenology and the Cognitive Sciences* 12 (4): 597–614.

Rawls, John. 1999. *The Law of Peoples: With "The Idea of Public Reason Revisited."* Cambridge, MA: Harvard University Press.

Rioux, Catherine. Forthcoming. "Hope: Conceptual and Normative Issues." *Philosophy Compass.*

Roberts, Peter. 1998. "Knowledge, Dialogue, and Humanization." *Journal of Educational Thought* 32 (2): 95–117.

Roberts, Robert C. 2003. *Emotions: An Essay in Aid of Moral Psychology.* Cambridge: Cambridge University Press.

Roberts, Robert C. 2007. *Spiritual Emotions: A Psychology of Christian Virtues.* Grand Rapids, MI: William B. Eerdmans.

Roberts, Robert C. 2009. "Emotions and the Canons of Evaluation." In *The Oxford Handbook of Philosophy of Emotion*, edited by Peter Goldie, 561–584. Oxford: Oxford University Press.

Roberts, Robert C. 2013. *Emotions in the Moral Life.* Cambridge: Cambridge University Press.

Rodger, Elliot. 2014. "Manifesto: My Twisted World." https://assets.documentcloud.org/documents/1173619/rodger-manifesto.pdf/.

Rogers, Melvin L. 2015. "Between Pain and Despair: What Ta-Nehisi Coates Is Missing." *Dissent*, July 31, 2015. https://www.dissentmagazine.org/online_articles/between-world-me-ta-nehisi-coates-review-despair-hope.

Scanlon, T. M. 2008. *Moral Dimensions: Permissibility, Meaning, Blame.* Cambridge, MA: Harvard University Press.

Scarantino, Andrea, and Ronald de Sousa. 2018. "Emotion." In *Stanford Encyclopedia of Philosophy*, edited by Edward N. Zalta, Winter 2018. https://plato.stanford.edu/archives/win2018/entries/emotion/.

Scherkoske, Greg. 2013. *Integrity and the Virtues of Reason: Leading a Convincing Life.* New York: Cambridge University Press.

Scholz, Sally. 2008. *Political Solidarity.* University Park: Pennsylvania State University Press.

Scholz, Sally. 2009. "Feminist Political Solidarity." In *Feminist Ethics and Social and Political Philosophy: Theorizing the Non-Ideal*, edited by Lisa Tessman, 205–220. Springer.

Schrank, Beate, and Astrid Grant Hay. 2011. "Hope and Embitterment." In *Embitterment: Societal, Psychological, and Clinical Perspectives*, edited by Michael Linden and Andreas Maercker, 17–29. Springer.

Segal, Gabriel, and Mark Textor. 2015. "Hope as a Primitive Mental State." *Ratio* 28 (2): 207–222.

Shelby, Tommie. 2005. *We Who Are Dark: The Philosophical Foundations of Black Solidarity.* Cambridge, MA: Harvard University Press.

Shepherd, Jack. 2012. "21 Pictures That Will Restore Your Faith in Humanity." *Buzzfeed*, June 20, 2012. https://www.buzzfeed.com/expresident/pictures-that-will-restore-your-faith-in-humanity.

Sherman, Nancy. 1999. "Taking Responsibility for Our Emotions." *Social Philosophy and Policy* 16 (2): 294–323.

Sherwin, Susan. 2012. "Relational Autonomy and Global Threats." In *Being Relational: Reflections on Relational Theory and Health Law*, edited by Jocelyn Downie and Jennifer J. Llewellyn, 13–43. Vancouver: UBC Press.

Sherwin, Susan, and Katie Stockdale. 2017. "Whither Bioethics Now? The Promise of Relational Theory." *IJFAB: International Journal of Feminist Approaches to Bioethics* 10 (1): 7–29.

Snow, Nancy E. 2013. "Hope as an Intellectual Virtue." In *Virtues in Action: New Essays in Applied Virtue Ethics*, edited by Michael W. Austin, 153–170. London: Palgrave Macmillan.

Snow, Nancy E. 2018. "Hope as a Democratic Civic Virtue." *Metaphilosophy* 49 (3): 407–427.

Snow, Nancy E. 2019. "Hope as a Moral Virtue." In *The Moral Psychology of Hope*, edited by Claudia Blöser and Titus Stahl, 171–197. Lanham, MD: Rowman & Littlefield.

Snyder, C. R. 2002. "Hope Theory: Rainbows in the Mind." *Psychological Inquiry* 13 (4): 249–275.

Snyder, C. R., Kevin L. Rand, and David R. Sigmon. 2018. "Hope Theory: A Member of the Positive Psychology Family." In *The Oxford Handbook of Hope*, edited by Matthew W. Gallagher and Shane J. Lopez, 27–43. Oxford: Oxford University Press.

Solnit, Rebecca. 2016. *Hope in the Dark: Untold Histories, Wild Possibilities*. Chicago: Haymarket.

Solnit, Rebecca. 2018. "Don't Despair: The Climate Fight Is Only Over If You Think It Is." *Guardian*, October 14, 2018. https://www.theguardian.com/commentisfree/2018/oct/14/climate-change-taking-action-rebecca-solnit.

Solomon, Robert C. 1976. *The Passions: The Myth and Nature of Emotions*. Garden City, NY: Doubleday Anchor.

Solomon, Robert C. 2007. *True to Our Feelings: What Our Emotions Are Really Telling Us*. New York: Oxford University Press.

Spelman, Elizabeth. 1989. "Anger and Insubordination." In *Women, Knowledge and Reality: Explorations in Feminist Philosophy*, edited by Ann Garry and Marilyn Pearsall, 253–274. New York: Routledge.

Srinivasan, Amia. 2018. "The Aptness of Anger." *Journal of Political Philosophy* 26 (2): 123–144.

Stahl, Titus. 2019. "Political Hope and Cooperative Community." In *The Moral Psychology of Hope*, edited by Claudia Blöser and Titus Stahl, 265–284. Lanham, MD: Rowman & Littlefield.

Stockdale, Katie. 2013. "Collective Resentment." *Social Theory and Practice* 39 (3): 501–521.

Stockdale, Katie. 2019. "Emotional Hope." In *The Moral Psychology of Hope*, edited by Claudia Blöser and Titus Stahl, 115–133. Lanham, MD: Rowman & Littlefield.

Stoddard, Sarah A., et al. 2011. "Social Connections, Trajectories of Hopelessness, and Serious Violence in Impoverished Urban Youth." *Journal of Youth and Adolescence* 40 (3): 278–295.

Strawson, P. F. 2008. *Freedom and Resentment and Other Essays*. New York: Routledge.

Stroud, Sarah. 1998. "Moral Overridingness and Moral Theory." *Pacific Philosophical Quarterly* 79 (2): 170–189.

Sullivan, Shannon. 2014. "The Hearts and Guts of White People." *Journal of Religious Ethics* 42 (4): 591–611.

Suttie, Jill. 2018. "Five Ways to Restore Your Faith in Humanity." *Greater Good Magazine*, August 28, 2018. https://greatergood.berkeley.edu/article/item/five_ways_to_restore_your_faith_in_humanity.

Sweet, Victoria. 2014. "Rising Waters, Rising Threats: The Human Trafficking of Indigenous Women in the Circumpolar Region of the United States and Canada."

SSRN Scholarly Paper ID 2447017. Rochester, NY: Social Science Research Network. https://papers.ssrn.com/abstract=2447017.

Tackett, Michael, and Maggie Haberman. 2019. "Trump Once Said Power Was about Instilling Fear. In That Case, He Should Be Worried." *New York Times*, February 4, 2019. https://www.nytimes.com/2019/02/04/us/politics/fear-trump.html.

Talaga, Tanya. 2018. *All Our Relations: Finding the Path Forward*. Toronto: House of Anansi.

Tappolet, Christine. 2016. *Emotions, Value, and Agency*. Oxford: Oxford University Press.

Taylor, George. 2005. "Racism as Original Sin: Derrick Bell and Reinhold Niebuhr's Theology." In *The Derrick Bell Reader*, edited by Richard Delgado and Jean Stefancic, 433–445. New York: New York University Press.

Taylor, Paul C. 2018. "Moral Perfectionism." In *To Shape a New World: Essays on the Political Philosophy of Martin Luther King, Jr*, edited by Tommie Shelby and Brandon M. Terry, 35–57. Cambridge, MA: Harvard University Press.

Teasley, Martell, and David Ikard. 2010. "Barack Obama and the Politics of Race: The Myth of Postracism in America." *Journal of Black Studies* 40 (3): 411–425.

Teroni, Fabrice. 2007. "Emotions and Formal Objects." *Dialectica* 61 (3): 395–415.

Tessman, Lisa. 2005. *Burdened Virtues: Virtue Ethics for Liberatory Struggles*. New York: Oxford University Press.

Tessman, Lisa. 2009. "Expecting Bad Luck." *Hypatia* 24 (1): 9–28.

Tiberius, Valerie. 2008. *The Reflective Life: Living Widely Within our Limits*. New York: Oxford University Press.

Times of India. 2019. "A Kidney Swap Involving Hindu, Muslim Families That Resurrected Faith in Humanity." May 30, 2019. https://timesofindia.indiatimes.com/city/chandi-garh/a-kidney-swap-involving-hindu-muslim-families-that-resurrected-faith-in-humanity/articleshow/69572820.cms.

Truth and Reconciliation Commission of Canada. 2015. *Final Report of the Truth and Reconciliation Commission of Canada: Summary: Honouring the Truth, Reconciling for the Future*. http://www.trc.ca/assets/pdf/Honouring_the_Truth_Reconciling_for_the_Future_July_23_2015.pdf.

UNHCR. 2019. "Global Trends: Forced Displacement in 2019." https://www.unhcr.org/globaltrends2019/.

UN News. 2020. "UN Chief Calls for 'Solidarity, Unity, and Hope' in Battling COVID-19 Pandemic." April 30, 2020. https://news.un.org/en/story/2020/04/1062972.

Urban Indian Health Institute. 2018. "Missing and Murdered Indigenous Women and Girls: A Snapshot of Data from 71 Urban Cities in the United States." https://www.uihi.org/wp-content/uploads/2018/11/Missing-and-Murdered-Indigenous-Women-and-Girls-Report.pdf.

Vasanthakumar, Ashwini. 2018. "Epistemic Privilege and Victims' Duties to Resist Their Oppression." *Journal of Applied Philosophy* 35 (3): 465–480.

Vidal, John. 2018. "'Boats Pass over Where Our Land Was': Climate Refugees in Bangladesh." *Guardian*, January 4, 2018. https://www.theguardian.com/global-development/2018/jan/04/bangladesh-climate-refugees-john-vidal-photo-essay.

Vinyeta, Kirsten, Kyle Powys Whyte, and Kathy Lynn. 2015. "Climate Change through an Intersectional Lens: Gendered Vulnerability and Resilience in Indigenous Communities in the United States." United States Department of Agriculture, December 2015. https://doi.org/10.2737/PNW-GTR-923.

Von Scheve, Christian and Mikko Salmela. 2014. *Collective Emotions: Perspectives from Psychology, Philosophy, and Sociology*. Oxford: Oxford University Press.

Walker, Margaret Urban. 1991. "Moral Luck and the Virtues of Impure Agency." *Metaphilosophy* 22 (1–2): 14–27. https://www.jstor.org/stable/24436913.

Walker, Margaret Urban. 2004. "Introduction." In *Moral Psychology: Feminist Ethics and Social Theory*, edited by Peggy DesAutels and Margaret Urban Walker, xi–xiv. Lanham, MD: Rowman & Littlefield.

Walker, Margaret Urban. 2006. *Moral Repair: Reconstructing Moral Relations after Wrongdoing*. Cambridge: Cambridge University Press.

Walker, Margaret Urban. 2018. "Hope(s) after Genocide." In *Emotions and Mass Atrocity: Philosophical and Theoretical Explorations*, edited by Thomas Brudholm and Johannes Lang, 211–233. New York: Cambridge University Press.

Walter, Natasha. 2018. "Three Ways for Activists to Stay Hopeful in These Grim Times Natasha Walter." *Guardian*, September 4, 2018. https://www.theguardian.com/commentisfree/2018/sep/04/ways-activists-stay-cheerful-refugee-women-hope.

Watts, Jonathan. 2018. "We Have 12 Years to Limit Climate Change Catastrophe, Warns UN." *Guardian* October 8, 2018. https://www.theguardian.com/environment/2018/oct/08/global-warming-must-not-exceed-15c-warns-landmark-un-report.

We Matter Campaign. n.d. #HopePact. https://wemattercampaign.org/activities/hopepact.

West, Cornel. 2018. "Hope and Despair: Past and Present." In *To Shape a New World: Essays on the Political Philosophy of Martin Luther King, Jr*, edited by Tommie Shelby and Brandon M. Terry, 325–338. Cambridge, MA: Harvard University Press.

Wheatley, J. M. O. 1958. "Wishing and Hoping." *Analysis* 18 (6): 121–131.

White, Jennifer, and Christopher Mushquash. 2016. "We Belong: Life Promotion to Address Indigenous Suicide Discussion Paper." *Thunderbird Partner Foundation* December 18, 2016. https://wisepractices.ca/wp-content/uploads/2017/12/White-Mushquash-2016-FINAL.pdf.

Williams, Bernard. 1981. *Moral Luck*. Cambridge: Cambridge University Press.

Willingham, Brian. 2016. "Finding Hope in the Flint Police Department." *New York Times*, November 21, 2016. https://www.nytimes.com/2016/11/21/opinion/finding-hope-in-the-flint-police-department.html.

Willis, Andre. 2017. "Notes Toward a Dissident Theo-Politics." *Political Theology* 18 (4): 290–308.

Woodruff, Paul. 2014. "Spectator Emotions." In *On Emotions: Philosophical Essays*, edited by John Deigh, 59–75. New York: Oxford University Press.

Yancy, George, and bell hooks. 2015. "bell hooks: Buddhism, The Beats, and Loving Blackness." *The Stone* (*New York Times* blog), December 10, 2015. https://opinionator.blogs.nytimes.com/2015/12/10/bell-hooks-buddhism-the-beats-and-loving-blackness/.

Yap, Audrey. 2017. "Credibility Excess and the Social Imaginary in Cases of Sexual Assault." *Feminist Philosophy Quarterly* 3 (4): 1–23.

Young, Iris Marion. 1990. *Justice and the Politics of Difference*. Princeton, NJ: Princeton University Press.

Znoj, Hansjörg. 2011. "Embitterment: A Larger Perspective on a Forgotten Emotion." In *Embitterment: Societal, Psychological, and Clinical Perspectives*, edited by Michael Linden and Andreas Maercker, 5–16. Springer.

Index